87-94

THE FICTION OF BERNARD MALAMUD

AMERICAN AUTHORS SERIES

Steinbeck: The Man and His Work edited by Richard Astro and Tetsu-maro Hayashi, 1971

Hemingway in Our Time edited by Richard Astro and Jackson J. Benson, 1974

The Fiction of Bernard Malamud edited by Richard Astro and Jackson J. Benson, 1977

The Fiction of Bernard
MALAMUD

Edited by
Richard Astro and Jackson J. Benson

Corvallis:

OREGON STATE UNIVERSITY PRESS

Library of Congress Cataloging in Publication Data
Main entry under title:

The Fiction of Bernard Malamud.

    Bibliography: p.
    1. Malamud, Bernard—Criticism and interpretation—
Addresses, essays, lectures. I. Astro, Richard.
II. Benson, Jackson J.
PS3563.A4Z63   813'.5'4   77-23232
ISBN 0-87071-446-5

PREFACE

LATE DURING THE SUMMER of 1949, Bernard Malamud, age 35 and a lifelong New Yorker, arrived in the Pacific Northwest to take a teaching position as an instructor in the English Department at Oregon State College. He was greeted at the train station in Albany, Oregon, by the Director of Composition at the small technologically and agriculturally oriented land-grant institution who drove the new instructor the few miles to Corvallis, a quiet community of about 10,000 in the heart of Oregon's farm-filled Willamette Valley.

As a New Yorker, Malamud had attended City College of New York and Columbia University where he received the B.A. and M.A. degrees and had taught English for nearly ten years at two area high schools. He had done some writing of his own and had published short stories in *American Prefaces, Threshold,* and the Washington *Post.* But in Corvallis, there seemed only time for the four sections of freshman English he would teach in a conservative and inflexible composition program which stressed, according to Department guidelines, "the writing of short expository themes, and the study of those elements of grammar, punctuation, spelling, and diction which are prerequisites to the writing of effective expository prose in any professional field." Under the watchful eye of the same composition director who was his first Corvallis acquaintance. Malamud endured the ordeals of group writing examinations, grading technical reports, and filing his themes in the Department "theme room."

Teaching four sections of composition every academic term is itself enough to dull the spirit. Doing so over a long period of time in a rigid, traditional program is almost unendurable. Faculty members who have taught in such programs quickly lose their vitality and even their equilibrium. But not so Bernard Malamud. For, while teaching four sections of composition a term and doing a good job of it, Malamud found time to write two important novels (*The Natural* and *The Assistant*) and the very fine volume of short stories, *The Magic Barrel*, for which he was awarded the National Book Award in 1959.

By the middle 1950's Malamud had become a novelist of some reputation, except in the administrative offices of the Oregon State English Department. Though he was promoted to assistant professor in 1954 and to associate professor in 1959, he was given large doses of composition classes to teach with only an occasional introductory literature course to break the monotony. Finally, in the spring of 1961, Malamud left Oregon State. He had come to Corvallis an unknown writer. He left a national figure, a novelist of genuine accomplishment in a time when few writers were successful in understanding, describing, and making plausible the bizarre facts of contemporary life.

The Fiction of Bernard Malamud was the third in a continuing series of conferences on major figures in modern American literature sponsored by the Department of English at Oregon State. It brought to the campus a group of notable scholars to talk about Malamud's craft and the importance of his fiction. The papers which follow are printed here as they were delivered at the Corvallis conference, with only minor editorial changes by some of the authors so that their essays are suitable for a reading audience. To the essays we have added an introductory piece by Jackson Benson and what we believe is the most complete checklist of Malamud criticism on record compiled by Donald Risty of San Diego State University.

The result is a volume which focuses in a broad way on Malamud's place in American literature, and in which a number of critics examine what they regard as the most noteworthy elements of his art. The Oregon State symposium and this volume are then the University's tribute to one of America's most important contemporary novelists and to the most distinguished faculty member ever to teach in its English Department. In the process, as Leslie Fiedler notes so well, we have transformed a man some among us once regarded as a "loveable misfit" or a "pain-in-the-ass" into a "cultural monument."

I would like to express thanks first to my colleagues, Michael Sprinker of Oregon State University and to Jackson Benson of San Diego State University. Jack and Mike made working on this conference a pleasure, for between us we created what we think was something of value. And we had fun in the process. My sincere thanks also go to President Robert MacVicar, Dean Gordon Gilkey, and Professor Robert Phillips of Oregon State University who believed in an idea and who encouraged us as we brought that idea to life. My thanks also to Ken Munford, Rita Miles, Marilyn Holsinger, and everyone else at the OSU Press who helped make the publication of this volume painless. My very special thanks to Sharon Springer of the English Department who helped with a thousand details. Finally, I would like to thank my wife Betty who was there when I needed support and encouragement.

RICHARD ASTRO
Oregon State University
Corvallis, Oregon
July 1976

CONTENTS

CONTRIBUTORS

Leslie Field—Associate Professor of English, Purdue University. Editor of *Bernard Malamud and the Critics* (NYU, 1970) and the *Twentieth Century Views Malamud* (Prentice-Hall, 1975), as well as books on Thomas Wolfe and Robert Penn Warren. Essays have appeared in *Bucknell Review, South Atlantic Quarterly, The Southern Literary Journal,* and *Modern Fiction Studies.* Advisory editor of *Modern Fiction Studies.* Senior Fellow and Lecturer, Bar-Ilan University, Israel, 1969-1970.

Leslie Fiedler—Samuel Clemens Professor and Chairman of the Department of English at the State University of New York at Buffalo. Associate Fellow of the faculty of Calhoun College, Yale University, and member of the Developmental Faculty of Empire State University. Among his eighteen books, several (including *Love and Death in the American Novel, Waiting for the End,* and *The Return of the Vanishing American*) are landmark pieces in American literary scholarship. Author of numerous critical and review articles, poetry, and short fiction which have appeared in such journals as *Kenyon Review, Partisan Review, Encounter, Per Monat,* and *Prevues.*

William J. Handy—Professor of English, University of Oregon. Author of *Kant and the Southern New Critics* (Texas, 1963) and *Modern Fiction: A Formalist Approach* (Southern Illinois, 1971). Articles have appeared in such journals as *Texas Studies in English, Texas Studies in Literature and Language, Kenyon Review,* and *The University of Houston Review.* Has served as visiting professor at the University of Missouri, University of North Dakota, and the University of Washington.

Ihab Hassan—Vilas Research Professor of English and Comparative Literature at the University of Wisconsin-Milwaukee. Formerly, Chairman of the English Department and Director of the College of Letters at Wesleyan University. Author of *Radical Innocence: Studies in the Contemporary American Novel* (Princeton, 1961), one of the most important studies of the genre. Also author of books on Henry Miller and Samuel Beckett, and postmodern literature. His most recent book is *Paracriticisms: Seven Speculations of the Times* (Illinois, 1975). Author of over one hundred articles and reviews as well as the chapters on "The New Consciousness" and "Fiction: Since 1945" in *The Literary History of the United States,* eds. Spiller et. al.

Peter L. Hays—Associate Professor and Chairman of the English Department at the University of California, Davis. Author of *The Limping Hero* (NYU Press) and of articles on modern fiction in such journals as *English Language Notes, Papers in Language and Literature, Studies in Short Fiction,* and *Modern Fiction Studies.* Contributor to *Hemingway in Our Time* (Oregon State, 1974).

Donald Risty—M.A. student, San Diego State University. This is his first major publication. Holds the B.A. from the University of California, Berkeley.

Ben Siegel—Professor of English and former head of the department at the California State Polytechnic University at Pomona. Director of the Annual Conferences in Modern American Writing at Cal Poly's Center for Continuing Education. Books include *The Puritan Heritage: America's Roots in the Bible, Biography Past and Present,* and a book on I. B. Singer. His latest book on Sholem Asch appeared in 1976. Author of articles on Philip Roth, Daniel Fuchs, and Saul Bellow as well as on Malamud.

EDITORS

Richard Astro—Chairman of the Department of English and Assistant to the Dean of Research at Oregon State University. Author of *John Steinbeck and Edward F. Ricketts: The Shaping of a Novelist* (Minnesota, 1973) and editor of books on Steinbeck and Hemingway. Articles on Steinbeck, Hemingway, Malamud, Fitzgerald, and others have appeared in *Modern Fiction Studies, Steinbeck Quarterly, Western American Literature,* and *Twentieth Century Literature.* Currently Director of the Oregon State University-National Endowment for the Humanities Development Grant Program.

Jackson J. Benson—Professor of English, San Diego State University. Author of *Hemingway: The Writer's Art of Self-Defense* (Minnesota, 1969) and editor of *The Short Stories of Ernest Hemingway: Critical Essays* (Duke, 1975). Articles on Steinbeck, Hemingway, and Faulkner have appeared in such journals as *Rendezvous, Twentieth Century Literature,* and *Journal of Modern Literature.* Currently at work on the definitive biography of John Steinbeck.

Jackson J. Benson

AN INTRODUCTION: BERNARD MALAMUD AND THE HAUNTING OF AMERICA

I. Moo Day for Malamud

Oregon in april is a big country of wet, green valleys and snow-laden mountains. As an event, this conference should have been a Western. The participants are all professionals, hired guns brought in from out of the East, Midwest, and California via United Airlines and Hertz, for the shootout at the O.S.U. student union.

When you hit a strange town the night before a showdown, you find a saloon and tell a few lies. But the motel lounge has more people in leisure suits than Levis, and the band is playing soft rock. At two tables in the rear, we peer at each other in the semi-darkness. At the next table I see Leslie Fiedler for the first time. He is squinting over a Mexican cigar, a Jewish Walter Huston. Near me at the other table is Ihab Hassan. Trim, in a continental-cut suit, he is obviously the dude with the derringer. He is puzzled, so I try to explain who I am, but the soft rock is too loud for any intricate bragging. The band leader begins telling jokes and doing impressions: "Round 'em up! Head 'em out!" A bearded man in a denim jacket and cowboy boots stands up on the far side of the room and yells, "Shut up and play some more music!" I find out the next day that he is a graduate student in English at the University of Oregon.

The next morning we nervously pace the motel lobby, fingering our manila folders, waiting for the cars to take us into the Oregon State campus. Corvallis is a small college town that has become a city while still managing to look like a small college town. We ride past a profusion of green lawns, trees, and shrubs. Old, white clapboard houses are mixed with cedar, earth-day modern. The campus streets are crowded with cars, but the campus itself is clean and pretty—ivy-covered dark-brick buildings are surrounded by blooming trees and vast expanses of grass. Sun streams down through broken clouds and is reflected on the puddles from a recent rain. Behind the Memorial Union is the old School of Forestry building, the new quarters of the English Department.

To the right of the main entrance to the Memorial Union, at the bottom of the inside stairs, there is a copy of the U.S. Constitution under glass on a granite pedestal, donated to the university by the head of a lumber company. We assemble in a conference room at the end of a huge baronial hall draped with flags which runs the length of the second floor of the Union. While waiting, it strikes me that this kind of conference on a major author has become a sort of modern art form. There is reckless creation in bringing from all over the country a half-dozen literary critics, mostly unknown to each other except by reputation, to the same room to talk about the same topic. It may be the academic equivalent of setting off colored smoke bombs or draping tall buildings in parachute cloth.

There are about a hundred of us—students, high school teachers, local college faculty and wives, and some faculty from out of state—sitting in folding chairs, sipping coffee out of styrofoam cups, and listening to Richard Astro's welcome. He introduces the President of the University, who gives us greetings. A tall, pleasant looking man, he looks unmarked but is obviously an old survivor. He is a scientist who during his tenure has promoted the humanities at an agricultural and technical school. He seems genuinely pleased that we are honoring Bernard Malamud who, during a previous generation, had served so long (and without much honor) on the Oregon State faculty. (I think of Malamud sitting in the midst of all this lush greenery writing of New York tenements—a strong reversal of Bret Harte sitting in London writing of California forests.) The president is forced to add, with an apologetic smile, that he will be unable to stay for the conference itself, since this is "Moo Day," a new traditional day of campus celebration. His part in the ceremony is to milk a cow, presumably a yearly fitness test. The situation is complicated, however, by the fact that no one has been able thus far to locate a cow on campus ready for milking.

But our subject is at hand. We will have our Western. Our Moo Day will be for Malamud.

II. Malamud Among the Moderns

Ihab Hassan has taken on the task of trying to place Malamud within the larger picture of contemporary fiction. His discussion moves tentatively, through multiple perspectives. It is a paper of questions, thoughtful musings, and personal doubts. He wonders, "How does Malamud manage to exclude from his fiction a crucial element of the postmodern sensibility? How does he transcend the problematic of fiction, which haunts so many contemporary novelists?" Is Malamud not therefore a "historical" novelist, engaging a human reality and a universe of discourse that are not really of our time?" Hassan reviews three features of postmodernism in American fiction: first, our writers are authors of fantasy; second, they pretend not to create a world, but instead pretend to plagiarize or play; and third, their play, in turn, "leads to parody and reflexiveness; the latter leads to self-unmaking or autodestruction."

Where does Malamud stand in respect to these features? Hassan suggests that he keeps himself at an ironic distance from all of these "happenings and unmakings" of recent fiction. For Malamud, art still works; it can still "take and give the human measure of things." His vision lacks the radicalism of more characteristic postmoderns. Instead, Malamud, in such works as *The Tenants* which examine the viability of art, offers only a "soft impeachment" of it. Yet, although Malamud may be more "modern" than "postmodern," more "classical" than "radical," it may be that postmodernism has not taken us very far beyond modernism after all and that with all his limitations, Malamud

may prove in the end as "luminary of our exhaustions" as a writer such as Barth.

For Hassan, the impression of Malamud's work:

> is of an imagination working through small, quotidian events,
> through human quirks and the quiddities of history, through the con-
> fined places of the spirit, through the entrapments of art or money or
> sex or guilt or race—pressing always toward liberation into some
> universal human space.

And it is the liberation of that which is inside, this effort toward
human transcendence in Malamud's work, which sets the stage
for Hassan's final thoughts. Is it closing time for the West? Is it
closing time for the novel? He cannot say, but he does look for
change not only in the modes of human expression but in the
very nature of human desire itself. The far future, he senses, will
not belong to West or East, nor even to the earth as a whole, but
to those "immensities still locked within us."

Hassan's canvas is so large, I find it difficult to react. And
who among us has read so widely that he can challenge Hassan's broadest impressions? Yet, limiting myself to what I know,
I wonder if Malamud does not better fit Hassan's description
of postmodernism than he thinks. When he speaks of a trend
"from 'closed' to 'open' forms, from 'realism' to 'surrealism,' from
'myth' to 'parody,' and from 'ironic tragedy' to 'self-ironic comedy,' " I think to myself that this is really a rather good description of Malamud's progress from the earlier *The Natural* and
The Assistant to the later *The Tenants* and *Pictures of Fidelman*. I wonder also if the indictment of art in *The Tenants* is
not more severe than Hassan thinks it to be and if this novel is
not, indeed, an example of what he calls "autodestruction"?

Yet, leaving aside *The Tenants* and *Pictures of Fidelman*,
I must agree that the bulk of Malamud's work is an extension of
the old, perhaps even old-fashioned. But what tradition does he
belong to? As I have read Malamud, I too, along with other
readers, have been reminded both of earlier Jewish-American
writers and a number of Europeans, particularly Dostoevsky,
Kafka, Joyce, and Beckett. But in his interview in *The Paris
Review*, Malamud has said about influences that "as a writer,

I've been influenced by Hawthorne, James, Mark Twain, Hemingway, more than I have been by Sholem Aleichem and I. L. Peretz." This, along with his long experience as a teacher of American fiction, suggests that he may be descended from the American tradition more than any other.

Part of the old-fashioned feeling I get in reading Malamud comes from being reminded of the Romance heritage of American fiction, particularly Hawthorne. Taking this as a clue and looking back over my Hawthorne for confirmation, I find that the two writers do indeed have a number of themes and techniques in common. They both possess the ability to combine, with great skill, reality and the dream, the natural and supernatural. That dream-reality mixture so powerful in Malamud stories such as "Idiots First," "The Silver Crown," or "The Magic Barrel" may owe more to Hawthorne stories like "My Kinsman, Major Molineux," "Young Goodman Brown," and "The Birthmark" than to Kafka, who is so frequently cited in this regard as a model. Malamud also shares with Hawthorne certain other modes and subjects, such as the "mysterious stranger," the "ghostly search," the "test of faith," the "peculiar mark or habit," and perhaps most importantly, that theme of Hawthorne's "Ethan Brand" which could be called "hardness of heart."

Old Hawthorne, who started us down the road of moral allegory, and there are very few, even among the "Naturalists," who haven't followed along. That, I suspect, is what bothers Hassan—not that Malamud's fiction "works," but that his fiction can still attempt to be literature in the old sense, to bring delight in the teaching of the soul to have faith and man to care for man. Malamud's appeal and any claim he may have to greatness appear to rest on this differentness from the others: a steady devotion to what might be called the Old Testament questions— Why should we be good, when there is no reward for goodness? How can we have faith, when there are no signs to confirm our faith? How can we love, if our love is met only with scorn or violence?

If the central image of Crane or the early Dreiser is a man lost in a sea of indifference, subject to the ebb and flow of the tide; if the central image of Hemingway is man's search for a clean, well-lighted place where he can pull himself together and face the omnipresent darkness with some dignity; then perhaps Malamud's central image is of Morris Bober in his prison, his tomb, his store, sitting in his backroom and offering a glass of tea, with lemon to Breitbart, the weary peddler, who carries his light bulbs on his back from place to place through the darkness, calling out, "Lights for sale!" If the conviction rate for robbery is three per cent and the failure for small business is more than thirty per cent, why, in heaven's name, should anyone want to be a Morris Bober? Or, to ask the question again within the more general framework of Malamud's fiction, given the current climate of belief, what's the good of being good?

In these images of Dreiser, Hemingway, and Malamud, there appears to be some kind of progression within the nihilistic context of literary Naturalism toward—what would you call it?—confidence? Possibly it is simply the discovery that knowing the worst, man can still aspire to something beyond physical survival. Obviously, for Malamud life is something more than a joke, literature something more than an empty game. One way of characterizing him within this progression might be to say that he has spent his time looking for the key to the prison described by Dreiser and stoically endured by Hemingway. Perhaps Malamud's work is part of the pendulum that swings from meaning, to non-meaning, back to meaning again, an answer to the nihilism of the late Fifties and Sixties similar to T. S. Eliot's answer to the nihilism and materialism of the late Teens and Twenties. Does this make Malamud old or new?

Malamud's place within, or as moving beyond, American Naturalism brings us into the context of the next conference presentation. In turning from Hassan to Bill Handy, we move from the tentative to the assertive, from the general to the very specific. It is somewhat of a jolt to find ourselves torn from the intergalactic night between stars in Hassan's final image and thrust into George Hurstwood's gas-filled hotel room at the beginning of Handy's address. For Handy begins with a comparison of Malamud to Dreiser and the worlds in which the characters of each writer live. Superficially, the situations appear to be similar: the characters of both writers struggle and suffer within worlds of difficult circumstances. Yet, Dreiser's characters are motivated almost entirely by the need to survive, while Malamud's characters are influenced by the obligations of human relationships. From this comparison as a foundation, Handy suggests a common pattern of development for each of the central characters of Malamud's "major novels":

> Each of Malamud's protagonists in *A New Life, The Assistant,* and *The Fixer* experiences . . . an awakening to the possibility of a fuller existence than the one he has been living and that that awakening begins a quest for existence, one which comprises the dramatic struggle central to each novel.

One would find it hard to argue with this proposition. Each of these protagonists does display a "propensity for reflection" which allows him to grow in awareness as he attempts to extricate himself from "what he discovers is a meaningless existence." In response, however, the question that comes to my mind is, what about the differences in kind also involved in these transcendencies? Handy speaks of a relationship as the catalyst for change, yet is not the relationship between S. Levin and Pauline Gilley significantly different in kind from that of Frank Alpine and Morris Bober? And what is the relationship that helps Yakov Bok—is it with Shmuel, with the Tsar, or with a combination of characters? And, isn't there a difference both in kind and in intensity of "reflection" in Frank Alpine and Yakov Bok?

Along with Handy, I believe that Malamud's Naturalism is less a philosophy than a background of human circumstance. Yet, I am not sure that his characters can be best explained as being on an "existential quest." Nor can I think of him merely as some sort of advanced Naturalist, as a writer who has modified his Naturalism with the possibility of humanism. To think so, of course, would certainly make him a "modern" within Hassan's scheme. No, all of this seems too limiting. For one thing, I am not inclined to take Naturalism very seriously. That is, most of our American Naturalists seem to be subversive humanists and disappointed Romantics (compare the Nobel Prize speeches of Faulkner, Hemingway, and Steinbeck in this regard) who maintain these attitudes in the face of all the evidence they mount to the contrary. What are "The Blue Hotel," "The Monster," *An American Tragedy,* and *Sister Carrie* after all, but moralistic allegories? What is Hemingway, after all, but a moralist who is sometimes allegorical, while maintaining a Manfred-like pose in the face of forces of darkness aligned against him?

Categories like Naturalism, post-Naturalism, Modernism, and post-Modernism all seem to fade into the background in response to the strength of American Romanticism. It would seem more profitable, when we consider the characteristics of Malamud's writing itself (rather than his time, his peers, or his possible sources), to plug him into the main line.

III. Malamud and the American Tradition

My argument for Malamud as an American writer, in the traditional sense, would go something like this. (Needless to say, my thinking along these lines has been stimulated by the work of others, particularly, as I recall, essays by Sam Bluefarb, Ben Siegel, and Theodore Solotaroff.) From *The Scarlet Letter* and *Billy Budd,* down through *The Red Badge of Courage,* to *Light in August, The Old Man and the Sea,* and *Henderson the Rain King* (to point to a few of the most obvious examples), the central tradition of American fiction, as many of us would agree, has been moralistic and often allegorical. The value system carried within this tradition has usually been broadly humanistic, rather than narrowly religious, emphasizing such concerns as the liberation of the individual human spirit and the need for love, faith, and respect in human relationships. The allegory employed in this tradition is not, of course, the "pure" allegory of systematic personification and metaphor, but a more modern or "realistic" allegory wherein secondary meanings and their interrelationships are developed suggestively in an approach that is often ambiguous and frequently ironic.

As allegory, our fiction has sought to objectify the persistent spiritual conflict within the American psyche. It has done so by creating symbols and metaphors (in the characters and physical environment surrounding the central character) which suggest values and conditions which have a part in the internal struggle. The objectification by allegory may be in terms of landscape, the swamp, for example, that faces Nick Adams in "Big Two-Hearted River" (or Susskind's cave in "The Last Mohican"); of objects, Joe Christmas' shoes in *Light in August* (or the crown in "The Silver Crown"); or of other characters, Quint in *The Turn of the Screw* (or Angel Levine in the story of the same name).

Because he is so vitally concerned with matters of conscience, the allegorical use of character is especially important in Malamud's fiction. The use of a character near the protagonist to represent conscience, a device commonly used by Malamud, is nearly as old as literature itself, and there is ample precedent in the American tradition. As examples the relationships of Queequeg, Chingachgook, and Nigger Jim to Ishmael, Natty Bumppo, and Huck Finn come to mind, probably because of the presence of Leslie Fiedler on the conference program. The members of the former group serve as more than companions or confidants to the central characters of the latter group. They become in some degree objectifications of that which is inside the central characters in each case. They provide, literally and figuratively, color. Each leads to and is the physical emblem of a crucial formation of conscience which is at the heart of his white (undifferentiated on the outside) counterpart. The Innocent Adam is given a moral identity as well as dramatic substance.

In Malamud's fiction objectification by character operates on two levels—for the central character by other characters, and for the reader by the central character. In most of his fictions, there is at least one character who provides "the test," who brings the lingering internal question to the surface, who forces the central character to the question of conscience: bumbling innocence is caught up by the collar and vague, good intentions are not enough—"Who are you?" and "What do you stand for?"

Malamud uses several different patterns in dramatizing this confrontation, each presenting to the reader a slightly different moral. One sort of test is that presented by the "loathly lady," as Edwin M. Eigner and others have labeled this figure. Many, if not nearly all, the women that Malamud central-character males have romantic encounters with show themselves to have some severe defect. The test, which is among other things a criticism of the "girl-of-my-dreams" syndrome, consists of a challenge to the depth of the protagonist's love—will he reject the woman because she does not match his superficial criteria? (That is, what is the depth of his moral perception?) If he does, then we have a valid indictment of his total value system. A few Malamud characters fail, such as Roy Hobbs in *The Natural* who—to oversimplify—finds Iris Lemon's beauty marred by her status as a grandmother (while at the same time overlooking her character entirely). Others pass. "Hefty . . . eyeglassed, and marvelously plain," middle-aged Olga teaches Mitka in "The Girl of My Dreams" the essence of love and thereby revives his stultifying soul. And the most important aspect of S. Levin's decision to stick with Pauline Gilley is that he no longer lusts after her under the spell of romance.

Although not entirely, these tend to be encounters from the outside. The encounters that interest me the most and which I believe make up the most powerful fictions in the Malamud canon and which most obviously tie him to the tradition are those which allegorize the inside, pitting the central character symbolically against himself. Most especially I am haunted by a group of stories which, because of their striking visual images, have become fixed in my mind—they give me nearly the same nightmares as an adult that I got from the Brothers Grimm as a child. One such story and surely one of Malamud's best is "The Last Mohican," wherein Susskind performs the functions of Chingachgook to Arthur Fidelman's Pathfinder.

Although Fidelman feels himself self-sufficient and does not want to be guided through the Eternal City, he is forced, through Susskind's uncanny ability to track him down, to make an inventory of his soul and come to terms with himself. Fidelman cannot escape the confrontation, for as we see early in the story, Susskind is really a part of Fidelman, a part that he would like to ignore, but cannot.

Getting off the train in Rome (where else would a Jew go to find his soul?), Fidelman "experienced the sensation of suddenly seeing himself as he was, to the pin-point, outside and in." Then becoming aware "that there was an exterior source to the strange, almost tri-dimensional reflection of himself he had felt as well as seen," he notices a stranger, "give a skeleton a couple of pounds," staring at him in such a way as to suggest that he, Fidelman, had been "mirrored (lock, stock, and barrel) in the other's gaze for some time." Susskind, as the stranger turns out to be, identifies himself subtly in the ensuing conversation as, in effect, the Wandering Jew, that part of Fidelman which represents his heritage and his conscience. Fidelman, proper, is a modern, "semi-assimilated" Jew who finds his counterpart embarrassing in his eccentric appearance, his claim of kinship, and his explicit Jewishness. He thinks of him as a bum, a panhandler, a "schnorrer" (what is the condition of a man's soul when he identifies it as a "schnorrer"?), and Susskind, in turn, demands more than just token attention. He wants, in fact, exactly half of Fidelman's resources—Fidelman has two suits, and Susskind wants, as only seems natural, one of them.

Near the middle of the story, the confrontation of conscience is made explicit:

"Am I responsible for you then, Susskind?"
"Who else?" Susskind loudly replied.
"Lower your voice . . . Why should I be?"
"You know what responsibility means?"
"I think so."
"Then you are responsible. Because you are a man. Because you are a Jew, aren't you?"

Fidelman makes the usual plea, "I am a single individual and can't take on everybody's personal burden," but it won't do.

There is no escape possible, no rationalization good enough to release him from his obligation to himself, his heritage, and through that obligation, to others.

Several other stories recreate similar haunting relationships and situations and press home a similar moral. In "Angel Levine" Manaschevitz meets his "Nigger Jim" in a black, Jewish angel whom he must learn to accept as fully "human" and thus Jewish before his wife can be made whole again. In "The Jewbird," Harry Cohen is confronted by a Jewish version of Poe's raven, an echo of Cohen's own lost soul, and ends up in a furious self-denial, beating and casting out the Jewbird—his heritage and conscience—onto the street to die of assorted concussions and a broken heart. There may be, in the words of Manischevitz, "Jews everywhere," but there are "anti-Semeets," in the words of the Jewbird, everywhere also.

Acceptance of the conscience by the central character in such stories requires not only faith, but an expression of mercy, love, charity, or forgiveness to confirm that faith. Manischevitz must not only believe in his Black Angel, but must perform an act of love in his acceptance which, contradicting previous training and belief, wrenches his soul. He musters the courage necessary, however, breaks out of the prison of his prejudices, and extends himself beyond the boundaries of what he was before, thus saving his wife. But Harry Cohen is unable to accept the image of his heritage in unconventional form. His failure (so reminiscent of the Romantic tale) to accept the Jewbird is a rejection of himself and, by extension, of his son. Ironically, it is Cohen's intolerance and American-Dream concern for status (he complains of the bird's dirtiness and his smell and is irritated by the bird's "old country" mannerisms) which allow him to cut short his concern for his son, whom he hopes to get into an Ivy League college.

Similar acts of faith and demonstrations of love are required of Leo Finkle in "The Magic Barrel," of Albert Gans in "The Silver Crown," of Howard Harvitz in "Man in the Drawer," of Gruber in "The Mourners," and of Mendel in "Idiots First." The terms of these stories are not entirely parallel, but in each case there is an allegorical representation of part of the protagonist in another character who, in turn, challenges the central character's humanity. Furthermore, Malamud's best novels—*The Assistant, The Fixer,* and *The Tenants*—follow roughly the same pattern. As a matter of fact, *The Fixer* is not only allegorical within the terms described, but goes further in being what could be termed a "morality play" in which a whole cast is brought from the inside, out, and the outside, in.

Most of the central characters in these stories and novels are Jews who are no longer Orthodox and are partly assimilated into non-Jewish society in one way or another. Even Leo Finkle in "The Magic Barrel," who is shortly to be ordained as a rabbi, originally lacks the faith, the love, and the depth of soul to be truly "Jewish" by Malamud's definition. And because these Jews are partly assimilated or doubtful, they are able to haunt us, just as they are haunted; we are able, by their successes and failures, to assess our own moral strength and spiritual capacity. We, too, are in this sense "assimilated Jews"—metaphorically, that is the modern condition of the American: alienated, doubtful, and self-centered.

"Haunting" is the word that seems to describe best the central effect of Malamud's work and which, in turn, names the quality that most clearly ties him to the writers of our past. Without shame, he has brought to life once again the curious tale as told by Poe, Hawthorne, Melville, and James. (His novels, in respect to this quality, seem but extensions of his stories.) Lucidly, modestly, he is able to touch the conscience and excite the visual imagination through his odd, twisted tales of fateful small happenings. For a moment, the agonized turnings of the human soul in conflict with itself are laid bare. A sudden shock of insight, often clothed protectively by irony, the story ends, and the world goes on its way.

Seldom profound, infrequently complex, he seems to get much of his power by daring to be old-fashioned, by daring to be almost trite, almost quaint, almost sentimental. Indeed, he plays with us by his deliberate and nearly constant skirting of critical disaster. But, having captured and phrased anew the haunting melodies of our past, why is it that his music often seems so thin? In an age of immensities, he seems determined to irritate the reader with his persistent tinkling in minor scales. Where are the bass tones of the Romantics past, those organ notes of God-like aspiration and thunderous despair? Perhaps Malamud, a post-Modern at least in time, is both weaker and stronger for being ultimately more like Hawthorne than his own contemporaries—stronger in that the strains of allegory and moral conviction are deeper, weaker in that the strains cannot be repeated with a similar force out of the time that originally produced and sustained them. The universe has grown too large, and man has shrunk too small.

IV.   The Jewish-Hyphenated-American-Writer

Was there ever a discussion of Malamud that did not include an argument about the relevance of his Jewishness? Leslie Field's speech, "Bernard Malamud and the Marginal Jew," may become the definitive essay on the topic, or at least definitive from a conservative point of view. Field—who startles me by matching almost exactly my mental picture of S. Levin (dark, bearded, and to my Wasp eyes, rather melancholy)—is Orthodox, a devoted supporter of Israel, and, in the past, a Malamud enthusiast. But this is an essay of second thoughts, and they are dark second thoughts.

He suggests that Malamud, and other Jewish-American writers, have been corrupted by "assimilationist tendencies" and the movement toward a universal humanism. These tendencies can only destroy that which is distinctively Jewish in their work:

> Malamud's roots are Jewish roots. The original soil nurtures a writer in such a way that in any age his writing is immersed in that which concerns Jews most directly. Transplanted, the writer may become a hybrid. His Jew of the *Torah*, the Law, the rabbinical teachings may become the Jew of general humanism, of universalism. In fact his Jew may become indistinguishable from the non-Jew as he becomes homogenized in a larger, non-Jewish world. He may emerge as Everyman as his identification with his own peoples' overriding concerns becomes peripheral or marginal.

What are these overriding concerns for the contemporary Jew? The Holocaust and the rebirth of the State of Israel—they constantly affect, in one way or another, the thinking and feeling of Jews today. Are these events at the heart of Malamud's fiction? Of course, Field replies, the answer must be "No." He accuses Malamud of being timid, of backing off. In effect, Malamud wants to use the Jewish milieu without paying the price of dealing with the reality of modern Jewish experience.

When Field finishes, his argument touches off a spirited series of challenges from the audience. The tender center of discussion, beyond Field's rather harsh indictment of Malamud, appears to be the conflict between the claims of a general humanism (expressed as universalism in literature) and the contemporary movement toward "ethnic identity." Why does Malamud as a writer have to assume a very special Jewish role as prescribed by Field? Haven't other peoples suffered as much or more than the Jews? Several members of the audience call upon their knowledge of what "Berny" had in mind (is this parallel to changing Seymour to Sy?), which, in *A New Life,* was not Jewish. (The next day, Leslie Fiedler gets up and in his speech mourns the fact that *A New Life* is not Jewish enough—a real-life transition that unfortunately I am unable to use here.)

Field's talk and the debate it stirs up raise a number of difficult questions regarding Malamud's Jewish identity (and any obligations that may presume to entail), his use of Jewish materials, and the relationship to those materials by both a Jewish and a non-Jewish audience. These are questions that for the most part Malamud himself would prefer to avoid, understandably, as "reductive" and would apparently prefer that critics avoid them as well. But his special achievement is really in large part based on his use of Jewish characters and settings, as well as our peculiar reactions to them. Avoiding the subject is really impossible, while reaching any consensus of reaction to Malamud's uses of the subject would also seem impossible.

As a non-Jew, I am attracted to Malamud's "universalizing" of the Jew. And, in general, I agree with what I detect in Malamud's work and in his interviews as an antipathy toward narrow

religious belief (either Jewish or Christian). Yet, I feel a hesi-
tancy in participating in what almost seems a family argument.
I wonder if other non-Jews share my slight edge of discomfort
when talking about Malamud. So many of his critics have been
Jewish and so much of the criticism has been published in Jewish periodicals. I wait for a raspberry from the back of the room
as I mispronounce some Yiddish word I've never heard spoken
aloud.

But in the last few decades the Jew has become a special
sort of symbol for the rest of us, a cultural symbol upon which
Malamud's work depends rather heavily, and I think I can safely comment on that. In recent years there has been wide discussion of this change in attitude, especially as an explanation for
the dramatic increase in the popularity of Jewish writers since
World War II. The best statement of this change has been made,
I think, by Sheldon Norman Grebstein in a recent essay:

> In the Western imagination the Jew had always played a special
> role as wizard, magician, possessor of secret knowledge, but never
> before, until Auschwitz and Buchenwald, had such moral authority
> been conferred upon him. From hated, feared, or ridiculed figure,
> lurking on the fringes of the culture, he was transformed into the Man
> Who Suffered, Everyman.

At the same time, there has been an increase in the moral
awareness of our society. In the postwar years we have had an
unprecedented affluence for the majority, while television has
brought it home to us as never before how many people both
here and abroad are suffering from social and economic oppres-
sion. Further, beginning with our awareness of the Holocaust—
which for us must include not only Hitler's ovens, but the fires of
Hiroshima and Nagasaki as well—and running through the fear
and persecution of McCarthyism, the shame and confusion of
Viet Nam, and, more recently, the ugly reflection of our own
suburban souls in Watergate, we have been brought, time and
again, to a terrible confrontation with ourselves.

Through the course of these confrontations, and the result-
ing anguish of self-examination, we have become more and
more aware of the possibility that what we had thought were
social and political questions are really moral, even religious

questions. Thus, what we have been led to is not only a heightened awareness of suffering, but guilt and anxiety as that awareness impinges on the satisfactions of affluence. Within this context, the Jew has evolved into a symbol of conscience—outwardly, as a function of his persecution which reached its climax in the Holocaust, and inwardly, as a function of his religious character (Jews perceived in this latter aspect as a group having its definition in religion—a religion persistently adhered to regardless of terrible consequences throughout the span of Western history). The Jew as symbol in recent literature is seen, therefore, as both provoking questions of conscience and demonstrating himself the constant spiritual trial of conscience.

It is difficult to believe that Malamud deliberately chose Jewish subjects as a result of the gain in impact that the Jewish figure has had on the American psyche. That impact as manifested in the strength of reactions to *The Assistant* and *The Magic Barrel* (as versus reactions to *The Natural* and *A New Life*) may even have come to him as a surprise. Previously, writers who had extensively employed Jewish materials, while often respected, did not usually gain a very wide audience. Instead, his choice, as indicated by his early publications, seems to have come, naturally and simply, out of his own background and the need of every writer to exorcise the painful spirits of the past. We don't know as yet the chronology of composition, but the chronology of publication suggests that during the Forties and early Fifties, Malamud developed a basic set of Jewish characterizations which, by accident or design, fit in very well with the change in American attitudes. By the time of the story "The Magic Barrel" (1954), his characters function in such a way as to say, "Take away the outside appearances of a human being, and what you have left as heart and soul is a Jew." In suggesting this, of course, he has given his Jews a common identity with mankind, a commonality he has expressed directly on several occasions in such words as, "All men are Jews except they don't know it."

The suggestion that all men underneath are "Jews" can be an appealing idea for Americans. We tend to believe in a moral or spiritual equality even more than we believe in equality under the law or equality of opportunity. Take away the badges of wealth and position—the material thrust of the American dream—and underneath every man has equal access to God and to salvation—the spiritual thrust of the American Dream. Furthermore, the discovery of the "real" person or the real nature of things beyond, behind, and within appearances or the physical exterior is by far the most pervasive theme in our moralistic literature.

For any number of historical and cultural reasons, it is fitting that Malamud has dramatized the Jew as moral doppelgänger to the American. Jews and Americans (as, of course, overlapping groups) have this characterization in common historically: they worry. Both have been thought of as prone to constant self-examination. Both tend to be moralistic and tend to see life, symbolically and allegorically, in Old Testament terms—the struggle in man between good and evil, the struggle to fulfill a prophesized destiny. There is some irony in the fact that much of the prejudice against Jews in this country came not so much from religious hostility (the cries of "You killed our Christ!" which Leslie Fiedler remembers from childhood), as from super-energetic pursuit of the American Dream. The stereotype before World War II was largely one of acquisitiveness—Jews will make a place for themselves, acquire money, goods, and status regardless of the moral cost. They became the archetypal immoral materialists. Now they have become the archetypal moralists.

This pattern becomes even more strange when we stop to consider the underpinnings of the American Dream. Calvinistic doctrine held that the accumulation of worldly wealth was a sign of God's favor (roughly, that material success was a sign of spiritual success, and wealth was a sign, therefore, of a higher status which had spiritual authority). And this doctrine, in turn, was derived from the history of Judaism, the Old Testament. The counter idea that wealth is a source of evil and can destroy character was also carried to this country within Protestantism, having for us essentially New Testament origins, and grew in strength in the Nineteenth Century largely as the result of Pastoral Romanticism (out of Rousseau and others). The most notable direct expression in American letters of this stance was, of course, Thoreau's *Walden*.

The result of the conflict between these two reactions to wealth in American culture has been an ambivalent reaction to success—in a moment Dream can turn to nightmare. Richard Cory may glitter when he walks, but while we are starving in the darkness and waiting for the night, it is Richard Cory who puts a bullet in his head. Which goes to show that while the true light may flicker, it never glitters. Andrew Carnegie may have become a cultural hero of a certain kind, but he and other "Christian" captains of industry and commerce (pious and moralistic all) were hated as "Jews."

It is odd that our ambivalence toward our own Dream has been matched by our ambivalence toward the Jew and that the two have been tied together historically—circumstances which I believe Malamud, consciously or unconsciously, has taken advantage of in his work. Our early settlers, the Puritans among others, often saw themselves as latter-day, Old Testament Jews, a chosen people acting out a new Exodus from Pharaoh-like tyrants in Europe to find a new life in the Promised Land, the New Eden. But our question from the beginning—and it is Malamud's as well—has been, what kind of new life? What kind of fresh start? Opportunity to regenerate the spirit or replenish the pocketbook?

Were we Biblical Jews of the Spirit, or historical Jews as shrewd traders and money-lenders? The two sides of the American dream have appeared to work together in our experience, by and large, as a spiritual checks and balances system. In recent decades, however, with the decline of the moral force of American Protestantism, its increasing secularization, the scale has tipped sharply toward materialism. In our search for a moral counterweight, is it any wonder that our cultural imagination has been attracted by the Jew once again? The idea of the Jew appears to us, both by virtue of the Holocaust and the formation and success of Israel, one of the few moral forces that rather than declining, has demonstrated its power and durability. Haven't we been Jews all along? And what is Israel to us but our New Eden, America, once again?

V.   Yiddish Knight and Jewish Cowboy?

One thing that seems certain to add durability to Malamud's critical life is his use of a multitude of models and sources. While critics seem intent on approaching him as a Jewish-American writer, he seems intent on baffling their intentions by mixing Christian ideas, sayings, and saints into Jewsh situations, and by referring directly and indirectly, to the works of numerous writers out of several traditions. He is, in short, a college professor and he seems determined to broaden the range of his fiction, at least in its reverberations, and to provide work for his colleagues.

As moralist and allegorist, Malamud might almost be expected to show the interest he has shown in medieval literature. But a Yiddish knight? Not quite—so far, his allusions to Arthurian Romance have been for the most part confined to the non-Jewish novel, *The Natural.* But Peter Hays in his conference presentation "Malamud's Yiddish-Accented Medieval Stories" uses one such tale of knighthood, not to demonstrate a specific source, but to suggest that the medieval has been an important influence in the background of many of Malamud's fictional motifs and methods.

Hays reviews Crétien de Troye's "Lancelot, or The Knight of the Cart" and then effects a broad comparison of situations and movements which are paralleled in Malamud's work. Malamud's protagonists are frequently involved in that mixture of heroic and anti-heroic which characterize the fortunes of Crétien's knight. Often, like this Lancelot, the Malamud character is reviled, reproached, and "cut to ribbons" in his quest for love: "Where the medieval knight went in search of glory, conquest, and approval of a beloved, Malamud's protagonists search for an authentic self and life-style, an identity worthy of commitment."

What the many similarities of movement and theme show, Hays explains, is not that Malamud has depended on Crétien de Troye, but that both writers are storytellers whose tales are grounded in the "archetypal myths behind most fictions." As literary critics, we should "pay more attention to genus, as well as species, to storytelling in general, elements, motifs, and methods which are the stock in trade of any storyteller from Homer on."

If not "a Yiddish knight, with his *payess* tucked into his beaver," can we find ourselves a cowboy with a Jewish accent? Montana Les Fiedler expresses a feeling of identity with the circumstances of *A New Life*. This is a book about that wave of migration from East to West in the early Fifties of which he, himself, was a part, a migration of "certain upwardly mobile, urban, Eastern young academics, chiefly Jews, into remote small-town State Universities, Cow Colleges, and Schools of Education." The fable in the novel is based on this touching and comic Western movement, "an account of two provincialities meeting head-on in a kind of mutual incomprehension which makes tragedy impossible, since the greatest catastrophe which can eventuate is a pratfall."

By contrast with Kesey's *One Flew Over the Cuckoo's Nest* which is a real Western, embodying the archetype of idyllic love between two males in the wilderness, Malamud's *A New Life* is a travesty Western. It is a tale about a failed Westering which typically involves the misadventures of the dude or tenderfoot who can never adjust to the ground rules of the new territory in which he finds himself. As long as S. Levin remains the absurd anti-hero of the travesty Western, Fiedler states, the *shlemiel* "on whom kids pee and nervous housewives spill tuna-fish casseroles, I love him and believe in him." But unfortunately the novel gradually changes as self-pity and self-righteousness take over, and the book becomes "what may well be the least rewarding of all American sub-genres, the Academic Novel." Because of either lack of nerve or excess of ambition—Malamud wanting to write an Art Novel rather than a Travesty—the au-

thor fails the original conception of the book and its "potentiality for becoming the first real Jewish anti-Western."

Fiedler, of course, describes the novel that he would have
written or the novel he would have Malamud write. And while
such criticism annoys authors mightily, it is probably justified
here on the basis of the author's apparent indecisiveness result-
ing in a failure of form. Writing rather close to his own experience in this novel, Malamud appears to have been guided more
by instinct and emotion than by more objective, formal considerations. Of interest within the context of the conference is
that once again in Fiedler, Malamud is charged with possible
timidity, a charge made earlier by Hassan in regard to Malamud's traditionalism and by Field in response to what he perceives as Malamud's failure to involve himself more deeply in
present Jewish concerns. Does Malamud fail to go far enough,
to plumb deep enough, to follow through with his commitments
often enough, or does he simply go a different path than we
would have him follow?

VI.   Mirror Images and Reversals

Ben Siegel's paper, "Through a Glass Darkly: Bernard Malamud's Painful Views of the Self," serves as a fitting conclusion,
since of all the papers it is the most comprehensive in its examination of the fiction itself. Siegel's focus is on Malamud's use of a
broad range of related techniques by which his characters can
see themselves, sometimes revealing their own inner nature and
sometimes obscuring or distorting it. Self-appraisal may come
from dreams, visions, or visitations, or it may come from such
refractive surfaces as those of "mirrors and windows, spectacles
and paintings, photographs and the human eye," all these serving "to confront man with his inner compulsions, passions, frustrations."

Malamud's theme is ethical or non-ethical behavior as illus-
trated by characters, "solitary non-achievers," who "never cease
probing their deepest motives and acts" and who are aided in
large part in their search by visual images which expose to them

"their most private expectations and guilts." Self-discovery is, therefore, central to Malamud's fiction. Often, the main character is able to grasp some insight into himself through an encounter with a double. Yet, just as often,

> his wanderers are too bemused by inner and external needs to see others clearly. They fail also to comprehend dream warnings issued by their intuitive or subconscious selves. Yet these internal signals prove more reliable guides than do their willed judgments. A Frank Alpine or Seymour Levin who grasps this truth seems eligible for better things. A Roy Hobbs who rejects all inner portents invites more failure and frustration.

Siegel's scrutiny of this pattern runs from early novels and stories to the later *The Tenants, Rembrandt's Hat,* and *Pictures of Fidelman.* He concludes that Malamud insists throughout his work that "no matter how pathetic or foolish, the individual can, by suffering, compassion, and self-scrutiny . . . assert his humanity." Although long and sometimes difficult to follow as an oral presentation, Siegel's paper may have more success as a written essay than any of the other papers. Certainly, it offers the most to those students interested in the specific workings of Malamud's fictional techniques and their connection to theme.

His essay is the one that perhaps best matches my own thinking about that which characterizes Malamud's central effect—his doublings, his images and visions, his hauntings. Siegel also seems to share my feeling that Malamud's basic metaphor for man's condition is that which was established relatively early in Malamud's career in the situations of the characters in *The Assistant* and *The Magic Barrel*:

> Mostly beleaguered Jews clinging to dignity and self respect, they shuffle between dark, cramped tenements and bare, depressing shops. . . . Unhappiness takes a heavy toll. Many are tiresome, self-pitying *nudniks* or pests unable to forget they are wanderers in a hostile world. Yet they never cease trying to salvage small victories from large defeats. 'Naturalized' rather than 'assimilated,' overwrought and determined to be heard, they share an inflected, idiomatic Yiddish-English and the melancholy discovery that America, the Golden Land, has not ended their exile.

Entering the New Eden does not end the exile of the spirit; change in outside circumstances alone will not work. Man takes his prisons with him, and the only way out is through "self-discovery," an expansion of the spirit, becoming more human than before.

As Siegel and many other Malamud critics have noted, the writer's most common motif is imprisonment—usually self-suffocation of the soul. When Fidelman, Harry Cohen, Albert Ganz, or Yakov Bok—or any of the other trapped or tortured characters in Malamud's fiction—is challenged by part of his soul which has been neglected to remember his heritage, it is not a narrow religious orthodoxy that he is being reminded of, but the broader and more fundamental obligation to be fully a *mensch*. The obstacles to this in Malamud's work are familiar ones to students of American literature—the prisons we build for ourselves through our selfishness and the prisons we build for others through our intolerance. The building blocks for our prison walls come out of a corrupt and perverse reservoir of values, and the mortar that ties those values together is the negative part of that mythic system we loosely refer to as the "American Dream."

Indeed, Roy Hobbs, in Malamud's first novel, *The Natural*, is so thoroughly caught up in the myth that he doesn't even see any alternatives to self-gratification, to striving to become "The Best," that is, gaining the fame, the money, and the girl from the *Playboy* centerfold that certify success. In this novel Malamud uses the "national pastime," so often employed by businessmen, Boy Scout leaders, and Little League coaches as a metaphor for American life, as precisely that—a metaphor for American life. So, here you are, kids, along with a picture of one of your heroes on every trading card, is a little dose of greed, pride, and lust to get you started.

More common in Malamud's work, and I think more effective, is a reversal of the American Dream. This reversal provides the real source of power for one of the most impressive novels of the postwar period, *The Assistant*. Here we find Frank Alpine whose vague ambition to become a glamorous desperado leads him to participate in a stupid and brutal robbery of a pitifully poor neighborhood grocery. The senseless beating of the storekeeper leads him to a crisis of conscience—Morris Bober, the grocer, *is* in fact his conscience. Bober's influence grows over Frank to such an extent that Frank eventually becomes Bober, while gradually casting out the original Frank who was after American "success" (inspired by dime novels) through robbery. As Bober, Frank ends up with long hours, little pay, and almost no chance for "advancement" while in the service of others (and only a slim chance of getting the girl). While Frank has not gained anything more, he has become something more. The difficult question the novel asks of its readers is, who among you would be willing to take the place of Frank (who has himself taken the place of Morris), letting Frank become your conscience?

⌐ Malamud's best work follows in this same direction. In general, it acts somewhat like a negative for a film documentary of the materialistic American Dream. His images are an inverse reflection of almost every major aspect of our media-supported, contemporary value system leading to "success." According to these values, youth is the ideal, and the rest of life is a struggle to remain as young as possible. In Malamud's world, young people are either callous and ignorant (like Nat Pearl in *The Assistant* or Albert Gans in "The Silver Crown") or suffering and ignorant (like Frank Alpine in *The Assistant* or Leo Finkle in "The Magic Barrel"). Since according to Malamud it is only through experience that one can learn the necessary lessons to give life true substance, his younger characters of worth are all developing characters. Rather than a falling away from youthful glamour, life is for them an upward struggle toward self-knowledge and redemption.

And woe be those Malamud characters who are caught up in the glamour of *True Romance*. For they shall suffer the betrayal of Memo, as in *The Natural,* or the rejection of an Isabella, as in "The Lady of the Lake," or the bursting of an illusion by an Olga, as in "The Girl of My Dreams," or, as in *A New Life,* be worn down into a recognition of flat-chested reality by a Pauline Gilley. And what about Leo Finkle in "The Magic Barrel"? Malamud's track record suggests that anyone who falls in love with a picture, who thinks he will redeem a prostitute, and who rushes forward to begin the job with "violins and lit candles" on the brain, is in for a few small surprises.

Our media culture insists that life is a search for the bluebird of happiness (every Silver Cloud has leather upholstery). Malamud's fiction suggests that life is a search to make necessary suffering meaningful. Iris Lemon tells the uncomprehending Roy Hobbs, "Suffering is what brings us toward happiness." When asked about suffering as a subject in his writing, Malamud sensibly replied, "I'm against it but when it occurs why waste the experience?" This is almost precisely the realization which comes to Yakov Bok during the darkest time of his terrible ordeal, as he nearly gives in to the temptation of suicide: "What do I get by dying, outside of release from pain? What have I earned if a single Jew dies because I did? Suffering I can gladly live without, I hate the taste of it, but if I must suffer, let it be for something. Let it be for Shmuel."

Our culture holds that happiness and security come from wealth and the acquisition of goods. Malamud's fiction suggests that the struggle to acquire wealth or to keep it makes us insensitive, selfish, and unloving, and that there is no joy except in loving. There are not very many wealthy people in Malamud's fiction. Perhaps one of the most notable is Mr. Fishbein in "Idiots First" whose rigid rules for giving prevent him from being charitable. More often there are ordinary people who try to hoard what little they have at some cost to their humanity. It is Albert Gans's worry over the cost of the crown in "The Silver Crown" and his worry about a possible blow to his pride if he has been bilked of his money that finally hardens his heart against his father completely. And it is Carl Schneider's callous Yankee morality and tightness that causes him to withhold the customary "fee" from the desperate former tenant in "The Key." And finally, although Harry Lesser in *The Tenants* is not wealthy, he shows the classical symptoms of the miser in protecting his manuscript and its possible completion. With artistic pride and selfish independence from the fate of others, he hardens his heart to the possible financial ruin of his landlord.

By contrast to such callous rejections of others' needs, there are scenes of deep compassion and communion, as when Breitbart tells Bober the story of his life and the two weep together. Then, there is the by now famous scene at the conclusion of "The Loan." After Kobotsky tells his story of woe and his need for a little money to finish payment for a headstone for his dead wife, the baker's wife, Bessie, refuses, countering with the story of her own afflictions. Her brother had sacrificed himself to Hitler's ovens to allow her to escape to America where she is able now, after twelve years of back-breaking labor, to make a "little living." But in her refusal of Kobotsky, she creates her own small horror. Overcome by her own misfortune, a tale she has told often, she forgets the oven in the bakery: "Screeching suddenly, she ran into the rear and with a cry wrenched open the oven door. A cloud of smoke billowed out at her. The loaves in the trays were blackened bricks— charred corpses." From these loaves come no more loaves and no fishes. The baker who has been weeping for his friend, while his wife has been weeping for herself, finds himself helpless to give the money he would like to give. All he can offer is his love and eternal regard: "Kobotsky and the baker embraced and sighed over their lost youth. They pressed mouths together and parted forever."

As further reversal of the American Dream, the physical landscape within which these themes are developed is in complete contrast to the world of *House Beautiful*. In apposition to a penthouse-suburban culture of high style, glamour, and conspicuous consumption, we find ourselves in a gray, timeless void somewhere in the inner-city, where nearly everything is old, shabby, and in need of repair. Malamud's best work shows us the human soul in conflict with itself on a stage stripped bare of cosmetics, media myths, and the junk of affluence. He cuts away, cuts away, down to the bone, through flesh and bone to essence of human need, agony, and joy. Everything is so minimal—so little is needed, and yet so little is given. Just a "little living," just a little mercy, for Christ's sake. He can tear the reader's heart out for the pity of it.

Within this scene the conflict is nearly always the religious conflict of mortification of the self—of pride, and lust, and greed—in favor of serving others. Malamud's characters, from Roy Hobbs in *The Natural* to Harry Lesser in *The Tenants,* are caught up in the prisons of who they are and how, by their passions and failures, they define themselves. While they may be literally trapped in a barren tenement apartment, a worn-out neighborhood bakery or tailor shop, an actual jail cell, or even a whorehouse, their release, which may or may not be accompanied by physical freedom, can come only through an expansion of the spirit. All of this is in direct contrast, of course, to the freedom promised us through the purchase of condominiums, recreational vehicles, or courses in self-defense or meditation.

In this regard, on the surface S. Levin in *A New Life* seems to have but exchanged one prison for another. From the trap of a stultifying childhood and a youth of drunken futility in the urban East, Levin leaps toward the wide open spaces of the West, but physically finds himself trapped once again with a wife he doesn't love, two adopted kids he doesn't like, and "other assorted headaches." But the point is that while his circumstances have not really changed that much, he has. When Gilley, his enemy, asks him why he takes on such a load, Levin answers (with one of Malamud's best lines), "Because I can, you son of a bitch." In the same way Frank Alpine can stay with the store and put Helen through school, and Yakov Bok can turn down a pardon and insist on a trial—because they have found the capacity within themselves to do so.

People can change. This may be the most important thing that Malamud has to say, and it is a profoundly religious thing to offer. And it is this power of the human spirit as demonstrated on such a desolate landscape which is the ultimate source of Malamud's own power as a contemporary American writer. That the spirit can triumph and that change is possible are, after all, the promises of the New World, America. However, there are two conflicting possibilities in the dream of change: the freedom to find one's own spiritual destiny and the freedom to chart one's own financial and social destiny. Our problem, as recorded in our literary tradition, has been that we have more often than not confused one possibility with the other—ownership with self-mastery, physical space with spiritual growth.

However, whether we move from a dank and rat-infested basement in a New York slum to the vast reaches of the Far West, or from a jail cell in Europe to a New World without kings and Cossacks, we take ourselves with us. So that in Malamud's fiction we see that our range is ultimately spiritual and moral; our freedom is expressed in the reach of our commitments to others. Malamud's world is generally a very dark, naturalistic world wherein nearly everything is determined. Such an existence can only be faced with the wry, Yiddish acceptance that if something can go wrong, it will go wrong. But there is one thing in such a world that is not totally determined, and that is the human spirit. This is the bright exception to the dark certainty of mortal and material imprisonment.

A new life is possible in the New World, but only on the inside. That is the great qualification of the American Dream, the joker in the fresh deck and the new deal. That we take ourselves with us to the territory ahead is the painful lesson brought home time after time to the Malamud character who tries to better his situation by changing his external circumstances. If we try to pretend to be other than what we are, we wind up like Henry Levin in "The Lady of the Lake," embracing "only a moonlit stone," a beautiful dream devoid of human warmth. If we depend on appearances, we will surely lose the spirit, as Manischevitz loses his angel in "Angel Levine." Susskind follows us all, wherever we may go. Beware the Last Mohican. To his questions we must answer, "Yes, I am a man. Yes, I am a Jew. Yes, I am responsible."

VIII. Ham and Eggs, Hash Browns, and a Short Stack

Since coming to Corvallis I had been waiting for breakfast. I had been dreaming of those big breakfasts that I had had years ago. I used to drive up to Oregon and then at four in the morning stop at a small diner on my way out to stand hip-deep in cold water, under a gray drizzle, steelhead fishing. Heaps of crisp hash browns and stacks of wheatcakes. I couldn't find a diner within walking distance, so on Moo Day Plus One, my wife and I went into the motel dining room and sat down, joining Ben Siegel and Leslie Field. A gray-haired maitre de seated us. The tables were covered with white linen and laid out with silver and crystal. It was a morning-after morning and everyone had his own thoughts. I sat thinking about the "Berny" Malamud people had talked about yesterday and what it must have been like for him at Oregon State. I wondered how he felt when, after years of teaching composition, he received the National Book Award. I wondered how many men and women out there somewhere in the small towns, forests, and farms of Oregon looked back fondly on their freshman English teacher, realizing that he had become famous.

The waitress came, and I ordered the biggest breakfast on the menu. When it arrived a few minutes later, it looked as good as I had hoped. All except the ham. It had a silvery-rainbow glaze on it that made me suspicious, and I turned it over with my fork to look at the other side. Siegel and Field sat silently for a moment, and then Field said, referring to my dismayed look, "So what's the harm? 'I put in my mouth once in a while, when my tongue is dry, a piece ham.' Go ahead—enjoy." I didn't eat the ham, not because I was embarrassed, or trying to be courteous. It just didn't look good to me.

IHAB HASSAN

BERNARD MALAMUD: 1976
FICTIONS WITHIN OUR FICTIONS

PROSPECTIVE

THE TASK SEEMS STRAIGHTFORWARD, almost simple: to "speak"
of Bernard Malamud's fiction, and to "situate" it on the scene
before us. But the task will seem simple only if we blink at all
our frames: I mean those transparent forms or conventions
through which we project our being. To "speak" of Malamud,
to "situate" his fiction, is to enter into a world of fictions within
and askew of many other fictions.

Consider this conference, made up of words, of deeds,
made up of the very matter of our mortality. Though death is
perhaps the last event we still dare not call a fiction, our presence here forces itself into the frame of a novel, called *A New
Life*, and a film by the same name.

> S. Levin, formerly a drunkard, after a long and tiring transcontinent-
> al journey, got off the train at Marathon, Cascadia, toward evening
> of the Last Sunday in August, 1950.

And 363 pages later:

> Two tin-hatted workmen with chain saws were in the maple tree in
> front of Humanities Hall, cutting it down limb by leafy limb, to
> make room for a heat tunnel. On the Student Union side of the
> street, Gilley was aiming a camera at the operation. When he saw
> Levin's Hudson approach he swung the camera around and snapped.
> As they drove by he tore a rectangle of paper from the back of the
> camera and waved it aloft.
> "Got your picture!"

A picture has a frame. The two passages I have read happen to enclose a story, which "takes place" in "Easchester" in "1950." The novel appeared in 1961. In 1973, I published myself a little book in which I wrote: "There is little gloss in *A New Life* (1961). Somewhat forced, somewhat secondhand in its felt life, the book centers on a faintly sour academic, S. Levin, who leaves New York City streets in search of fuller possibilities in the Far West (Oregon?)." We convene in Corvallis, Oregon, in 1976, the Bicentennial Year of America, which is the myth of myths of the New Life. Can we still believe that the task of "speaking" about Malamud and "situating" his work is straightforward?

I do not mean to appear sophistical; I only wish to say that everything we view, we view through frames. These are concealed cognitive structures, fictions. We ignore their fictive character at the risk of becoming literalists—or mistaking our lassitude for consensus. So much we can grant without giving ourselves to a French orgy (hence Apollonian?) of "deconstruction." Thus, if I modestly expose some tacit fictions of this or any other conference, it is not only because I sense that certain familiar forms—say, the academic address, the critical article, the book review—are in process of quiet reconstruction. It is also because I am somewhat uneasy with my subject and want to admit my discomforts.

Why, then, did I consent to speak about Bernard Malamud? There is, of course, the matter of an honorarium, and an occasion to hold forth in public, and a chance to visit Oregon—temptations triple. But there is also a possibility that my discomforts, which center on four queries, may not be wholly personal. The queries are:

1. What does the act of "critical assessment" now mean, given the growing disposition of criticism itself to become a kind of fiction, given its paracritical infidelity to the text?

2. If Art is one of Malamud's three constant themes, is his concept of it largely modern, rather than postmodern, and so standing from us at a certain distance?

3. And what of Malamud's second major concern, Jewish Experience? In an era of terrorism and secession, in a time of fracture, how do we perceive Jewish literature?

4. Finally, considering Malamud's steady vision of Moral Regeneration, what kind of renewal can we now expect in America—or anywhere on this very odd planet?

I will not pretend to answer these queries. But I do feel their pressure on my text, which has split, as it were, into three vertical planes: a Foreground focusing on Malamud, a Background opening on the contemporary scene, and flickering in between, a Perspective of quizzical personal views.

Who knows but that Bernard Malamud may yet receive his due through all my shifting frames!

PERSPECTIVE

I wonder: Did Malamud receive his due while he was at Oregon State? Did he give Oregon State its due? And why is Bennington not organizing a conference on Malamud?

Perhaps the problem is homage, which we all desire even if we must join the dead to get it. The Ford Foundation would not support Black Mountain College when the need was dire. Yet it has supported historians to write the story of defunct Black Mountain College.

I do not exclude myself from this blindness of time. Though I fancy myself an amateur of change, I must take credit for writing surely one of the dullest reviews of a now-famous first novel, called V.

BACKGROUND

The Contemporary Scene of Fiction.

The scene is partly in the eyes of the beholder, and the whole scene is invisible to any single beholder. Having said so little, I can then add: the scene, in any case, is a palimpsest of novelistic events, old and new, modern and postmodern, traditional and experimental, coexisting in our fictional space. What do Mailer, Bellow, Updike, Barth, Pynchon, Oates, LeGuin, and Malamud really have in common? Even their shared American language is a plurality of tongues.

This is not all: The palimpsest is in time as well as in space. The "contemporary scene of fiction" is not an instantaneous or synchronic event. How many decades back does contemporary reach? And if we consent to the banalities of literary history, defining contemporary fiction as postwar fiction (post-Hiroshima?), can we then isolate a major historical trend in that period? There is a trend, of course from "closed" to "open" forms, from "realism" to "surrealism," from "myth" to "parody," and from "ironic tragedy" to "self-ironic comedy." This trend appears evident even in the careers of individual novelists: contrast Bellow's *Dangling Man* (1944) with *Humboldt's Gift* (1975), Mailer's *The Naked and the Dead* (1948) with *Why Are We in Vietnam?* (1967), Barth's *The Floating Opera* (1956) with *Chimera* (1972), and in one short, prodigal decade, Roth's *Letting Go* (1962) with *The Breast* (1972). Moving with the times, moving the times, each author seems to become more conscious of the play of fiction, the problematic of fiction as fiction and of reality as another kind of fiction.

FOREGROUND

Malamud is not Proteus. Yet compare *The Natural* (1952), gravid with archetypes, mythic in the manner of the Forties, with *The Tenants* (1971), which confronts Black and Jew with the strident slogans of the Sixties, and offers three distinct endings. Though the changes in Malamud's style or temper are scarcely cataclysmic, they testify to his continued quickness to American culture. In this, Malamud is perhaps closer to Bellow than to Mailer or Barth. For him, "the axial lines" of existence are, if not always straight, still decently strong: life can offer, as S. Levin says, "Order, value, accomplishment, love." Human dignity is not an illusion; humanism, though in tatters, will not go abegging. Art tends toward morality, Malamud asserts in his interview with Daniel Stern in the *Paris Review* (Spring, 1975): "Morality begins with an awareness of the sanctity of one's life, hence the lives of others—even Hitler's to begin with

—the sheer privilege of being, in this miraculous cosmos, and trying to figure out why. Art, in essense, celebrates life and gives us our measure." Such celebration demands the "privileges of form," the miracles of metaphor. "I love metaphor," Malamud says. "It provides two loaves where there seems to be one. Sometimes it throws in a load of fish." The novel is thus in no imminent or future jeopardy: "It'll be dead when the penis is," he quips. (This may not be so far in the future, if some have their way.) "The human race needs the novel. We need all the experience we can get. Those who say the novel is dead can't write them."

PERSPECTIVE

I do not quote Malamud ironically. I view him as he takes the human measure with much wonder and no derision. And I remind myself that classic as Malamud seems, he is a master who advises his students to take chances, to work in uncertainty, to experiment if experiment they must: "Let the writer attempt whatever he can. There's no telling where he will come out stronger than before. Art is in life but the realm is endless," he says.

Yet I also wonder: How does Malamud manage to exclude from his fiction a crucial element of the postmodern sensibility? How does he transcend the problematic of fiction, which haunts so many contemporary novelists? Is he not finally an "historical" novelist, engaging a human reality and a universe of discourse that are not wholly of our time?

A writer writes what he must. Malamud is entirely in his right to say: "Nobody can tell a writer what can or ought to be done, or not done, in his fiction. A living death if you fall for it." But this goes for readers too, readers who are writers, and readers who do not write. The marvelous constraints of literary language never quite reach that final, that obscure, region of our freedom where our instincts take value. We are free to ask if not always to judge.

And so, brutally, I ask: Why read Malamud now? Perhaps twenty years hence or twenty years ago—but why now?

BACKGROUND

Elements of a Postmodern Sensibility.

It is probably vain to continue speaking of an avant-garde in literature. The concept itself is historical. It applies mainly to late nineteenth and early twentieth century movements, and it may no longer
provide an adequate description of literary change. (There are hints of
dissatisfaction with the concept in Renato Poggioli's *The Theory of the
Avant-Garde;* and the hints become hysterical in Hans Magnus Enzens-
berger's "The Aporias of the Avant-Garde," reprinted in Philip Rhav's
Modern Occasions.) Furthermore, as a military metaphor, the avant-
garde implies linear combat; the enemy lies ahead. But in a cybernetic
age, the world is rounded by feedback, the enemy may lie all around, and
change takes the shape of a spherical wave. Finally, what avant-garde
we can now discern seems to have turned its aggressions inward; the
enemy is mainly within. This is particularly evident in the non-verbal
arts: Vito Hannibal Acconci, a body artist, bites and punishes himself in
galleries; Chris Burden arranges to have himself shot in the arm in public; and the Viennese, Rudolph Schwarzkogler, slowly amputates his
penis (Malamud: take note) before a moving camera, and bleeds to
death. Play or pathology, there is a somber moral here. Postmodern art
seems to feed upon itself; the message of the artist has become not only
his medium but his own body as well.

Even the writer now wants to experiment with the physical book,
wants to alter the book as one mutilates the flesh, hoping thereby to transform language into the spermatic word. Thus, for instance, William Gass,
in *Willie Master's Lonesome Wife,* pretends that his book has become
woman's flesh; typography becomes pornography. But like every artist,
Gass really woos his own words best. "Imagination," he writes in capital
and crooked letters, "is its medium realized. You are your body—you do
not choose the feet you walk in—and the poet is his language." Literature, speaking in the mother tongue, may be more loving of the word
and thus more conservative than other arts. Yet even literature now bril-
liantly entertains the forms of its unmaking—the forms of its silence, ex-
haustion, self-parody, or de-creation.

It is this noisy silence, or unmaking, this periodic, and now fanatic,
will of literature to question itself radically, to return to zero in order to

begin again, that characterizes contemporary change better, I feel, than
the historical concept of the avant-garde. For implied in this change is a
vast reconstitution of the human world, implied, as Michel Foucault
would say, is a new *épistémè*, affecting all those codes by which we perceive and articulate our being in history. Self and Society, Art and Language, and even Nature, may no longer appear to us the same.

But this is hardly the place to speculate about the invisible linea-
ments of an imagined posthumanism. It is maddening enough to define
postmodernism in literature. Let me, however, attempt precisely that.
Here, much too briefly, are three features of postmodernism in American
fiction:

1. FANTASY. Novels are made of words, and words are microfic-
tions, writers nowadays insist, though it seems obvious. Borges with his
gnostic enigmas and fabled labyrinths; Beckett with his Cartesian anti-
epics, rabble in the head droning their endless monologues; Nabokov
with his mirrored fictions, or transparent boxes within boxes, trying to
capture the pale radiance of eternity—all three point the way to sundry
American "surrealists" (Burroughs, Hawkes, Wurlitzer), "romancers"
(Vonnegut, Brautigan, Purdy), "ludic fabulists" (Coover, Matthews),
"surfictionists" (Federman, Sukenick, Katz), "patarealists" (Reed),
"dreck geometers" (Barthelme), "residents of ultimacy" (Barth), "true
lie-minded men" (Gass), and plain geniuses (Pynchon). Forgive the
labels; whatever these authors may be, they are neither naturalists nor
realists in the narrower acceptance of such terms. They are authors of
fantasy.

2. PLAY, PARODY, AND SELF-REFLECTION. Unlike their predeces-
sors, postmodern writers pretend not to "create a world" (of course they
do); they pretend to plagiarize or play. Lexical equilibrists, player kings,
Bossa Nova dancers, masters of game theory, programmers of the logos,
their verbal activity strives for a certain lightness. This lightness does
not only make for levity, slapstick, absurdism, or dark gray humor. Far
more perilously, it both accepts and tries to resist that "weightlessness of
all things," as Nietzsche put it, which results from the "death of God"
and the dissolution of values. Conscious of their game at the edge of nihilism, hyperconscious even ("cosmopsis," Barth says, is the postmodern
malady), they become supreme parodists. They parody popular forms:

the Detective Story (*An American Dream*), The Western (*Little Big Man*), Science Fiction (*Cat's Cradle*), the Historical Novel (*The Sot-Weed Factor*), Pornography (*Lolita*), and the Sentimental Idyll (*Trout Fishing in America*). In the end, they are their own best parodists, entertaining themselves in cracked mirrors. "Another story about a writer writing a story!" writes Barth in a story in *Lost in the Funhouse*. ". . . who doesn't prefer art that at least overtly imitates something other than its own processes?" In another story, the reflexive process becomes explicitly autoerotic. The author forces the reader to become a voyeur of the author's fictive masturbations. Once again, the body becomes both medium and message.

3. THE SELF-UNMAKING OF LITERATURE (OR RADICAL IRONY). Play leads to parody and reflexiveness, the latter leads to self-unmaking or autodestruction, and we are back where we began. But the "bad conscience" of postmodern Art before Life, and its complex ludic "resentment" (again, the terms are Nietzsche's), are felt by the novelist not only as an aesthetic, ethical, or political dilemma; they are perceived by him as an epistemological perplexity and an ontological conundrum as well. The extreme case is made by Raymond Federman when he says in *Surfiction*: "Thus, the primary purpose of fiction will be to unmask its own fictionality, to expose the metaphor of its own fraudulence, and not pretend any longer to pass for reality, for truth, or for beauty." The case is made even more extremely, which is to say figuratively, by Ronald Sukenick in *The Death of the Novel and Other Stories*: "The contemporary writer . . . is forced to start from scratch: Reality doesn't exist, time doesn't exist, personality doesn't exist. God was the omniscient author, but he died [Nietzsche again]; now no one knows the plot. . . . In view of these annihilations, it should be no surprise that literature, also, does not exist—how could it?" Thomas Pynchon, who creates supreme factifictions of our annihilations or entropies, with a paranoia sweeping heroically through mind, matter, and history, is also haunted by the act of metaphor: "a thrust at truth and a lie." Behind the hieroglyphs of concealed meaning—what? Pynchon remembers his Wittgenstein: "The world is everything that is the case," and again: "Of that which one can not speak, one must be silent."

So much for this particular strain of the postmodern sensibility, an eccentric strain perhaps, yet highly visible, and audibly silent.

FOREGROUND

I return to Malamud in my discontinuous attempt to place his fiction within other fictions of the age. "An ironic humor would seem to be his mother tongue," Daniel Stern says of him. Indeed, Malamud puts himself at an ironic distance from all the happenings and unmakings of postmodern literature. For him, comedy is reserve, "the guise of invention," and irony itself lives naturally in the cadences of human speech, in the densities of quotidian perception. The comedy is not absurd, the irony not radical. Art can still take and give the human measure of things though artists themselves may be obstructed. And therein lies "an interesting ambiguity," Malamud thinks: "the force of the creative versus the paralysis caused by the insults, the confusions of life."

This interesting ambiguity frames *Pictures of Fidelman* (1969). A self-confessed failure as a painter, Fidelman refuses the Yeatsian choice, "perfection of the life, or of the work"—he wants both, has neither. Fidelman ends, however, buggered with kindness by a Venetian glass blower, seeking the imperfections of human love. "In America, he worked as a craftsman in glass and loved men and women." In the first story, "The Last of the Mohicans," Malamud had made grotesquely clear the triple failure of his hero: as painter, as art critic, and as *mensch*. The ghostly refugee, Susskind, destroys Fidelman's manuscript on Giotto. "The words were there but the spirit was missing," Susskind cries before he disappears, "light as the wind in his marvelous knickers, green coattails flying . . . ." And in the last story, it is the same story over again: Beppo, the Venetian glass worker, slashes and burns Fidelman's poor pictures. "It's for your own sake," Beppo hoarsely says. "Show who's master of your fate—bad art or you." The pathos of the failed artist, his postures and impostures, his ribald cowardice, his sudden appeals to mercy—all these Malamud wryly exposes.

But Malamud seems also intent on revealing the outlandish hues of eroticism, coloring all the portraits of Fidelman. In

"Still Life," for instance, Fidelman accidentally seduces the love-
ly Annamaria by assuming a priest's garb. Divesting himself of
his cassock, though with his biretta on, "Pumping slowly, he
nailed her to her cross." Fidelman's moments of erotic glory,
however, are few; more often, he moves at the sad or seedy edge
of sex. In "Naked Nude," he cleans the latrines of an Italian
whorehouse while forging a Titian nude; in "A Pimp's Revenge," he turns procurer to complete a "masterpiece," which
he only botches. The shames of Art and Love seem always com-
plicit in the same bitter and antic gesture:

> While Scarpio is out talking to the guard, the copyist hastily sketches
> the Venus of Titian, and with a Leica Angelo has given him for the
> purpose, takes several new color shots. Afterwards, he approaches
> the picture and kisses the lady's hands, thighs, and breasts, but as he
> murmurs, "I love you," a guard strikes him hard on the head with both
> fists.

Setting out to paint a portrait of "Mother and Son," with a snap-
shot of his sister, Bessie, to substitute for his mother's dead face,
setting out, that is, to paint himself in his mother's/sister's in-
cestuous arms, he ends by painting himself with the nineteen-
year-old prostitute, Esmeralda:

> . . . the picture was, one day, done. It assumed a completion: this
> woman and man together, prostitute and procurer. She was a girl
> with fear in both black eyes, a vulnerable if stately neck, and a steely
> small mouth; he was a boy with tight insides, on the verge of crying.
> The presence of each protected the other. A Holy Sacrament.

But Fidelman, of course, must finally ruin the picture:

> When Esmeralda pulled open the curtain and saw the mess, moan-
> ing, she came at him with the bread knife. "Murderer!"
> F. twisted it out of her grasp, and in anguish lifted the blade into his
> gut.
>   "This serves me right."
>   "A moral act," Ludovico agreed.

PERSPECTIVE

I ask myself: Is the focus of Pictures of Fidelman *too soft—or rather too sharp? The "snap of comedy; the reserved comic presence—that beautiful distancing; the funny with sad; the surprise of surprise," as Malamud puts it, may tend to over-define his vision.*

A more serious objection: In making Fidelman a failed artist, Malamud has not really made the case against Art, has not explored the Morality of Art, at all. In fact, he has exempted himself as novelist from these perils and shames that the true artist may also suffer.

Think of Death in Venice, The Counterfeiters, A Hunger Artist; *think again of* Pictures of Fidelman. *Is the discrepancy there one of "literary stature," that trick of time which magnifies in pious eyes the measure of "greatness"? Or is it rather that Mann, Gide, and Kafka were engaged in a far more subversive, even sinister enterprise? By calling into doubt the Morality of Art, by exposing its corruptions, did they prevision the postmodern experiment—which Malamud has chosen to avoid?*

FOREGROUND

Consider now *The Tenants*. Once again, art is the focus in this story of interracial sex and struggle. Lesser, a Jew, and Spearmint, a Black, monomaniacs of different kinds, haunt a tenement to type their art and soul into the night. Levenspiel, ailing and greedy landlord, perhaps more human than either, cries out: "Art my ass, in this world it's heart that counts." Art and soul and heart—and ass. There are also two women, Irene and Mary, one a Jew, the other a Black, who maintain the mirror symmetry of the pattern. Yet in the end, of course, each artist lives with his nausea alone.

The question is: Which of the three endings of the novel? In one imagined version, the world ends (after twenty-three pages only) with fire:

... whining fire and boiling shadows rush up the smelly stairs. With-in the walls lit cockroaches fly up, each minutely screaming. Nobody say no, so the fire surges its inevitable way upwards and with a con-vulsive roar flings open Lesser's door.

In another dreamt version, the novel ends with a double hymen-eal to miscegenation: Lesser marries Mary, Spearmint, Irene:

Irene asks Lesser, as they dance a last dance together, "How do you account for this, Harry?"
"It's something I imagined, like an act of love, the end of my book, if I dared."
"You're not so smart," says Irene.

And in the third and "real" version—real only because it con-cludes the book in our hand called *The Tenants*—Lesser and Spearmint, each feeling the anguish of the other, murder one an-other. The last words are those of the landlord:

Mercy, the both of you, for Christ's sake, Levenspiel cries. Hab rachmones, I beg you. Mercy on me. Mercy mercy mercy mercy mercy mercy mercy mercy mercy [113 times].

Thus Malamud terminates his novel with fire, marriage, or mercy. Elliptic in poetry, astringent in humor, compassionate always, shifting from first to third person perception, from narra-tive to dialogue to reverie, this superbly written book is true both to its author's vision and to his sense of the altered times.

But does the novel also show an altered sense of the prob-lematic of art? On a certain level, the dialogue of Lesser and Spearmint may be seen as a conflict not only between two races, two histories, and two conceptions of life, but also between two stereotypes of Art. As men, Lesser and Spearmint need one another, repel each other, and together suffer. As emblems, the Jew stands for responsible Form, the Black for felt Experience. It is, of course, the latter who makes the scathing case against art:

Think of this sacred cathedral we're in, Willie, with lilting bong-ing iron bell. I mean this flower-massed, rose-clustered, floating is-land. I guess what I mean is what about art?
Don't talk flippy. I worry about it gives me cramps in my mother-fuckn liver. Don't say that dirty word.

Art is the glory and only a shmuck thinks otherwise.

Lesser, don't bug me with that Jew-word. Don't work your roots on me. I know what you talkin about, don't think I don't. I know you tryin to steal my manhood. I don't go for that circumcise shmuck stuff.

And again, later:

"If we're talking about art, form demands its rights, or there's no order and maybe no meaning. What else there isn't I think you know."

"Art can kiss my juicy ass. You want to know what's really art? *I* am art. Willie Spearmint, *black man*. My form is *myself*."

Yet Willie also approves of Keats, "a fine dude," and agrees with Coleridge that "Nothing can permanently please which does not contain in itself the reason why it is so and not otherwise." Willie's case against the ambiguity of art is thus itself ambiguous; to revolution he commits himself only verbally. In a sense, Irene quietly makes a more devastating case against art. Although she is herself, as a failed actress, attracted to artists, she uses one writer, Lesser, to leave another, Spearmint. Exasperated by the monomania of both, she asks Lesser at one point: "What sort of life is that for me? Why don't you fuck your book and save time all around?" In the end, or rather, in *one* end, Irene realizes that no book is as important as she is, and simply leaves for San Francisco.

As for Lesser, this is what he thinks:

With or without her he has to finish, create love in language and see where it takes him, yes or no. That's the secret, you follow the words. Maybe this man in the book will learn where it's at and so will Lesser. Although if you have to make a journey to track love down maybe you're lost to begin with. No journey will help.

The last part partly undercuts the first. Even monomaniacal Lesser, to whom Malamud refers simply as "the writer," can not resolve the paradoxes of his literary life. Author of one very good novel, he is also the author of one very bad. He believes and again disbelieves in salvation through Art. Lesser knows that each book he writes nudges him closer to death; and he knows as well that writing is his sole wager on immortality. A maker of fictions, he, more than anyone else in the book, wants to avoid mendacity.

I say "the book"—which book? The one Malamud has written? The one each of us reads? The one that the character called Lesser is writing? Or the one that the nameless writer, in the novel that Lesser is writing, is also trying to write? About this last, a fiction within a fiction within a fiction, Malamud writes:

> Anyway, this writer sets out to write a novel about someone he conceives to be not he yet himself. He thinks he can teach himself to love in a manner befitting an old ideal. He has resisted this idea for years; it's a chancy business and may not pay off. Still, if during the course of three books he had written himself into more courage, why not love? He will learn through some miracle of transformation as he writes, betrayal as well as bounty, perhaps a kind of suffering. What it may come to in the end, despite the writer's doubts, is that he invents this character in his book who will in a sense love for him; and in a sense love him; which is perhaps to say, since words rise and fall in all directions, that Lesser's writer in his book, in creating love as best he can, if he brings it off in imagination will extend self and spirit; and so with good fortune may love his real girl as he would like to love her, and whoever else in a mad world is human. Around this tragic theme the story turns.

Is Malamud then showing the face of Love in endless mirrors? Is he insisting on the Book as our Last Hero? Has he become enamored, like Echo, with the postmodern Narcissus? I much doubt it. As the title story in *Rembrandt's Hat* (1973) indicates, the artist *manqué* continues to wear his floppy emblem, his aura, "like a crown of failure and hope." In bad times, the insults and confusions to which he submits may exacerbate his condition, but the conception of Art itself, in triumph or tribulation, remains unchanged. And it is always the partial, or insufficient artist fumbling and stumbling toward his vocation, who presents, in Malamud's own idiom, the "soft impeachment" of Art. There is neither nihilism in Malamud's vision nor radical revision of the nature of human desire and its representations in the arts.

PERSPECTIVE

Often I think: Has postmodernism itself not failed in its representations of human desire? Has it really taken us very far beyond modernism? How many of us clench our teeth and brace our legs, as we plunge with the latest anti-novelist in his verbal toboggan, only to discover that our end is no farther or deeper or brighter than our beginning?

Certainly, there are limits to Malamud's stubborn, ironic art. For irony is less the "mother tongue," as Stern says, than the father's conscience of incongruity; irony structures too much both feeling and form in Malamud's fiction. But I am not certain that the limits of Malamud, sharp as they are in my own eyes, will finally prove less liminary of our exhaustions than, say, the work of John Barth.

There is a question here larger than our conception of Art. That wrecker's ball in The Tenants *means to bring down your house and mine. Perhaps the house of Western civilization is already cracking if not crumbling down. Can the ironic conscience of the Jew help shore up these ruins?*

BACKGROUND

Jewish Literature.

The time of literary history is neither existential nor sidereal time; it may be closer to the time of our most fastidious fashions. Does it not seem at least a century ago that the names of Henry Roth and Daniel Fuchs and Nathanael West began to ring in our consciousness, that Delmore Schwartz and Leslie Fiedler put forth a brilliant and combative claim for a new Jewish literature in America, that Saul Bellow and Bernard Malamud, preceding countless others, articulated that literature and gave it a permanent place in history? "In Bernard Malamud," someone wrote in *Radical Innocence* in 1961, "we find further testimony that the urban Jewish writer, like the Southern novelist, has emerged from the tragic underground of culture as a true spokesman of mid-century America." How quaint this now sounds—and at the same time how obvious, almost jejune.

There is no longer much doubt that Jewish fiction has expanded the frontiers of the American imagination, but doubt persists concerning the definition of a Jewish novel. For what *in literature* determines a Jew? Is it his sense of exile and history, his conscience, his knowledge of pain, his wry jokes, the cadences of his Yiddish speech, his immigrant experience, his character which may be part *schlimazel* and part *schlemiel,* his intricate family romances, his Zionism, his religion, his symbolic role as both scapegoat and savior, or simply his name? On such questions critics naturally cannot agree. There are those, like Robert Alter, who believe that the Jew in literature is a moral abstraction. Others, like Norman Podhoretz, think that he is the creation or fantasy of a particular author. But there are also critics who may agree with Marigold Johnson when she says in *The New Republic:*

> There are more Jews in New York than in all Israel; over 50 per cent of bookbuyers in America are Jewish. Such statistics are relevant to Malamud—not necessarily as a factor in his winning both the National Book Award and the Pulitzer, but because they mean he can take a lot for granted. He can write in the knowledge of a shared cultural idiom, play about with Yiddish shorthand imagery—above all, he knows he can tap that inexhaustible preoccupation with the conflicts and anxieties of being Jewish, and still speak with the voice of the assimilated man who has chosen to be an outsider.

I do not know how accurate this cultural perception really is. But as we read and reread Malamud today, the issue seems to me to have become subtly different. The issue has come to this: Has our attitude toward the Jew as literary symbol or archetype changed in the last two decades?

PERSPECTIVE

In 1958, Norman Podhoretz wrote: "To Malamud, the Jew is humanity seen under the twin aspects of suffering and moral aspiration. Therefore any man who suffers greatly and who also longs to be better than he is can be called a Jew." As it applies to Malamud, this statement seems to me unexceptionable. Yet this same statement raises in my mind questions which, troublesome or distasteful as they may seem, I can not ignore. Do Jews now suffer more than certain people, say, in Chad,

Brazil, or Bangladesh? Or is the element of moral aspiration in these latter people still too inchoate and remote from us to possess our imagination? In other words, can a work of the "Third World" have the impact of Wiesel's play, Zalmen, or the Madness of God? Is Fanon's Wretched of the Earth such a work? And turning to the Middle East, has the situation there become so full of ambiguities, ambiguities of power and of verity, so as to challenge our pieties and absolutes? Is Edward Said correct, for instance, when he says that "any individual mention of Palestine can be construed as a victory against the system" of censorship which prevails in our "open" American society? And how can one begin to deal with the emotional or political explosiveness of Chomsky's opinion, in Peace in the Middle East? that "the Nazi massacre, though unforgettable in its horror, no longer determines the choice of action [in the Middle East]? Rather, it is the living death of the refugee camps and the steady drift towards further misery yet to come that set the terms for policy." Finally, though there seems to be no end in sight to our international miseries, how are we to understand the recent, self-serving censure of Israel in the United Nations, understand it beyond partisan vindication or outrage?

I wonder and perhaps wander too far.

Yet I have not forgotten the statement of Podhoretz. The literary questions, you may recall, were these: how do we nowadays perceive Malamud's symbolic Jews? Has contemporary experience altered subliminally our relation to these symbols? Can the great archetypes—Isis, Kali, Christ, Prometheus, the Wandering Jew, to name only a few—ever really shift or change?

We owe allegiance, I think, to both myth and history, archetype and neotype, permanence and process. We could not live without that doubleness of time moving through our veins. Let us then freely admit it: the novel we read is and is not the same novel we read twenty years ago, and Malamud's "Jew" belongs as much to history as Morris Bober or Yakov Bok, and as much to myth as Roy Hobbs or Frank Alpine, though all finally belong to literature.

FOREGROUND

Asked "Are you a Jewish writer?", Malamud asked back: "What is the question asking?" He then went on to answer: "I'm an American, I'm a Jew, and I write for all men. A novelist has to or he's built himself a cage. I write about Jews, when I write about Jews, because they set my imagination going. I know something about their history, the quality of their experience and belief, and of their literature, though not as much as I would like. Like many writers I'm influenced by the Bible, both Testaments. . . . As a writer, I've been influenced by Hawthorne, James, Mark Twain, Hemingway, more than I have been by Sholem Aleichem and I. L. Peretz, whom I read with pleasure." Granted: an author may sometimes deceive himself or others about his work, and he may not be a shrewder critic of it than his shrewdest reader. Yet in this particular admission Malamud confirms the impression his work freely gives.

The impression is of an imagination working through small, quotidian events, through human quirks and the quiddities of history, through the confined places of the spirit, through the entrapments of art or money or sex or guilt or race—pressing always toward liberation into some universal human space. Critics have noted the motif of the prison in Malamud's fiction. He acknowledges it, "a metaphor for the dilemma of all men: necessity, whose bars we look through and try not to see . . ."; but he acknowledges it only to begin again that ceaseless effort "to transcend the self-extend one's realm of freedom." This guarded effort of renewal, this qualified transcendence, identify the primary movement in *The Assistant* (1957) and *The Fixer* (1966).

The Assistant, I believe, will prove a classic not only of Jewish but of American literature. Set in a milieu of immigrant shopkeepers and minority groups, the novel transforms downbeat city streets into some drab version of pastoral, into an exigent myth of renascence. Its luminous metaphors light the dismal store of the Bobers; its clear rhythms speak, beneath the inflections of Jewish speech, of universal human responsibility;

its dramatic ironies seem to come to rest, beyond the failures of love, knowledge, or the American Dream, in a bleak image of regeneration. Or is there regeneration? Frank Alpine, orphan, part thug and rapist, part ghostly assistant, dreams of St. Francis, loves Helen, and becomes a Jew. The miracle of the rose—plucked from a garbage can, tossed in the air, wood becomes flower. Frank, in brown rags and dancing out of the woods of the mind, gives it to Helen: "Little sister, here is your little sister the rose." But in reality, the sacrament becomes a "pain between his legs." The mystic, the lover, the sufferer are of one narrow imagination compact. But who can answer Helen Bober when she says of her father, and perhaps indirectly of Frank: "He could, with a little more courage, have been more than he was"?

Frank Alpine, I suggest, more than any character in Malamud's fiction, represents the qualified effort of human transcendence, and it is no accident that he is born a Christian. How bitterly qualified this effort really is, how much hope informs it, remains for every reader to determine. Yet collectively, as citizens of this qualified American Bicentennial, as inhabitants of "spaceship earth," how much does Frank Alpine offer us, how much does Malamud at his best?

PERSPECTIVE

How much does Malamud offer us at his best? How much do I?

A little cribbed in my praise, a little crabby in my censure, I am compelled to ask why my admiration of Malamud is not more fluent, and my criticism of him more candid. Perhaps it is because I no longer feel that a human intelligence ought to discipline itself by the fictions of another without creating its own answerable fictions. Or perhaps it is because I sense that in the mediated literary encounter between Malamud and myself, there is finally a knot of resistance, which leaves me respectful—yet eager to spin free!

I met Bernard Malamud only once, in the New York apart-
ment of a friend, Daniel Stern. It was a brief, pleasant, and cour-
teous meeting. Malamud asked me how I liked Mr. Sammler's
Planet, *which had just appeared. I answered that I had not yet*
read it. When I later read Bellow's novel, and did not like it very
much—certainly not as much as Herzog *or even* Humboldt's Gift
—I realized that Malamud's simple query could also serve as a
test of my attitude toward his own fiction—a test, if you wish, of
the tilt of my own temperament.

At the Sterns' I also met Elie Wiesel on several occasions,
with whom I felt an immediate personal and even theological
affinity. Why then have I never written about Wiesel, or Stern
for that matter? What does it really mean to write about another
living being? Is not such writing always a kind of framing? Or
is there a way to write about "another," a living yet absent "oth-
er," knowing all that we ought to know about ourselves?

Such questions echo through a critic's language even after
he turns paracritic.

BACKGROUND

The Novel and the Echo of the Universe.

The Israeli writer, Amos Oz, recently said: "With the exception of
Saul Bellow, I'm not terribly happy with the Jewish American novelists.
The others are too wise, their characters exchange punchlines instead of
talking to each other, their books are just clever sociology. They don't
have the echo of the universe, you don't see the stars in their writing." The
novels of Bernard Malamud are scarcely "clever sociology," though in their
most ambitious moments they do encompass American, indeed Western,
civilization within their comic vision. But few readers, I suspect, would
claim to hear in them "the echo of the universe."

That echo is sometimes heard in Mailer, in Bellow when his crotchi-
ness allows it, and lately in Pynchon. And in whom else? The question
stings our sense of the present and future adequacy of the novel. In South
America a remarkable fiction has been in the making for over three decades: Borges' *Fictions*, Cortazar's *Hopscotch*, Asturia's *The Mulatto and
Mister Fly*, Rosa's *The Devil to Pay in the Back Lands*, Fuentes's *A*

Change of Skin, and above all Marquez's *A Hundred Years of Solitude,* give a sense of the range, power, and complexity of that fiction. Perhaps it is only in South America or in Africa, if ever the baleful constraints of politics permit it, that a novel at once epic and experimental, full of cosmic wonder and human particularity, can still find articulation. Perhaps, and again perhaps; I remain skeptical.

Meantime, is it closing time in the West? Malamud himself is not reassuring. "My nature is optimistic, but not the evidence—" he says, "population, misery, famine, politics of desperation, the proliferation of the atom bomb. My Lai, one minute after Hiroshima in history, was ordained. We're going through long, involved, transformations of world society . . . ." Malamud is not reassuring—how could he be?—and about the novel he is elusive—how could he not be? Asked: "What does one write novels about nowadays?" he replies: "Whatever wants to be written."

Is it closing time for the Novel?

RETROSPECTIVE

I came to "speak" about Malamud, and to "situate" his fiction within our fictions.

Let it then be simply said: Bernard Malamud is among our finest writers. From his witching sense of the first sentence, through all his dramatic doublings and reversals, to his final ironic catharsis, there is an integrity of moral and artistic purpose that grips us mercilessly in the name of . . . mercy? And sometimes, as in the end of "The Magic Barrel," we are left at the edge of a true human mystery.

There is no great profit in comparing Malamud with other writers Jewish in name or literary persuasion. Nor is there great benefit in forcing Malamud to fit such categories as modernism or postmodernism, which may finally satisfy our need for taxonomy more than art. But there is also no authentic way to consider Malamud's fiction without reference to those urgencies and distractions that frame our being and challenge the being of Art.

I do not know, though once I thought I did, if it is closing time for the novel. Yet as I look farther into time, I know that I must hope for a change not only in the modes of artistic representation but also in the nature of human desire itself.

I do not know if it is closing time in the West. But as I struggle against every intimation of decadence in the present, I sense that the far future belongs not to the East nor to the West, not to the North nor to the South, perhaps not even to the whole earth, but to immensities still locked within us, of which America, even on this ambiguous anniversary of its abstract conception, may serve as metaphor.

Yet even America no longer seems large enough as metaphor. In a cosmic frame, may not the Wandering Jew represent the human race itself, born in exile, chosen to consciousness, wandering through the intergalactic night, carrying its own enigma to the farthest stars?

W. J. Handy

THE MALAMUD HERO: A QUEST FOR EXISTENCE

On the surface, Malamud's three major novels, *A New Life* (1961), *The Assistant* (1957), and *The Fixer* (1966), have much in common with the novels of the naturalist writers, novels which portray their protagonists engaged in a struggle with the forces of their cultural and physical environments and ultimately victimized by those forces. Yet neither Sy Levin of *A New Life*, nor Frank Alpine of *The Assistant*, nor Yakov Bok of *The Fixer*, can be regarded finally as a victim, as, for example, Dreiser's George Hurstwood or Clyde Griffiths are victims. Malamud himself commented on the question in a 1964 interview in the *National Observer*:

> A bad reading of my work would indicate that I'm writing about losers. That would be a very bad reading. One of my most important themes is a man's hidden strength. I am very much interested in the resources of the spirit, the strength people don't know they have until they are confronted with a crisis.

A comparison of the respective visions of man's existence held by the two writers is instructive. Both Dreiser and Malamud see human existence as characterized by struggle and suffering, and both reveal a deep sense of sympathetic understanding for what it means to carry out a human existence. But Dreiser's naturalistic focus leaves no possibility for considering man as anything more than an object among objects. Every protagonist in Dreiser's fiction is portrayed as incessantly acted upon by the forces of environment and ultimately victimized by those forces. Dreiser's concept of man, as that concept determines the values of each of his major characters, is singularly consistent throughout his work. For all of Dreiser's characters the dominant consideration in life is material success and its accompanying rewards. What one could become in a world dominated by men of wealth and power, by men schooled and skilled as opportunists, what one could become in such a world directed the plans and hopes and actions of each of the novel's central figures. Ultimately Dreiser's vision of man is pessimistic. He wrote out of the unhappy conviction that man is caught in a mechanistic and biological existence where even one's hopes and desires are determined by environment and happenstance. Yet it must be emphasized that Dreiser wrote also out the conviction that sympathetic understanding of man's lot is at least one discernable value, if, indeed, the only value.

Malamud's vision, on the other hand, is not limited to man's existence in a naturalistic world. His characters are indeed victimized by the forces of their cultural environment. But the Morris Bober or Sy Levin or Frank Alpine or Yakov Bok whose suffering has meant a discovery of new limits to what it means to be a human being can hardly be regarded as pathetic victims as is the case with Dreiser's Hurstwood or Carrie, or Clyde Griffiths.

The profound difference between the two writers lies in their respective visions of the worlds which their characters live in. Characteristically the novel presents a world. One remembers the emphasis placed on the concept of "world" as an all-embracing differentia of the novel by Rene Wellek and Austin Warren in their authoritative *Theory of Literature* in 1942:

> This world or *kosmos* of a novelist—this pattern or structure or organism, which includes plot, characters, setting, world-view, tone— is what we must scrutinize when we attempt to compare a novel with life or to judge, ethically or socially, a novelist's work.

The aesthetics of fiction have done little in the last 25 years to elaborate Wellek and Warren's emphasis on "world" as fiction's differentia, perhaps because what was understood by the "world" of fiction was quite clearly either the world of place, i.e., Dreiser's or Bellow's Chicago or Malamud's Brooklyn, Czarist Russia, or the American Northwest; or the world of consciousness, i.e., the mind of Joyce's Leopold Bloom or Faulkner's Quentin Compson.

Malamud's vision of human existence is much broader, much more inclusive than Dreiser's. For Malamud, man lives not only in the naturalistic world where the strongest motivating force is survival and where only the fittest survive. For Malamud, man lives also in the world of human relationships, the world of interpersonal relationships which the existentialist psychoanalyst Ludwig Binswanger calls "Mit-welt," literally "with-world." The motivating force here has nothing to do with survival; rather, it has to do with that unique reality we call relationship—that reality which is the central focus, for example, of Martin Buber in his celebrated *I and Thou*. And further, Malamud's characters are characteristically reflective, each possessing the desire and the innate capacity for conscious awareness of his existence. Binswanger sees self-awareness as an ontologically distinct reality or world, one which he terms "Eigenwelt" or one's own world.

The profound difference, then, between Dreiser's and Malamud's vision of human existence is evident. Dreiser presents his characters as living in one world, the only world he envisioned, the naturalistic world. Dreiser's pronouncements in his autobiographical essay, "What I Believe" leave no doubt about the scope and limitation of his vision of man's existence:

> As for myself, I really view myself as an atom in a greater machine, just as is the cell in the greater body of which it finds itself a part. But as for myself being a free and independent mechanism with spirit of its own? Nonsense! Science knows nothing of a soul or spirit.

As for the world of human relationships being a reality apart from the naturalistic world, Dreiser flatly rejects the possibility:

> And when you pass into the realms of animals and vegetables—of whom man, by reason of a built-up process of offense, and defense, is supposed to be the overlord—what other incentive or incentives do you find there? Love? For the propagation of the species, the progeny of the individual—yes. But for anything other than the progeny of the individuals of the species as against the welfare of the individuals and the progeny of all other species? No.

What I wish to suggest is that there is a characteristic pattern in Malamud's presentation of the "world" or "worlds" of his novels. Each of his protagonists is placed squarely in the naturalistic world at the outset, and for each the process of extricating himself from what he discovers is a meaningless existence becomes a quest for a new life—however vaguely realized in its initial conception.

The pattern is reminiscent of Camus' well-known image of man's awakening in his philosophical essays, *The Myth of Sisyphus*:

> It happens that the stage sets collapse. Rising, streetcar, four hours in the office or the factory, meal, streetcar, four hours of work, meal, sleep, and Monday Tuesday Wednesday Thursday Friday and Saturday according to the same rhythm—this path is easily followed most of the time. But one day the "why" arises and everything begins in that weariness tinged with amazement. 'Begins'—this is important. Weariness comes at the end of the acts of a mechanical life, but at the same time it inaugurates the impulse of consciousness . . . For everything begins with consciousness and nothing is worth anything except through it.

The point is that each of Malamud's protagonists in *A New Life, The Assistant* and *The Fixer* experiences just such an awakening to the possibility of a fuller existence than the one he has been living and that that awakening begins a quest for existence, one which comprises the dramatic struggle central to each novel.

In *A New Life* Sy Levin, introduced in the opening lines as "formerly a drunkard," is presented as having experienced the characteristic Malamud protagonist's awakening to the possibility of a new existence at some period before his arrival at his new teaching post. That is, the decision to find a new life in the Northwest has already been made, and the decision to find a new existence has been deeply experienced. In an early conversation with Pauline Gilley, his new chairman's wife, he somewhat timidly tries to reply to her questions about the change in his life:

> "Have you been to many places?"
> "The opposite is true."

Later,

> He went on although advising himself not to. "My life, if I may say, has been without much purpose to speak of. Some blame the times for that, I blame myself. The times are bad but I've decided I'll have no other."

Two significant themes are introduced in this early dialogue, themes that suggest Malamud's pattern in establishing the dramatic situation that confronts each of his protagonists once the "awakening" experience has occurred. The first is the realization that his "life has been without much purpose," a realization that Camus so dramatically establishes as the starting point for the possibility of a new existence. The second is the protagonist's acceptance of the conditions—that although "the times are bad," he "will have no other."

In a later meeting with Pauline Gilley, the intimate encounter in the forest, Levin is impelled to reveal to her something of his inmost self by recounting the experience of his awakening from a "life without much purpose":

> For two years I lived in self-hatred, willing to part with life. I won't tell you what I had come to. But one morning in somebody's filthy cellar, I awoke under burlap bags and saw my rotting shoes on a broken chair. They were lit in dim sunlight from a shaft or window. I stared at the chair, it looked like a painting, a thing with value of its own. I squeezed what was left of my brain to understand why this should move me so deeply, why I was crying. Then I thought, Levin, if you were dead, there would be no light on your shoes in this cellar. I came to believe what I have often wanted to, that life is holy.

But the awakening to the possibility of a new life in each of Malamud's protagonists is presented as merely the beginning of the quest. In *A New Life*, Sy Levin's struggle is epitomized in his further explanation to Pauline:

> That was the end of my drinking though not of unhappiness. Just when I thought I had discovered what would save me—when I believed it—my senses seemed to die, as though self-redemption wasn't possible because of what I was—my emptiness the sign of my worth. I denied the self for having denied life. I managed to get and hold onto a little job but as a person I was nothing. People speak of emptiness but it was a terrifying fullness, the soul has gas. It isn't exactly apathy, you have feeling but it's buried six feet. I couldn't respond to

experience, the thought of love was unbearable. It was my largest and most hopeless loss of self before death. . . . One Sunday night after a not otherwise memorable day, as I was reading in this room, I had the feeling I was about to remember everything I had read in my life. . . . Sensing an affirmation, I jumped up. That I was a free man hit in my mind even as I denied it. I suddenly knew as though I were discovering it for the first time, that the source of freedom is the human spirit. . . . Afterwards I experienced an emotion of well being so intense that I've lived on it ever since.

Implicit in Levin's experienced awakening to the possibility of a new life is his decision to leave the world of New York City and begin his new life in the Northwest. And what is most significant in the change of worlds is his new-found capacity to celebrate the external world of his environment. Nowhere in modern fiction is such a celebration of place more enthusiastically experienced. On his first ride from the station to his new post at Cascadia College, his openness to the qualities of the world of the Northwest is his most real experience. Malamud's presentations of Levin's experience of his new world function not so much as descriptions of a setting as they do to objectify the new free consciousness of Levin:

> Levin relaxed and enjoyed the ride. They were driving along an almost deserted highway, in a broad, farm-filled valley between distant mountain ranges laden with forests, the vast sky piled high with towering masses of golden clouds. The trees softly clustered on the river side of the road were for the most part deciduous; those crawling over the green hills to the south and west were spear-tipped fir.
> My God, the West, Levin thought. He imagined the pioneers in covered wagons entering this valley for the first time, and found it a moving thought. Although he had lived little in nature Levin had always loved it, and the sense of having done the right thing in leaving New York was renewed in him. He shuddered at his good fortune.
> "The mountains to the left are the Cascades," Pauline Gilley was saying. "On the right is the Coastal Range. . . . The Pacific lies on the other side of them, about fifty miles."
> "The Pacific Ocean?"
> "Yes."
> "Marvelous."

And when he sees "in the distance, a huge snow-capped peak rising above the rosy clouds reflecting the setting sun,

floated over the darkish blue mountain range," his response
reveals the felt intensity of his new world:

> "Extraordinary," muttered Levin.
> "Mt. Chief Joseph," Pauline said. "I knew you'd like it."
> "Overwhelming. I—"
> His heart was still racing from the sight. . . .

And again when walking in a forest, "he heard strange noises
in the sky, and looking up, beheld for the first time in his life a
flight of geese. The fluttering, honking formation of birds was
like a ship borne by the wind into the high invisible distance."
The contrast with his old life is presented by Malamud as also
a part of his conscious awareness:

> Never before had he lived where inside was so close to out. In a
> tenement, each descent to the street was an expedition through dank
> caves and dreary tunnels.

Levin's reflections on his new life suggest not only his propensity for reflection characteristic of the Malamud hero; they suggest also the traditional dream of the East Coast American to
find a new life in the West. A few months after his arrival in
the Northwest, Levin reflects:

> Imagine, Levin from Atlantic to Pacific—who would have thought
> so only a few years ago?—seeing up close sights he had never seen
> before: big stone mountains ahead, thick green forests, unexpected
> farms scattered over the hillsides, the ghostly remains of forest fires,
> black snags against the sky. . . . He was discovering in person the
> face of America.

Yet Levin's new life was not without its drawbacks. He
"saw himself fleeing with both heavy bags when he learned . . .
that Cascadia College wasn't a liberal arts college." And his
disappointment was immediate when he discovered that he
was to teach composition, not literature. His new life had further limitations, most occasioned by his inability to respect his
immediate superior, the director of composition, who preferred
teaching composition to literature, who objected to his beard,
"some of your students may think you're an oddball;" whose
chief interest was in producing a picture book of American literature, since, as his wife, Pauline, confessed, "there's no doubt

he's lost some of his interest in literature," and who became finally Levin's chief antagonist in his new life by fulfilling his declaration: "What we don't want around are troublemakers." Yet Levin's acceptance of the conditions of his new world was unquestioned. As he reflected in his liaison in the barn with a local barmaid:

> It was overwhelming how his life had changed in a month. You gave up the Metropolitan Museum of Art and got love in a haystack. "My first barn," Levin murmured.
> "I'll get my blanket and then we can lay down," Laverne said.
> "In front of the cows?"

The significant change, however, was not so much in Levin's external life, in what was happening to him in his new world, but in his internal life, in the change that he had hoped for in his early declaration to Pauline: "One always hopes that a new place will inspire change—in one's life." Malamud presents Levin as attempting to bring about that inner change by intellectual determination: "He often read over sentences he had copied, such as 'To change intention changes fortune'—Montaigne, and 'The new life hangs on an old soul.'" And the result is a measure of success. Malamud writes:

> What was new with Levin in the September weeks before classes began?
> His world—inside he was Levin, although the new Levin, man of purpose after largely wasted years.

The Levin "of purpose" is, of course, not yet the Levin whose sense of purpose has not been tested by conflicting encounters that comprise the main body of the narrative: the struggle against insurmountable opposition to reform the curriculum of the English Department and the struggle to discover the real basis of his relationship with Pauline.

It is in the final encounter with Gilley that the change in Levin is most strongly revealed. Gilley's bitter diatribe against his wife ironically reveals something of Pauline's hopes for a new life and the failure to find it in her marriage. Gilley predicts failure for Levin and Pauline, justifying at the same time his own stance toward his own failure in his marriage relationship:

. . . she'll blame you for as much as she blames herself, because you married her—in my case when she was twenty—and don't do what she calls "bring me out," meaning make out of her something she couldn't make out of herself though you may have broken your back trying to think up new ways to do it.

Gilley's list of "new ways" reveals his stance toward his wife, the real way he regards her, most evident in his mechanical manipulation of the relationship:

I've suggested courses, taken her on trips, kept her on a decent budget even when I couldn't so well afford it, given her a position in the community, a car, fine home, children just as real and lovable as anyone else's, although adopted, and in general tried everything I know to make her happy.

His most telling revelation appears in his unaware disclosure that his wife was not so much part of a relationship as she was an object in his concept of relationship:

And when she's through with that complaint she will have worked herself up into a nervous jag, so that unless you get out of the house early you'll be having an argument with her that may run through the day and into the night, just in time let's say when you might be thinking of a little natural satisfaction.

Something of Pauline's misery in the relationship is suggested as Gilley continues:

The next day it'll take her half the morning to wake up because she hasn't slept well, which happens more times than you think.

The climax of the encounter occurs when Gilley asks what for him would be the "overwhelming question":

An older woman than yourself and not dependable, plus two adopted kids, no choice of yours, no job or promise of one, and other assorted headaches. Why take that load on yourself?

Levin's response objectifies the change in Levin's quest for existence:

Because I can, you son of a bitch.

The final scene suggests the direction Levin's new life, and Pauline's, will take. What Malamud presents in his fictional image is not a new life in a new place but a new life in a new relationship:

"Gerald wouldn't keep that promise [i.e., to never again seek a teaching position], if he had made it to you."

"That's the point," Levin said.

She rested her head on his shoulder. "Trust me, darling, I'll make you a good wife."

Her body smelled like fresh baked bread, the bread of flowers.

"Wear these." He gave her the gold hoop earrings he had kept for her.

She fastened them on her ears.

"God bless you, Lev."

"Sam, they used to call me back home."

"God bless you, Sam."

The final image recalls Gilley's earlier destructive act of photographing his wife and Leo Duffy. Now once again Gilley "swung his camera around and snapped." The act reveals that no change has occurred in Gilley's existence:

> As they drove by he tore a rectangle of paper from the back of the camera and waved it aloft.
>
> "Got your picture."

There is a remarkable similarity between Malamud's presentation of the awakening to the possibility of a new existence which was experienced by Sy Levin and that experienced by Frank Alpine. Both revelations occur as a result of new formed relationships, the former between Levin and Pauline Gilley, the latter between Frank Alpine and Moris Bober. In an imagined conversation with the grocer, the assistant reveals something of his existence in a naturalistic world and the awakening experience which began his quest for a new existence:

> One day while they were talking in the back, he would begin, as he had once done, about how his life was mostly made up of lost chances, some so promising he could not stand to remember them. Well, after certain bad breaks through various causes, most likely his own mistakes—he was piled high with regrets—after many such failures, though he tried every which way to free himself from them, usually he failed; so after a time he gave up and let himself be a bum. He lived in gutters, cellars if he was lucky, slept in lots, ate what the dogs wouldn't or couldn't, and what he scrounged out of garbage cans. He wore what he found, slept where he flopped and guzzled anything.
>
> By rights this should have killed him, but he lived on, bearded, smelly, dragging himself through the seasons without a hope to go

by. How many months he had existed this way he would never know.
Nobody kept the score of it. But one day while he lay in some hole
he had crawled into, he had this terrific idea that he was really an
important guy, and he was torn out of his reverie with the thought
that he was living this kind of life only because he hadn't known he
was meant for something a whole lot better—to do something big,
different. In the past he had usually thought of himself as an average
guy, but there in this cellar it came to him he was wrong. That was
why his luck had so often curdled, because he had the wrong idea of
what he really was.

But Frank Alpine's attempts to intellectualize just what a
new life should be and his actual experience of his intellectual-
ized decisions result in the tormented struggle that comprises
the greater part of the work. Malamud presents his initial decision to lead the exciting life of a criminal as the first instance
of his having "the wrong idea of what he really was." In the
robbery of the grocer, Frank's response to the actual experience was in direct contrast to his idea of what the experience
would be. When Morris is being threatened by Frank's accom-
plice, Ward Minogue, who was "waving a pistol at the grocer's
head," Frank is presented as "leaning against the sink . . . to
control his trembling." And Malamud's image for Frank's dis-
may objectifies the on-going thematic conflict in his new life:

A cracked mirror hung behind him on the wall above the sink and
every so often he turned to stare into it.

The fictional image recalls T. S. Eliot's objectification of the
same theme:

Between the idea and the reality
Falls the shadow.

Frank's actual response to the pitiable condition of the grocer
was to "hastily rinse a cup and fill it with water." Malamud's
simple fictional statement again poignantly reveals Frank's
most real attitude toward the victimized grocer, i.e., that attitude which he discovers he really possesses as he is witness to
his own response:

He brought [the water] to the grocer, spilling some on his apron
as he raised the cup to his lips.

And when Ward Minogue raised his gun to strike the grocer, Frank is shown "staring into the mirror, waving frantically, his black eyes bulging."

In his well-known *Partisan Review* essay, "What Is Existentialism," Professor William Barrett writes:

> According to Buber, I find reality only when I am able to say Thou to another person, and in so saying my own is really born.

Malamud depicts Frank Alpine's experience of robbing the Jewish grocer as not so much a dramatic event to be narrated as a presentational event to be experienced, the theme of which is Frank's discovery of his own response toward another:

> His plans of crime lay down and died. He could hardly breathe in his unhappiness. . . . . In the back nauseated by the sight of the Jew's bloodied head, he realized he had made the worst mistake yet, the hardest to wipe out.

Malamud's presentation of the robbery episode is only in part a naturalistic one. In the difference between the stances taken toward their victim by Ward Minogue and Frank Alpine, we see Malamud's first shift in subject matter—from naturalistic characters in a naturalistic world to one humanistic character whose felt concern was for another's suffering and his own guilty part in it. When Frank Alpine returned two days after the robbery, his motivation was hardly that of a naturalistic protagonist:

> Morris went outside to pull in the two milk cases. He gripped the boxes but they were like rocks, so he let one go and tugged at the other. A storm cloud formed in his head and blew up to to the size of a house. Morris reeled and almost fell into the gutter, but he was caught by Frank Alpine, in his long coat, steadied and led back into the store. Frank then hauled in the milk cases and refrigerated the bottles. He quickly swept up behind the counter and went into the back. Morris, recovered, warmly thanked him.

The incident, the return of Frank Alpine to assist the grocer and Frank's continued assistance to Morris in his struggle for the survival of his store and his family, comprise the narrative of the novel. Malamud's central subject matter, however, is not so much the presentation of the external events accompanying the relationship of Frank and Morris, as it is the presentation of the relationship itself, i.e., Frank's desire for a "new life." Malamud again uses the concept directly:

> Alone afterward [Frank] stood at the window, thinking thoughts about his past, and wanting a new life.

Frank's desire for a "new life" is presented as a quest for a new existence in a new free self, but, for Malamud, it is to be a self born in and through relationship with another. The thematic center of the novel is precisely here. Not only does the assistant become the grocer, but something of the same kind of exchange occurs on the spiritual level.

In all three novels one of Malamud's central themes is the possibility of change in the process of carrying out a human existence. Malamud has commented on this theme in his interview with William Kennedy in the *National Observer*:

> A man is always changing and the changed part of him is all-important. I refer to the psyche, to the spirit, the mind, the emotions.

Malamud is on sound psychological ground in his presentation of the change which may occur as a direct result of a rewarding relationship. The humanist psychologist Carl Rogers, who is the chief spokesman for the Chicago School of Psycho-therapy, writes:

> It is possible to explain a person to himself, to prescribe steps which should lead him forward, to train him in knowledge about a more satisfying mode of life. But such methods are, in my experience, futile and inconsequential. . . .
>
> The failure of any such approach through the intellect has forced me to recognize that change appears to come about through *experience in a relationship*.

Rogers was speaking of the role of the therapist in effecting change in what he calls "becoming a person," but he adds that "these [research] findings justify an even broader hypothesis regarding all human relationships." And he concludes:

> There seems every reason to suppose that the therapeutic relationship is only one instance of interpersonal relations, and the same lawfulness governs all such relationships.

In Rogers' description of the necessary conditions which characterize the mature or spiritually fulfilled person in the relationship, he could be describing the character of Morris Bober. Rogers writes:

> If I can create a relationship characterized on my part: by a genuineness and transparency, in which I am my real feelings; by a farm acceptance of and liking for the other person as a separate individual; by a sensitive ability to see his world and himself as he sees them; then the other individual in the relationship [and here he could be describing the change in Frank Alpine]: will experience and understand aspects of himself which previously he has repressed; . . . will become more similar to the person he would like to be. . . .

Morris Bober is presented throughout the work as Malamud's image of a man who has achieved spiritual fulfillment, a man who understands human suffering and who accepts it as a norm of existence. For example, his relationship with Breitbart is just one instance of his capacity for seeing another in what Martin Buber calls the "I-Thou relation."

> When Breitbart first came to Morris' neighborhood and dropped into the store, the grocer, seeing his fatigue, offered him a glass of tea with lemon. The peddler eased the rope off his shoulders and set his boxes on the floor. In the back he gulped the hot tea in silence, warming both hands on the glass. And though he had, besides his other troubles, the seven-year itch which kept him awake half the night, he never complained. After ten minutes he got up, thanked the grocer, fitted the rope onto his lean and itchy shoulder and left. One day he told Morris the story of his life and they both wept.

Even those whom Morris has little respect for, Karp, the liquor store owner, or Schmitz, the German grocer whose competition Morris fears most, are treated by him in the "I - Thou" relation. When Morris, seeing, in passing, Karp's thriving business, wished "the liquor store would burn to the ground . . . although it shamed him," he is anguished when later the liquor store does burn to the ground. His sympathetic response, however, grows not so much out of his guilt for wishing Karp bad fortune as it does out of his genuine feeling for another's suffering:

> As the firemen began with the grappling hooks to tear out the burned fixtures and heave them onto the sidewalk, everybody fell silent . . .

A car drew up and parked beyond the drugstore. Karp got out with
Louis and they crossed the hose-filled street to their store. Karp took
one look at his former geshaft, and though it was for the most part
insured, tottered forward and collapsed. . . .

Afterward Morris couldn't sleep. He stood at his bedroom window in his long underwear, looking down at the pile of burned and
broken fixtures on the sidewalk. With a frozen hand the grocer
clawed at a live pain in his breast. He felt an overwhelming hatred of
himself. He had wished it on Karp—just this. His anguish was terrible.

Once Frank Alpine begins his work as Morris' assistant in
the store, he begins at the same time his spiritual apprentice-
ship to Morris in his quest for a new life. In an early exchange
with Morris, Frank tries to reveal something of his struggle for
meaning in his life. Again, the scene is reminiscent of Sy Levin's similar revelation to Pauline Gilley:

"I've often tried to change the way things work out for me but I
don't know how, even when I think I do. I have it in my heart to do
more than I can remember." . . . He gazed at the grocer then at the
floor. "All my life I wanted to accomplish something worthwhile—
. . . but I don't. I am too restless—six months in one place is too
much for me. Also I grab at everything too quick—too impatient. I
don't do what I have to—and I move out with nothing. You understand me?"

"Yes," said Morris.

Frank fell into silence. After a while he said, "I don't understand myself. I don't really know what I'm saying to you or why I'm
saying it."

"Rest yourself," said Morris.

"What kind of life is that for a man of my age?"

He waited for the grocer to reply—to tell him how to live his
life, but Morris was thinking, I am sixty and he talks like me.

"Take some more coffee," he said.

"No thanks." Frank lit another cigarette and smoked it to the
tip. He seemed pleased yet not eased, as though he had accomplished
something (What? wondered the grocer) yet had not. His face was re-
laxed, almost sleepy, but he cracked the knuckles of both hand and
silently sighed.

Morris' capacity for sympathetic understanding of another's suffering or another's troubled condition extends to everyone he finds himself in contact with—from the "Drunk Woman"

who still gets a measure of credit in the store to Al Marcus, the paper products salesman, who was dying of cancer but who refused to give up his daily life of work, "although he had a comfortable pile":

> Everybody knew how sick he was, and a couple of the storekeepers earnestly advised him to quit working, but Al, smiling apologetically, took his cigar out of his mouth and said, "If I stay home, somebody in a high hat is gonna walk up the stairs and put a knock on my door. This way let him at least move his bony ass around and try to find me."

Malamud objectifies Morris Bober's capacity for the I - Thou relation in a simple statement:

> No matter how bad business was, Morris tried to have some kind of little order for him.

The scene is important in the developing overall theme of the work when it is once again enacted after Morris' death—this time by Morris' assistant and Breitbart, the light bulb salesman, now a poor peddler whose business had been destroyed years earlier by his own brother. The scene concludes the image of Frank in the store, now himself the grocer, spiritually as well as physically:

> After he had mopped the kitchen floor and swept the store, Breitbart appeared, dragging his heavy boxes. Lowering the cartons of bulbs to the floor, the peddler took off his derby and wiped his brow with a yellowed handkerchief.
>
> "How's it going," Frank asked.
>
> "Schwer."
>
> Breitbart drank the tea and lemon that Frank cooked up for him. . . .

Of the three novels under consideration, none presents its protagonists caught in the destructive forces of a naturalistic world more emphatically than does *The Fixer*. The scenes and episodes which present Yakov Bok's miserable condition through two and one-half years of imprisonment constitute a major part of the work. Some of Malamud's most powerful writing is to be found in these presentations of his protagonist, a man victimized by chance forces over which he had no control.

Time was summer now, when the hot cell stank heavily and the walls sweated. There were mosquitoes, and bugs hitting the walls. Yet, better summer; he feared another winter. And if there was a spring after the winter it would mean two years in prison. And after that? Time blew like a steppe wind into an empty future. There was no end, no event, indictment, trial. The waiting withered him. He was worn thin by the struggle to wait, by the knowledge of his innocence against the fact of his imprisonment; that nothing had been done in a whole year to free him. He was stricken to be so absolutely alone. Oppressed by the heat, eaten by the damp cold, eroded by the expectation of an indictment that never came, were his gray bones visible through his skin? His nerves were threads stretched to the instant before snapping. He cried out of the deepest part of him, a narrow pit, but no one appeared or answered, or looked at him or spoke to him, neither friend nor stranger.

His desperate pacing in his cell is his pathetic response to his fear that "he might go crazy doing nothing," that "he hadn't the wit, he told himself, to be this much alone."

Gradually we see that it is not Yakov's suffering itself that is Malamud's central concern; rather, it is the implications of the suffering that are uppermost thematically.

Like Frank Alpine who makes a decision to change his life, however confused his beginning, and like Sy Levin who crosses the country in search of a new life, Yakov Bok leaves the shtetl "to get acquainted with a bit of the world," "to know what's going on in the world." In an early scene in the Jewish community, Yakov expresses a strong desire to abandon the life of withdrawl from the world—conflicts that life in the shtetl represents. His kindly father-in-law argues with Yakov's decision to leave the shtetl:

". . . but what I don't understand is why you want to bother with Kiev. It's a dangerous city full of churches and anti-Semites."

Yakov's answer reveals his dissatisfaction with his life in the shtetl and his desire to seek a new life:

"I've been cheated from the start," Yakov said bitterly. "What I've been through personally you know already, not to mention living here all my life except for a few months in the army. The shtetl is a prison, no change from the days of Khmelnitsky. It moulders and the Jews moulder in it. Here we're all prisoners. I don't have to tell you, so it's time to try elsewhere I've finally decided."

And like Frank Alpine and Sy Levin, Yakov Bok does not realize that underlying the decision to seek a new life is an impulse stronger than his ability to account for it intellectually. That is, in each novel the decision for change is gradually revealed to the consciousness of the hero as the beginning of a quest, not merely for a new life in a new environment, but for a new life in a new free self. It is, of course, an irony in the light of his imprisonment that Yakov wishes to leave the shtetl because "the shtetl is a prison." Yet it is a deeper irony that the peaceful life of the shtetl would indeed prevent him from finding the meaning in his life that he vaguely seeks. In all three novels it is the seeking after living that is affirmed.

In Malamud's presentations of his protagonists involved in strikingly different worlds in carrying out their existences—the world of the Brooklyn grocery store, the world of a Northwest university, and the world of early twentieth century anti-Semite Czarist Russia—in all three presentations, one undeniable characteristic of human living is suffering. That is, what each novel finally affirms is that the freedom to live, to discover a new life, is not merely the freedom to experience, but also, ironically, the freedom to struggle and the freedom to suffer. As Yakov concludes:

You lived, you suffered, but you lived.

Morris Bober, in his answer to Frank Alpine's questions about what he considers the characteristic suffering of Jewish people, again expresses Malamud's theme:

If you live, you suffer.

And when Frank asks, "What do you suffer for, Morris?", the reply is one climatic point in the novel:

"I suffer for you," Morris said calmly.

Morris suffers, that is, for man, whose existence, as Malamud presents it, is characterized by suffering. One recalls Karl Jaspers' assertion:

Suffering tells me that I exist.

The point is also Malamud's theme: Suffering introduces the
possibility of the awakening to a new life.

One of the best presentations, however whimsical, of what
suffering means is given in the scene in which Yakov is reflecting on his reading of the Old Testament, which he was allowed
to have for a time. The contrast he sees is that between human
experience and God's experience. The effect of the passage is
to express, with levity rather than lament, the differentia of
human experience as struggle and suffering:

> The purpose of the covenant, Yakov thinks, is to create human ex-
> perience, although human experience baffles God. God is after all
> God; what he is is what he is: God. What does he know about such
> things? Has he ever suffered? How much, after all, has he experi-
> enced? God envies the Jews: it's a rich life. Maybe He would like
> to be human, it's possible. . . .

What it means to be a human being is further differentiated
through Yakov's reflection that perhaps the limitation in the
nature of the God of the Old Testament is precisely that God
cannot be a human being:

> Then he read longer and faster, gripped by the narrative of the joy-
> ous and frenzied Hebrews, doing business, fighting wars, sinning and
> worshipping—whatever they were doing always engaged in talk
> with the huffing-puffing God who tried to sound, maybe out of
> envy, like a human being.

The passage reflects, in spite of Yakov's whimsy, one aspect of
the concept of man upon which the novel is based, namely that
for Malamud the living of life including its struggling and suffering is not simply the fate of man but the privilege of man.

> Yakov's suffering in his prison cell is intensified by his despair: He
> walked all day and into the night, until his shoes fell apart, and then
> walked in his bare feet on the lacerating floor. He walked almost in
> liquid heat with nowhere to go but his circular entrapment, strik-
> ing himself on his journey—his chest, face, head, tearing his flesh,
> lamenting his life.
>
> His crooked feet hurt unbearably. Yakov lay down in exhaustion
> on the floor. Torture by his own instrument—pain of body on deep
> depression.

It is at this point that Yakov's situation begins almost imper-
ceptively at first, to undergo a fundamental change. He be-

gins to experience moments of release from his misery. Malamud presents definite steps in his developing consciousness. The first indication of his new desire to live is in his new interest in food, not for subsistence merely, but for the enjoyment of the experience of eating:

> The minute after he had eaten he was hungry. He had visions of Zhitnyak appearing one day with a huge plate of well-seasoned chicken soup, thick with broad yellow noodles, a platter of meat kreplach, and half a haleh loaf from which he would tear hunks of sweet foamy bread that melted on the tongue. He dreamed of rice and noodle pudding with raisins and cinnamon, as Raisl had deliciously baked it; and of anything that went with sour cream—blintzes, cheese kreplach, boiled potatoes, radishes, scallions, sliced crisp cucumbers. Also of juicy tomatoes of tremendous size that he had seen in Viscover's kitchen. He sucked a ripe tomato till it dribbled from his mouth, then, to get to sleep, finally had to finish it off, thickly salted, with a piece of white bread.

And then the imagined experience is transferred at once to a real experience as Yakov gives conscious form to a real experience. His action reflects his existential decision to come out of his withdrawal in his misery and suffering in order once again to experience his existence:

> After such fantasies he could hardly wait for the guard to come with his breakfast; yet when it came at last he restrained himself, eating very slowly. First he chewed the bread until its hard texture and grain flavor were gone, then bit by bit swallowed it down. Usually he saved part of his ration for nighttime, in bed, when he got ravenously hungry thinking of food. After the bread he ate the gruel, sucking each barley grain as it melted in his mouth. At night he worked every spoonful of soup over his tongue, each pulpy cabbage bit and thread of meat, taking it in very small sips and swallows, at the end scraping the bowl with his blackened spoon.

The point is that at such moments his focus is not on his desperate situation; rather for such moments he is free from the imprisonment of his suffering. In a statement of his convictions during the *National Observer* interview, Malamud said, again in the analogy between physical and spiritual imprisonment:

> I feel that a man's way out is his imagination and his will. He frequently does the impossible.

Then in a new section, marked "7" in Chapter VI, in which Malamud shifts the viewpoint to the second person, Yakov begins to employ Spinoza's concept of freedom, which he had earlier explained to Bibikov, as a device for securing his own. He envisions the possibility of moments of freedom from his imprisonment by attempting to create conscious experiences which he could experience in his imagined constructions. That is, he begins to create his own existence:

> You wait. You wait in minutes of hope and days of hopelessness. Sometimes you just wait, there's no greater insult. You sink into your thoughts and try to blot out the prison cell. (If you're lucky it dissolves and you spend a half hour out in the open, beyond the doors and walls and the hatred of yourself.) If you're lucky and get out to the shtetl you might call on a friend, or if he's out, sit alone on a bench in front of his hut. You can smell the grass and the flowers and look at the girls, if one or two happen to be passing by along the road. You can also do a day's work if there's work to do. Today there's a little carpentering job. You work up a sweat sawing wood apart and hammering it together. When it's time to eat you open your food parcel—not bad. The thing about food is to have a little when you want it. A hard-boiled egg with a pinch of salt is delicious. Also some sour cream with a cut-up potato. If you dip bread into fresh milk and suck before swallowing, it tastes like a feast. And hot tea with lemon and a lump of sugar. In the evening you go across the wet grass to the edge of the wood. You stare at the moon in the milky sky. You breathe in the fresh air. An ambition teases you, there's still the future. After all, you're alive and free. Even if you're not so free, you think you are.

In a climactic scene in the episode depicting Yakov's achievement of freedom to celebrate his given world, his existence in a prison cell, Malamud presents contrasting images of Yakov's day in the cell, images first of a death-in-life existence, then images of a spiritually alive existence:

> During the day there were the regular checks through the spy hole, and three depressing searches of his body. There were cleaning out ashes, and making and lighting the stove. There was the sweeping of the cell to do, urinating in the can, walking back and forth until one began to count; or sitting at the table with nothing to do. There was the going for, and eating of, his meager meals. There was trying to remember and trying to forget. There was the counting of each day; there was reciting the psalm he had put together. He also watched the light and dark change. The morning dark had a little

freshness, a little anticipation in it, though what he anticipated he could not say. The night dark was heavy with thickened and compounded shadows. In the morning the shadows unfurled until only one was left, that which lingered in the cell all day. It was gone for a minute near eleven he guessed, when a beam of sunlight, on days the sun appeared, touched the corroded inner wall a foot above his mattress, a beam of golden light gone in a few minutes. Once he kissed it on the wall. Once he licked it with his tongue.

We see that now although still imprisoned, Yakov, ironically, has become a person capable of a fuller and richer life experience that he was capable of in the shtetl.

Each of Malamud's three major novels is concerned with the *being* of the central character, with his decision to discover a new life, with the subject matter of the search, which in every case begins with the search for self. And in each novel, despite ironies, usually ludicrous, the hero succeeds—never however in terms in which he had envisioned his quest.

Peter L. Hays

MALAMUD'S YIDDISH-ACCENTED MEDIEVAL STORIES

CRITICS HAVE ALREADY DETAILED specific elements in Bernard Malamud's fiction which are common in the literature of the Middle Ages. Leslie Fiedler and others have noticed the use of the Fisher King in *The Natural*,[1] where Malamud obviously contrives to make Roy's contests with the Whammer and, later, with Vogelman and Youngberry, medieval jousts with distinct overtones of Freud and of the ritual combat between the aging winter king and the young *daimon* of spring. Thus Malamud desscribes Roy (King) as "Sir Percy lancing Sir Maldemer, or the first son (with a rock in his paw) ranged against the primitive papa";[2] he is a knight "in full armor, mounted on a black charger, . . . with a long lance as thick as a young tree" (p. 231). Roy's night with Memo is described in terms similar to those used by medieval romancers to portray the test of the perilous bed.[3] Roy Mellard has commented on Malamud's use of pastoral elegy and Edwin Eigner on the motif of the loathly lady in Malamud's fiction.[4] Thus, I think it safe to say that Malamud has read and absorbed much of the literature of the medieval period and has echoed elements of it in his work.

What follows is a further look at Malamud's work from the perspective of medieval literature, specifically Chrétien de Troye's "Lancelot, or The Knight of the Cart" (the latter, in Malamud's fiction, Yakov's wagon or Levin's brown 1946 Hudson). This is, however, not a one-to-one influence study, but rather an attempt to see Malamud in historical context.

Chrétien's tale, like many of those which tell of the Matter of Britain, begins with a fierce knight, Meleagant, entering Ar-

thur's court and hurling down a challenge. He will release the
many captives he holds from Arthur's kingdom if Arthur will
send Guinevere out under the protection of a knight brave
enough to fight Meleagant. Through a rash boon, granted by his
threatening to quit, Sir Kay wins Arthur's permission to escort
the Queen. However, the blustering seneschal is quickly
trounced, wounded, and captured by Meleagant. Gawain, ahead
of the rest of the pursuing court, encounters a mysterious knight
flogging a nearly dead horse. The nameless knight begs a spare
horse of Gawain, and proceeds ahead where Gawain again
finds him, this time unhorsed, the borrowed horse killed, the area
trampled and strewn, broken shields and lances evidencing his
unsuccessful attempt to rescue Guinevere.

The cart of the title then appears, driven by a dwarf, both
carts and dwarfs held in low repute in those times, dwarfs frequently considered Platonically as evilly misshapen men (cf.
Melot in *Tristan* and his descendant Otto Zipf in *The Natural*),
and carts, like tumbrels, used to display malefactors to the derision and scorn of the populace. That a knight of Arthur's—a bold,
valiant hero—should be unhorsed and fail at rescuing the distressed damsel is shame enough, but to have opprobrium heaped
on ignominy, he must now trade his charger for an ox-drawn
tumbrel. The vehicle, however, is going his way, and so after
hesitating a moment, from considerations of the disgrace he will
be in, Lancelot, for so it is, gets aboard. Then Gawain catches
up, is invited by the dwarf to join his friend in the cart, but de-
clines, saying, " . . . it would be dishonourable to exchange a
horse for a cart."[5] And, indeed, the unnamed Knight of Cart,
for he is not identified as Lancelot until nearly 3400 lines later,
is reviled by townspeople and knights alike for whatever deed it
was that caused him to ride the cart.

Hereafter, the narrative proceeds in more conventional
medieval romance fashion. Gawain and Lancelot come to a castle where Lancelot insists on sleeping in a bed he is told is too
good for one disgraced as he is; it is the perilous bed, and of
course he survives it. He and Gawain separate, and Lancelot at
one point is so lost in rapture and reverie for Guinevere that he

doesn't hear warnings not to cross a boundary stream and is un-
ceremoniously knocked off his horse into the water while the
animal is placidly drinking.

The cold bath restores Lancelot to his senses and he defeats
his attacker, but note how Chrétien has made his hero, as Wolfram will later with Parzival, mighty yet vulnerable, accomplished yet foolish. And these incidents are repeated, prowess
alternating with self-doubt and foolish behavior. An attractive
hostess tests Lancelot by having her armed servants pretend to
strip and ravish her, then calling on unarmed Lancelot for help.
Seeing four armed men, he hesitates, which is reasonable enough
for any mortal, but not as we have idealized Lancelot and his
more-than-human successors, the heroes of romance.

Subsequently, he lifts the lid of a stone sarcophagus, a lid
requiring the strength of ten to move it, from the tomb prophe-
sied to contain ultimately the one who will free the inhabitants
of the land from their captivity. Thus Chrétien foreshadows
Lancelot's ultimate victory and underscores his role as savior, all
the while having characters heap verbal abuse on Lancelot for
his tumbrel ride.

The crucial incident occurs when Lancelot comes to the
bridge which separates him from the castle in which Guinevere
is held. A raging torrent is bridged only by a sword "as long as
two lances" (p. 308), with two lions or leopards guarding the
further extreme. Since his armor is too clumsy, Lancelot re-
moves guantlets, greaves, and footwear, and crawls across, slic-
ing hands and feet to ribbons. The cats are false visions, but he
must immediately fight Meleagant and is losing until he spies
Guinevere watching him and is inspired to win. Meleagant's
father intercedes and stops the combat. Guinevere, however, instead of being grateful to Lancelot for coming to her rescue and
enduring pain and nearly death, acts coldly, snubbing him. She
is *la belle Dame sans merci* because Lancelot has violated the
code of courtly love: a lover should be willing to bear anything
for his mistress, and Lancelot, mere superhuman that he is, hesi-
tated two seconds before getting into the dwarf's cart.

Other less-than-heroic incidents include Lancelot's awkwardly trying to hang himself with his belt from his saddle bow when he believes Guinevere is dead and his twice being captured by lowly vassals. The first time, Lancelot is returned to the king, his feet tied together beneath his horse. The second time, he is held captive by a lady jailer, who once lets him out on a parole to attend a tournament where Guinevere, to test his loyalty, asks him to fight badly and lose.

In Malamud's fiction, the protagonists suffer like predicaments. Thus, just as Lancelot, the Knight of the Cart, is thoroughly reviled for the crime of love, so are Frank Alpine, Sy Levin, and Arthur Fidelman. As Lancelot is reproached by his lover, so Roy is by Harriet, Memo, and Iris; Frank is by Helen; Yakov is by Raisl and Zinaida; and Fidelman is by Annamaria, Esmeralda, Margherita, and Beppo. Like Lancelot, Malamud's heroes are cut to ribbons in their quests for love and fortune. Also like Lancelot, Malamud's heroes persist. Where the medieval knight went in search of glory, conquest, and approval of a beloved, Malamud's protagonists search for an authentic self and life-style, an identity worthy of commitment. Like Lancelot, they often conceal their identities—Roy Hobbs hides his past, Frank Alpine covers his face with a mask, Sy Levin covers his with a beard, and Bok becomes Dologushev.

Chrétien's tale is one of generations; thrice we encounter fathers and sons, twice wise fathers and unruly sons (like Meleagant and his honorable father, Bademagu), once a kind father matched by kind, brave sons. Similarly Malamud's stories look backward to both real and adoptive parents, and forward to children: Sam Simpson and Pop Fisher, and Iris's daughter and pregnancy by Roy; Sy's worthless parents and Pauline's adopted children and the child by Levin which she is carrying; Frank's orphaned existence, Helen's parents, especially Morris, as well as Detective Minogue and Ward, Breitbart and his son, Julius Karp and Louis, and Sam Pearl and his children, Nat and Betty; Jakov with Shmuel, his father-in-law, the guard Kogin and his son, Zina Nikolaevna and her father, Zhenia Golov and his mother Marfa, and Raisl and her son Chaim—even the Czar as Russia's Little Father.

Perhaps more significant are the rebirth themes. The rescue that Lancelot accomplishes is like that of Hercules' rescue of both Theseus and Alcestis, and like Orpheus' near-rescue of Eurydice. The land where Meleagant holds Arthur's subjects captives is a "kingdom whence no foreigner returns." Clearly a symbolic land of the dead, it lies across a water barrier difficult to cross, like the Rivers Styx and Lethe, and the magic streams of Celtic fairy lore. There Lancelot conquers the prince, Meleagant, and forces the captives' return, as Heracles had with Alcestis. Similarly, Roy Hobbs disappears from both the public and the reader's view after he is shot by Harriet Bird, only to be reborn as a Knight in the uniform of Pop Fisher's baseball team. Frank Alpine buries himself in the tomb of the store and falls into Morris' grave, but through the inspiration provided by Helen and Morris, the homeless, valueless wanderer acquires a place, an adopted family, a set of values, and a religion. He dies as robber, and is reborn as assistant to Morris, and becomes his spiritual son (and, presumably, his son-in-law). Levin "for two years lived in [drunken] self-hatred, willing to part ith life. . . . ,"[6] but goes west for "a new life." Yakov is entombed in the living death of years of solitary confinement, dying as an unpolitical pacifist, being reborn as an activist in spirit, a revolutionary willing in dream to kill Czar Nicholas five years before the historical deed.

In the works of both authors, characters are motivated by love, and there are echoes of St. Paul.[7] Malamud and Chrétien would probably agree heartily that "Love bears all things, believes all things, hopes all things, endures all things" (1 Corinthians 13:7) and "that suffering produces endurance, and endurance produces character, and character produces hope . . ." (Romans 5:3-4). They would also agree with Romans 12:9: "Let love be genuine."

I do not intend a lengthy comparison of Chrétien and Malamud, nor to use the work of either Lord Raglan or Joseph Campbell as touchstones to test which writer's heroes more closely approach the definition of a mythic hero. Obviously Chrétien's Lancelot comes closer. But there are parallels: the basic quest pattern central to medieval romance and only slightly less so in the stories of *The Natural, The Assistant, A New Life, The Fixer, Pictures of Fidelman,* and possibly even *The Tenants;* the mixture of the heroic, even the tragic, with humor and bathos; the concern for psychological realism (expected in this century, unexpected in the twelfth); the mixture, too, of realism and surrealism, of the humanly possible and the magical. Thus, the predators guarding the far end of the sword bridge are illusions only, and a magical ring given Lancelot by the Lady of the Lake reveals as much to him. There is magic, similarly, in Malamud, from prestidigitation to illusion to visits by the Devil and by fairy godmothers (transmogrified into black angels named Levine). Harriet Bird is an otherworldly being whose connection to the occult is suggested both by her dryadic dance and by her ritual use of silver bullets (*The Natural,* pp. 35, 40-41). Roy is a magician (*The Natural,* pp. 112-113) who has returned from death (figurative if not literal). Although more prevalent in the short stories, magic continues in Malamud's longer works. The wooden rose Frank carves for Helen becomes real (*The Assistant,* p. 245), Bok's visions become part of his daily reality, and surrealism plays a part in Chapter Five of *Pictures of Fidelman.* What Jean Frappier says of Chrétien applies as well to Malamud:

> Though he felt and exploited the spell of the fantastic, he recognized the classic qualities of balance and reason. . . . He sought to illuminate the mysteries of the heart and conscience. He treated of love, sometimes with a tincture of comedy, sometimes with tragic emphasis. He liked to knot and unknot situations humanly significant. . . . He did not reject the joys of this transitory life, but he conceded nothing to baseness, demanded of his heroes greatness of soul, and exalted the virtue of sacrifice. What he condemned was futile excess and lack of balance. . . . He preferred those characters who make themselves, who develop power and self-knowledge through trials.[8]

Certainly the same can be said of Bellow, Hemingway, Faulkner, Melville, and of many other authors. Almost any two authors, however distant from each other in time and culture, if they deal with basic human concerns in recognizable form, can be compared and found similar, especially when they use the quest motif as well as mixtures of laughter and tears. Is all that I have said so far, then, a sham, a mere exercise in specious criticism? I hope not. Malamud's references to medieval literature are explicit and his allusions little less so. I am sure that he has read medieval literature, and I believe that he has read Chrétien.[9] But criticism of Malamud has put him firmly in another tradition as well, that of Yiddish literature.[10] The Malamud hero is a *schlemiel,* a bungler, more used to failing than succeeding, a hero who comments on his own ineptitude with self-deprecating humor, but who, through his suffering, learns a new humanity. Ruth Wisse describes those characteristics which define the *schlemiel* as having "the potential for suffering, submitting to loss, pain, humiliation, [and] for recognizing himself as . . . only himself." These apply equally well to Lancelot, as does her statement that: "The character courageous enough to accept his ignominy without being crushed by it is the true hero of Malamud's opus. . . ."[11]

Is Lancelot, then, really a Yiddish knight, with his *payess* tucked into his beaver? No, though the question is not as ridiculous as it sounds. Besides the possibility that Chrétien himself was a converted Jew, it is known that there were Yiddish minstrels in medieval Europe who traveled between the isolated Jewish communities, telling tales of Dietrich von Bern, Hildebrand, King Arthur, and Gawain.[12] Nor should my linking of Malamud's bunglers with the supremely heroic Lancelot be that surprising. Max Schulz, commenting on Malamud and paraphrasing Frank Kermode, says that "the tendency of any . . . fiction, once it forgets fictiveness . . . is to regress into myth." In a similar vein, Earl Rovit reminds us that "the use of elements of folklore in fiction is, of course, the rule rather than the exception. Indeed, storytelling is probably the oldest and still the lustiest vehicle for folklore itself."[13] What we too often forget in our scholarly analyses of authors is that they are storytellers. While I am not happy with the connotations of "regress" as Schulz uses it, he is absolutely correct in seeing archetypal myths as the basic and fundamental stuff of which fiction is made. Such a statement is, of course, obvious in writers like Joyce, Faulkner, Melville; it is also true, though somewhat attenuated, in writers like Henry James, for Christopher Newman, Isabel Archer, and Lambert Strether are all on quests, and the confrontation of naive America with corrupt Europe is simply another variation on the conflict of spring king and winter king.

Thus, while critical students of Malamud may validly continue to examine him in either the medieval or the Yiddish tradition or both, or still another, we as literary critics should also pay more attention to genus as well as species, to storytelling in general, to the elements, motifs, and methods which are standard for any storyteller from Homer on. Critics should not overlook the fact that even sophisticated modern novelists are essentially storytellers. Structuralists now tell us this, and so do those folklorists who are taking as their objects of inquiry whole literary works and not just parts of previously identified folklore. For too long we have dissected (and vivisected) writers in order to identify elements which, though no doubt significant, are fractions of the authors' works, frequently minor fractions at that. We're like Melville's sailors who charted whales as islands in the open sea or Lilliputian cartographers mapping puddles as lakes. With a writer as intelligent and syncretic as Malamud,[14] it is absolutely essential to see him not just as a modern writer who combines elements of myth, medieval romance, and Yiddish humor, as well as the influence of Hawthorne, Dostoevski, Dreiser, Chekov, and Hemingway, but also as a writer working in the age-old tradition of the tale, a writer like Twain and Faulkner, working out of the oral as well as the written tradition of at least two continents, and we must analyze his works and evaluate him with his peers in this broader context of storytelling.

NOTES

[1]Leslie Fiedler, *No! in Thunder* (Boston: Beacon Press, 1960), p. 105, first published in *Folio*, 1955; °Earl Wasserman, *"The Natural*: Malamud's World Ceres," *The Centennial Review*, 9 (Fall 1965), 438-460; Jonathan Baumbach, *The Landscape of Nightmare* (New York: New

York University Press, 1965), pp. 107-111; Sidney Richman, *Bernard Malamud* (New York: Twayne, 1966), pp. 28-49; Robert Shulman, "Myth, Mr. Eliot and the Comic Novel," *Modern Fiction Studies,* 12 (Winter 1966-67), 400-403; *Frederick W. Turner III, "Myth Inside and Out: *The Natural,*" *Novel,* I (Winter 1968), 133-139.

²Bernard Malamud, *The Natural* (New York: Harcourt, Brace, 1952), p. 32. Subsequent quotations will refer to this edition and will be paginated parenthetically in the text.

³ Cf. Wolfram's *Parzival,* stanza 567; Chrétien's *Lancelot,* pp. 518-538.

⁴*James M. Mellard, "Malamud's Novels: Four Versions of Pastoral," *Critique,* 9 (1967), 5-19. *Edwin M. Eigner, "Malamud's Use of the Quest Romance," *Genre,* 1 (January 1968), 55-74.

⁵Chrétien de Troyes, "Lancelot," *Arthurian Romances,* ed. & trans. W. W. Comfort (London: J. M. Dent, 1914, 1958), p. 275, V. 396. Subsequent references in my text will be paginated parenthetically and will refer to this edition.

⁶Bernard Malamud, *A New Life* (New York: Farrar, Straus & Cudahy, 1961), p. 201.

⁷See Peter L. Hays, *The Limping Hero* (New York: New York University Press, 1971), pp. 45-47, for a discussion of Malamud and St. Paul; Chrétien quotes St. John in the introduction to "Perceval" (pp. 48-51) but attributes the quotation to St. Paul, and Urban Holmes in the first-named source in Note 9 below argues for Chrétien's familiarity with St. Paul's writings (pp. 14-15).

⁸Jean Frappier, "Chrétien de Troyes," *Arthurian Literature in the Middle Ages,* ed. Roger Sherman Loomis (Oxford: Clarendon Press, 1959), p. 161.

⁹In addition to Chrétien's prominence in accounts of medieval literature, and the fact that he is one of our main sources on Lancelot, Perceval and the Grail legend, Malamud might also have been intrigued by the theory advanced by Urban T. Holmes, Jr., beginning in 1948, that Chrétien was a convert from Judaism. Holmes' contention is based on the large Jewish community at Troyes in the twelfth century and on Chrétien's name, which, literally, is "Christian." Cf. Urban T. Holmes, Jr., "A New Interpretation of Chrétien's *Conte Del Graal,*" *University of North Carolina Studies in the Romance Languages and Literatures,* No. 8 (1948), 30-31; Holmes and Sister M. Amelia Klenke, *Chrétien, Troyes, and the Grail* (Chapel Hill: University of North Carolina Press, 1959), pp. 51 et passim; and Holmes, *Chrétien de Troyes* (New York: Twayne, 1970), pp. 22-23. Interestingly, Holmes argues that Chrétien has blended various sources in *Perceval,* the matter of Britain, the Bible, the Kabbalah, numerology, and the Midrashim—that is, both written and oral tradition.

---

*The essays marked with an asterisk are reprinted in *Bernard Malamud and the Critics,* ed. Leslie A. Field and Joyce W. Field (New York, New York University Press, 1970).

[10]For example, in the volume *Bernard Malamud and the Critics,* cited above, there appear these essays:

"The Jewish Literary Tradition," Earl H. Rovit, pp. 3-10; originally published as "Bernard Malamud and the Jewish Literary Tradition" in *Critique, 3* (Winter-Spring 1960), 3-10.

"The Old Life and the New," Theodore Solotaroff, pp. 235-248; originally published as "Bernard Malamud's Fiction: The Old Life and the New," *Commentary, 33* (March 1962), 197-204.

"The Hero as Schnook," Alan Warren Friedman, pp. 285-303; originally published as "Bernard Malamud: The Hero as Schnook," *Southern Review, 4* (October 1968), 927-944.

"Jewishness as Metaphor," Robert Alter, pp. 29-42; originally published in Alter's *After the Tradition* (New York: E. P. Dutton, 1969), pp. 116-130, and before that in *Commentary, 42* (September 1966), 71-76.

A second volume of essays by Leslie and Joyce Field, *Bernard Malamud* (New York: Prentice-Hall, 1975), nearly doubles the list of essayists examining Malamud in ethnic context:

"Bernard Malamud's Ironic Heroes," Sanford Pinsker, pp. 45-71; originally printed as "The Schlemiel as Moral Bungler—Bernard Malamud's Ironic Heroes" in Pinsker's *The Schlemiel as Metaphor—Studies in the Yiddish and American Novel* (Carbondale: Southern Illinois University Press, 1971), pp. 87-124.

"Bernard Malamud and the Jewish Movement," Sheldon Norman Grebstein, pp. 18-44; originally published in *Contemporary American-Jewish Literature: Critical Essays,* ed. Irving Malin (Bloomington: Indiana University Press, 1973), pp. 175-212.

"Portrait of the Artist as Schlemiel," Leslie Field, pp. 117-129.

[11]Ruth R. Wisse, *The Schlemiel as Modern Hero* (Chicago, University of Chicago Press, 1971), p. 111.

[12]Cf. Charles A. Madison, *Yiddish Literature* (New York: Frederick Ungar, 1968), p. 4; Sol Liptzin, *A History of Yiddish Literature* (Middle Village, New York: Jonathan David Publishers, 1972), pp. 4-5; Irving Howe and Eliezer Greenberg, *A Treasury of Yiddish Stories* (New York: Fawcett Premier, 1968), p. 30.

[13]Both authors are quoted from their essays appearing in *Bernard Malamud and the Critics,* cited above: Schulz, p. 186; Rovit, p. 5.

[14]Cf. Sam Bluefarb, "The Syncretism of Bernard Malamud," in the second volume of essays collected by the Fields, *Bernard Malamud,* cited above, pp. 72-79.

BERNARD MALAMUD AND THE MARGINAL JEW

". . . Say, Morris, suppose somebody asked you what do the Jews believe in, what would you tell them?"

The grocer stopped peeling, unable at once to reply.

"What I like to know is what is a Jew anyway?"

Because he was ashamed of his meager education, Morris was never comfortable with such questions, yet he felt he must answer.

"My father used to say to be a Jew all you need is a good heart."

"What do you say?"

"The important thing is the Torah. This is the Law—A Jew must believe in the Law."

"Let me ask you this," Frank went on. "Do you consider yourself a real Jew?"

Morris was startled, "What do you mean if I am a real Jew?"

"Don't get sore about this," Frank said, "But I can give you an argument that you aren't. First thing, you don't go to the synagogue —not that I have ever seen. You don't keep your kitchen kosher and you don't eat kosher. You don't even wear one of those little black hats like this tailor I knew in South Chicago. He prayed three times a day. I even hear the Mrs. say you kept the store open on Jewish holidays, it makes no difference if she yells her head off."

"Sometimes," Morris answered, flushing, "to have to eat, you must keep open on holidays. On Yom Kippur I don't keep open. But I don't worry about kosher, which is to me old-fashioned. What I worry is to follow the Jewish Law."

"But all those things are the Law, aren't they? And don't the Law say you can't eat any pig, but I have seen you taste ham."

"This is not important to me if I taste pig or if I don't. To some Jews is this important but not to me. Nobody will tell me that I am not Jewish because I put in my mouth once in a while, when my tongue is dry, a piece ham. But they will tell me, and I will believe them, if I forget the Law. This means to do what is right, to be honest, to be good. This means to other people. Our life is hard enough.

Why should we hurt somebody else? For everybody should be the best, not only for you or me. We ain't animals. This is why we need the Law. This is what a Jew believes."

"I think other religions have those ideas too," Frank said. "But tell me why it is that the Jews suffer so damn much, Morris? It seems to me that they like to suffer, don't they?"

"Do you like to suffer? They suffer because they are Jews."

"That's what I mean, they suffer more than they have to."

"If you live, you suffer. Some people suffer more, but not because they want. But I think if a Jew don't suffer for the Law, he will suffer for nothing."

"What do you suffer for, Morris?" Frank said.

"I suffer for you," Morris said calmly.

Frank laid his knife down on the table. His mouth ached. "What do you mean?"

"I mean you suffer for me."

The clerk let it go at that.

"If a Jew forgets the Law," Morris ended, "he is not a good Jew, and not a good man."[1]

I quote this passage from *The Assistant* in entirety because for years critics have used snippets of it in their attempts to probe the essence of Jewishness in Bernard Malamud's writings. Many have gone beyond this as they try to demonstrate that Malamud epitomizes the Jewish-American writer in the United States today.

Even a cursory examination of Malamud's work reveals that Jewishness and the Jewish milieu are central to it. We have Morris Bober, the Jewish grocer of *The Assistant;* S. Levin, the Jewish English instructor of *A New Life;* Yakov Bok, the persecuted Jew of *The Fixer;* Arthur Fidelman, the Jewish art critic and would-be artist of *Pictures of Fidelman,* and Harry Lesser, the Jew as author of *The Tenants.* One could make an exhaustive list of Jews in Malamud's short stories. These Jews and the Jews of the novels are not simply stage setting, not simply incidental Jews; they are Jews involved in things Jewish. Morris Bober, as we have seen, defines his Jewishness when Frank Alpine presses him. Yakov Bok's Jewish experience at the end of *The Fixer* is summed up this way:

One thing I've learned, he thought, there's no such thing as an unpolitical man, especially a Jew. You can't be one without the other, that's clear enough. You can't sit still and see yourself destroyed.

Afterwards he thought, where there's no fight for it there's no freedom. What is it Spinoza says? If the state acts in ways that are abhorrent to human nature it's the lesser evil to destroy it. Death to the anti-Semites! Long live the revolution. Long live liberty![2]

Leo Finkle, the rabbinical student and protagonist of the excellent short story "The Magic Barrel," agonizes about his faith as he rejects marriage broker Pinya Salzman's offers to him of eligible mates. Finkle finally insists upon Salzman's disreputable daughter in what is perhaps one of the most enigmatic scenes in a Malamud story. And so on through Bernard Malamud's world of Jewish blackbirds, idiots, *luftmenschen,* and landlords.

But if the Jew and Jewishness are central to Malamud, the gnawing question arises: What kind of Jew and Jewishness? It's something that has concerned critics for some time. Obviously, Malamud's fiction is interwoven with bits and pieces of Judaism. But what of the essence of Judaism, whatever that may mean? Does Bober's explanation to Frank Alpine constitute that which is central to Jewishness? Does Yakov Bok's closing statement in *The Fixer?* Or what of stories such as "The Lady of the Lake," in which the conflict arises from the protagonist's denial of his Jewishness and his fair lady's ultimate rejection of him because she has a concentration camp number on her arm and must therefore preserve her special Jewish identity. Ostensibly, she would have married him had he not attempted to pass for a non-Jew. And, finally, what kind of Jewishness is represented in the concluding lines of "Angel Levine": " 'A wonderful thing, Fanny,' Manischevitz said. 'Believe me, there are Jews everywhere.' "[3]

Few critics claim that Malamud is concerned solely with the Jew in his writing. Nor do they accept the notion that those elements of Jewishness which concern Malamud constitute *all* of Jewishness. One would be terribly presumptuous to insist that such and such defines the Jew to the exclusion of everything else. After all, over the years Jews and non-Jews have wrestled with the definition of Jewishness. For that matter, periodically in the United States, Israel, and elsewhere in the world where we have sizeable clusters of Jews, the Jews themselves have become immersed in great debates on "Who Is A Jew?" Is the Jew defined strictly by orthodox Jewish law as a child of a Jewish mother? Or is a Jew one who attends a synagogue or a temple? Or one who recognizes Israel as his or her actual or spiritual homeland? Or one who feels himself or herself part of Jewish history? Or simply one who professes he or she is a Jew?

This whole vexing area concerning who is a Jew or what is Jewishness is fraught with frustration for those who are concerned with definition and identity. Therefore, it won't do to set up an ersatz argument and say that perhaps Malamud is a Jewish-American writer because he writes about Jews and some elements of the Jewish milieu; however, because he ignores other elements which you or I may consider significant, he is really not a Jewish-American writer. It may be constructive to probe a bit in order to see just what kind of Jewish world it is that Malamud has given us. What has been included and what has been left out? And if we do get a clearer picture of this Jewish world, does it ultimately tell us more about the ideas and esthetics in Bernard Malamud's fiction than we already know and feel? I believe it does.

Malamud himself has decisively rejected the label of Jewish-American writer. His colleagues Saul Bellow and Philip Roth have also done so with equal vehemence. I submit, however, that the denials are often too quick and Pavlovian. As one of their own fictional characters might say: "Why not to protest? I'm entitled." But we may also legitimately ask whether they protest too much and whether in fact in their almost automatic retorts they are not really revealing an ambivalence central to themselves and their writings. In one place Roth says: "I did not want to, did not intend to, and was not able to speak for American Jews. . . . I spoke *to* them, and I hope to others as well."[4] And Bellow frequently proclaims that his books are not Jewish: "They're books and I resent sometimes being thrust into a bag."[5] Quite recently when Bellow was pressed, he admitted "that he is not 'fully awake' to the needs of Israel and his heritage."[6]

Malamud has not been the public figure that either Roth or Bellow has been. He has granted few interviews. But his position comes through clearly in the few exchanges he has had concerning Jews and Jewishness.

➤ In April, 1968, Malamud was in Israel on a brief lecture tour. When asked about his role as a Jewish-American writer, he said: "What has made the Jewish writers so conspicuous in American literature is their sensitivity to the value of man." "Personally," he concluded, "I handle the Jew as universal man. Every man is a Jew though he may not know it. The Jewish drama is a . . . symbol of the fight for existence in the highest possible terms. Jewish history is God's gift of drama."[7]

In 1973, Joyce Field and I had an opportunity to interview Malamud through a series of letters. Here is a brief excerpt from our exchange:

> *Question*: Saul Bellow, Philip Roth, Bruce J. Friedman, and other contemporary American novelists have rejected the label "Jewish-American Writer." In one way or another you have also. Nevertheless, you and others are still being classified this way. How do you respond to this categorizing of you and your work? Would you reject the term Jewish-American Writer categorically?

> *Answer*: The term is schematic and reductive. If the scholar needs the term he can have it, but it won't be doing him any good if he limits his interpretation of a writer to fit a label he applies. Bellow pokes fun at this sort of thing by calling "Bellow-Malamud-Roth" the Hart, Schaffner, and Marx of Jewish American literature.

> *Question*: Whether or not you accept the label of Jewish-American Writer, would you not agree that your writing reveals a special sense of a people's destiny that more often than not cannot be fully grasped in all its nuances and vibrations by those who are not fully sensitized to that people or its destiny? On one level, for example, it has been said that one must be a Russian in order to respond completely to the nineteenth-century notion of salvation through suffering that is dramatized so well by Dostoevsky. Or that only blacks can truly appreciate the plight of black America. Could one not also say that only those who understand the *Yiddishkeit* of the characters or the *Yiddish* milieu are able to respond fully to the silent communication between a Morris Bober and a Breitbart or between a Yakov Bok and his father-in-law, and so on?

> *Answer*: I'm sensitive to Jews and Jewish life but so far as literature is concerned I can't say that I approve of your thesis: that one has

to be of a certain nationality or color to "fully grasp" the "nuances and vibrations" of its fiction. I write on the assumption that
any one sensitive to fiction can understand my work and *feel* it.

It is not easy for Jews in the arts to define the Jewishness
in the literature, music, and painting they create. A short time
ago a large group of Jews addressed this very problem at the
first national Jewish celebration of "The Jewish Cultural Arts,"
a bicentennial event. In three days of discussion "they had a
difficult time defining Jewish culture. Many were uncomfort-
able about attributing the source of their creativity to their Jewishness." Others had no such problems, and they often talked of
the Nazi *Holocaust* and the rebirth of Israel as "important fac-
tors in awakening their Jewish consciousness."[9]

What is the definition of the hyphenated literatures we
espouse in America? What is Italian-American or Black-Ameri-
can or Jewish-American?

Isaac Bashevis Singer is a good starting point. No one
wants to classify Singer. Here we have an American writing in
Yiddish (primarily about an earlier East-European Jewish life),
but who is translated into English almost immediately, and a
writer who is increasingly being read and studied in English
departments across the country. Is Singer or is he not a Jewish-
American writer? He is Jewish and is American and he is a
writer. But Norman Mailer is Jewish and is American and is a
writer. Do we put Norman Mailer and Isaac Bashevis Singer
in the same bag? Or what of a writer who is a black American
but whose writing has nothing in common with James Baldwin
or Ralph Ellison, and who, in fact may write only about a fictive mountain and stream world of Colorado? One could mar-
shal examples from American writers of Polish, Italian, Span-
ish, and Japanese ancestry, too. We have something of a similar dilemma involving the hyphenated American writer. Why
does Faulkner represent Southern-American writing whereas
William Sydney Porter (O. Henry), also a Southerner, does
not?

— In the case of the Jewish-American writers, we have some
of the same problems in defining who or what is a Jew. But I

believe it is generally accepted that someone who has Jewish forefathers and whose writing seems to be immersed in something called the Jewish heritage or Judaism or the special burden of Jewish history, and who is living and writing in the United States — this someone is a Jewish-American writer, whether our Bellows, Roths, and Malamuds accept the label or not. Even if this writer takes himself off to Israel, France, or wherever, and he continues to write, he may still be considered a Jewish-American writer.

When a writer who is black or Jewish or Chinese has become so assimilated or integrated into the predominant White Anglo-Saxon Protestant American society that he not only no longer recognizes himself as a minority person, a person distinct from the majority, and when the writer's subject and style cannot be distinguished from those considered a part of our "mainstream" American, then that writer must no longer be considered a part of the distinct or separate or hyphenated group.[10]

Sheldon Grebstein, in an essay entitled "Bernard Malamud and the Jewish Movement," made a convincing case for the "Jewish Movement" in American letters. He began by saying: "Only those too perverse or fuzzy-headed to recognize cultural facts now refuse to acknowledge the existence of a Jewish Movement in contemporary American writing, and especially the writing of fiction." Why, Grebstein asks, did the movement come about? His answer is instructive:

> In part, it was engendered by a void, born to occupy the space left by the decline or demise of other movements . . . But more important, the Jewish Movement responded to an urgent cultural need. In short, and this is now a truism, the Jewish writer was made the beneficiary of Hitler's death camps. We Americans, spared the war's worst horrors, had to know more about those piles of corpses, teeth, shoes, we saw in the newsreels. Whether out of guilt, morbid curiosity, or both, the Jew became important to us. In the Western imagination the Jew had always played a special role as wizard, magician, possessor of secret knowledge, but never before, until Auschwitz and Buchenwald, had such moral authority been conferred upon him. From hated, feared, or ridiculed figure lurking on the fringes of the culture, he was transformed into the Man Who Suffered, Everyman.

To Americans especially, ever respectful of eyewitness reports and ready to listen to the man who was there, the Jew compelled attention. . . . Who could better instruct us than the Jews, those most expert and experienced sufferers? Others had taken a beating, yes, but what other group in human memory had been marked out for genocide?[11]

Grebstein then focused on three elements of Jewishness one finds in Malamud, whom he considers the foremost practitioner of Jewish-American fiction today: 1) the theme of meaningful suffering; 2) the use of Jewish humor; 3) the use of a distinctive Jewish voice.[12]

Other critics have examined a variety of other Jewish elements in Malamud's writing. Earl Rovit, for example, in "Bernard Malamud and the Jewish Literary Tradition," says that the Jewish-American writer usually has not used Yiddish folklore in his writing. But Malamud's ironic vision, he claims, is in "the tradition of the Yiddish teller of tales," even though his means of telling tales is not. Rovit explores Malamud's uses of esthetic form to resolve "unresolvable dramatic conflicts" and demonstrates that Malamud is both part of and apart from the Jewish tradition.[13]

Robert Alter, using a different approach, states that although Malamud's protagonists are Jewish, he doesn't write *about* Jews and doesn't "represent a Jewish milieu." To Malamud Jewishness is "an ethical symbol," a moral stance. Alter sees in Malamud's writing qualities deriving from Jewish folklore, most notably the juxtaposition of reality and fantasy, and the folk figure of the *schlemiel-schlimazel,* used by Malamud as the symbol of the Jew, a person who is involved in the world and becomes its victim. Alter traces what he considers Malamud's "central metaphor of Jewishness," the prison, which, he argues, is the perfect emblem for both the human and the Jewish condition.[14]

Samuel I. Bellman castigates those critics who have a one-theme reading of Malamud—his "judaization of society." Bellman would not place Malamud in a Jewish tradition. He sees three basic and *equally* important themes running through Malamud's work: conversion (universalizing the Jewish problem), a decaying and rotting world, and a new life. He says that not all of Malamud's material is derived from Yiddish sources. His varied sources include Jessie Weston, James Joyce, Henry James, and Edgar Allen Poe. And to Bellman there are apparently "chunks of poorly-digested derived material."[15]

Cynthia Ozick, in "Literary Blacks and Jews," sees Malamud probing and depicting the very heart of a grotesque Jewish context in his latest novel *The Tenants*. She traces the changes in Malamud's thinking from his early story, "Angel Levine," to the recent novel in which the black man Willie Spearmint is pitted against the Jewish white man Harry Lesser. Along the way she interweaves a real-life dialogue between authors Irving Howe and Ralph Ellison, her counterparts to Malamud's fictional characters. Ozick points out that Malamud has given us in his latest novel a portrait of "a ferocious, a mythic, antisemite." She recounts a brief fantasy that Malamud wrote into *The Tenants:* "Some day God will bring together Ishmael and Israel to live as one people." But she reminds us that Malamud realizes that this "miracle" is after all just a dream, a fantasy. Reality is otherwise: Jewish culture must be destroyed by the *goyim*, blacks as well as whites. And Ozick concludes that "*The Tenants* is a claustrophobic fable: it's theme is pogrom."[16]

One reads the critics of Bernard Malamud's fiction and one becomes acutely aware of the Jewish pieces that each critic gleans and then contributes to a Malamud Jewish mosaic. Some focus on new-found roles for second and third generation American Jews in a pluralistic society, some on the sense of an immigrant past. Others examine satire, humor, the *schlemiel*, religion, myth, ritual, folklore, and so on. Some ignore the Jewishness in Malamud's fiction; most do not.

The debate continues in an attempt to identify the Jewish writer and Jewish writing. Josephine Knopp, for example, in her *Trial of Judaism*, talks of a code of *mentshlehkayt* or humanity or of man's "basic goodness" as being an important criterion in the Jewish novel. She associates this code with a few important writers today, including Elie Wiesel, Isaac Bashevis Singer, Saul Bellow, and Bernard Malamud.[17]

But one should perhaps listen to Meyer Levin as he talks about the Jewish writer in America. He, too, talks of the big three—Bellow, Malamud, and Roth. Each, he believes, relates to the Jewish milieu in a special way. He resents those writers "who fear they will lose status if the word *Jewish*" is associated with their writing. Moreover, he goes on, the writers who reject Jewish or Jewish-American classifications for their writing are telling us a great deal about their own inner struggles as they cope with material of their lives which eventually filters down into their fiction.

A number of writers, Levin says, including himself:

> . . . felt that they had been drawn into the Jewish experience more strongly; this was now our predominant experience, particularly as *The Holocaust* developed and as Israel developed. Therefore a more proper category for us was at least American Jewish writer and probably at best a Jewish writer.

When Levin was asked specifically whether he considered Bellow, Roth, and Malamud Jewish-American novelists, he answered this way: They have not "escaped" by calling themselves simply American novelists. They are Jewish novelists also.

And as for Malamud, specifically, and how his writing measures up to something called Jewish, Levin passionately pulls things together:

> [Malamud is] a peculiar case. . . . *The Assistant* was written out of love. . . . It is a Jewish book. . . . His stories afterward . . . bear the flavor of Yiddish literature transplanted here. . . . They have a slight dust over them. I feel as if I am reading a good Jewish writer whose work has been translated into the American scene. So he has not allowed himself to really confront the things that might be more important to him except when he tried it in . . . *The Tenants*. . . .

Levin goes on:

> I think that Malamud has been perhaps *timid* about approaching the American Jewish or Jewish scene. . . . There is virtually nothing said in his material about Israel, about the American-Jewish community's intense and active relationship to Israel. He is alienated

perhaps from the Jewish community and his characters seem to be alienated—so that each works on their little problem or theme. But it has been one of my complaints that this entire group of writers is writing as if American absorption socially with Israel didn't exist. And yet if you go into any Jewish community in this country, you will find that the principal social activities, if not religious activities, revolve around helping Israel, saving Israel, or even anger against Israel, or trying to deny that Americans should have anything to do with Israel. But you cannot describe an American Jew (and these are the people that he writes about), you cannot do this fully and honestly psychologically, without entering into their consciousness of Israel and *The Holocaust*. . . .

Moreover, Levin insists:

No American Jew, no Jew, can get through a single day without somewhere reverberating in his mind some problem, question, attitude in the relation to *The Holocaust* and in relation to Israel. And that any fiction that depicts our generation as Jews or as partial Jews or as renegade or not-wishing-to-be Jews or as self-hating Jews or Jews who passed and changed their names even and live in an all non-Jewish society . . . no character of that kind can go through the day without this passing through his consciousness.

Thus, Levin observes, Malamud is a Jewish writer really writing about many aspects of Jewishness, but at the same time ignoring the real concerns of Jews today. He seems to be saying that Malamud in his fiction does not deal with the real flesh and blood Jew in America today, but the marginal Jew.

James Joyce, Levin explains, was very much aware of this Jewish consciousness when he depicted Bloom, the assimilated Jew. And as for writers today like Salinger and Mailer, Levin concludes, they are more honest than people like Bellow, Roth, and Malamud in that they at least try in their writing to move away from the Jewish world, the Jewish milieu. They don't insist upon having it both ways: that is, an emasculated Jewish world which is then renamed an American world.[18]

In 1950 an important book was published. Coming as it did a few years after the Nazi *Holocaust,* two years after the birth of the State of Israel, and almost at the beginning of America's short-lived and uneasy love affair with Jewish-American fiction, it can perhaps give us historical perspective for the marginal Jew in Jewish-American writing.

Simon Halkin, in his *Modern Hebrew Literature,* surveys 200 years of Hebrew literature, from 1750 to 1950. Along the way he recalls what a number of scholars have always realized concerning a split within the psyche of the modern Jewish writer. At the outset Halkin indicates clearly that he does not intend to write a "history" of modern Hebrew literature. "I regard modern Hebrew literature as the most faithful and comprehensive record of *Jewish life* during" the modern Jewish period, Halkin says. [italics mine] Thus does Halkin prepare one for a history of the Jewish people *and* their literature during the "modern" period, an approach to literature not without its successful precedents.

He argues as follows: about 50 years before the French Revolution, pockets of Jews dotting the West reached a high economic status. What followed was, it seems, recognition of sorts by the predominant cultures in various Western countries; thus followed also a cultural and, to a lesser extent, social emancipation. Finally, after they had "proved" themselves, Jews were granted political emancipation in certain Western, Central, and Eastern European countries. From this social, economic, political, cultural complex concerning the modern Jew, there emerged around the middle of the eighteenth century a rejection of the centuries-old "Jew-in-seclusion" mode of life. The primarily secular Age of Enlightenment, or *Haskalah,* replaced it.

From these beginnings, Halkin goes on to explore the "dilemma of *Haskalah* literature." Simply stated, it is the perennial problem of Jewish writers everywhere, whether they write in Israel, the U.S.S.R., or the United States, whether their native language is Hebrew, Russian, or English, and it concerns Bernard Malamud as it did Kafka before him. The problem goes something like this: How does one reconcile traditional and assimilationist tendencies? Or, if one's Jewishness is distinct, is it not true that a movement toward a universal humanism or other aspects of "enlightenment" will destroy the distinctiveness of one's Jewish writing?

Halkin then focuses on the emerging new "humanism" in Jewish writing and the first stirrings of Zionism as they were reflected in literature. He traces faith and religion as they were used and became a basis for much of the best of modern Jewish writing. Finally, virtually on the eve of the formation of the State of Israel, *The Holocaust* is seen as the latest and most pervasive influence on Hebrew writing.[19]

Halkin's survey is basically a run-through of diaspora literature. If in Halkin's overview one includes a Bernard Malamud, it becomes evident that he too is very much a part of the latter-day dilemma of the *Haskalah*, or "literature of the enlightenment." That is, Malamud's roots are Jewish roots. The original soil nurtures a writer in such a way that in any age his writing is immersed in that which concerns Jews most directly. Transplanted, the writer may become a hybrid. His Jew of the *Torah*, the Law, the rabbinical teachings may become the Jew of general humanism, of universalism. In fact his Jew may become indistinguishable from the non-Jew as he becomes homogenized in a larger, non-Jewish world. He may emerge as Everyman as his identification with his own peoples' overriding concerns becomes peripheral or marginal.

At one time I argued that Malamud must be placed squarely at the center of Jewish tradition. In an essay entitled "Malamud, Mercy, and *Menschlechkeit*," Joyce Field and I insisted that despite the complexities and nuances involving the Jewishness of Malamud's fiction, we finally believed that the Bobers, Boks, Lessers, and many other Malamud characters were ultimately revealed as people who became positively involved in the Jewish milieu. We further insisted that Malamud's major characters eventually stepped out of a nebulous history into the Judaic tradition of Abraham, Isaac, Jacob—and the covenant with God. Possibly we made too many leaps then to place Malamud within the Jewish tradition so centrally.[20]

At a little later date I formulated some additional thoughts on Jewishness. It was on our Day of Atonement, when memories of previous *Yom Kippurs* (especially the 1973 Arab-Israeli *Yom Kippur War*) were painfully etched on our minds, that I received a ninety-minute cassette from a well-meaning Christian neighbor. A bit later, with the fast day still lingering as if suspended in chambers of my consciousness, I listened to the tape. Then I put it aside, but I continued to hear the after-echoes. It fused with *Kol Nidre*—that mystical *Yom Kippur* chant—and would not disappear. Two days later I wrote (but never mailed) a letter to my neighbor. I soon realized that I was trying to answer all the well-meaning neighbors, the proselytizing Jews who had converted to Christianity, and even the Bernard Malamuds who tend at times to fuse Judeo-Christian concepts.

I came to regard the unmailed letter with an odd sense of affection and called it my "Dear Betty" or "*Yom Kippur*-Plus-Two-Days-of-Reflection" letter. I even fictionalized a name for the converted Jew who had made the tape. His name became Mr. Cohen and hers was Betty. So I penned the following to Dear Betty and others:

> People are weary of hearing about *The Holocaust*, Israel, Soviet Jewry, and anti-Semitism. But they never tire of telling the Jews that all their problems would be solved if they would simply stop being Jews. "Be something else," they are told. "Anything else. Just stop being Jews. Or at the very least, admit that there is really no difference between Jews and non-Jews. After all, All Men are Jews, or is it All Men are Christians except that they don't know it?"
>
> Perhaps some of the chief offenders are those ubiquitous proselytizers, the Jew-turned-Christian. We find them among the Hebrew-Christian sects, Jews-for-Jesus, etc. They operate on the street corner and the campus. They have their store front missions and their lecture tours; their newsletters and their magazines. And now the electronic age has spawned the cassette.
>
> On this particular cassette Mr. Cohen talks endlessly to Jews, Christians, and anyone else who will listen to his concept of religious enlightenment. He's the ancient mariner with a modern message. And although he tries mightily, nowhere, dear Betty, in his sermon that you passed on to me, has he fathomed the essence of Judaism *or* Christianity. It would be as if a person just having converted to Judaism tried to proselytize his "unenlightened" former brethren by relating his unhappy journey through his former sterile life as a nominal or peripheral Christian. He could start with the trappings— simpering Jesuses on gaudy Sunday School cards, stories of muscular Christianity à la Crusades, church socials and bingos, the hackneyed Sunday sermon, etc. You know and I know that these things are no

more to be considered Christianity than Cohen's silly comments about Jewish food and the Jewish *Yom Kippur* are the essence of Judaism.

I don't recognize my Jewish life, my faith in anything Cohen said. And his *Yom Kippur Sermon* is an insult, coming as it does at the time of our real *Yom Kippur*, our Day of Atonement, at the end of our days of awe and introspection and awareness. Does Cohen have any notion at all of what it is to be a Jew? Does he really know, has he really felt our long history—which goes back many years before the birth of Jesus? Does he know what a Jew feels about Abraham, Isaac, Jacob? The story of Moses and the Exodus? *The Holocaust?* The birth of Israel? He says he does, and he alludes to some of these people and events along the way, but he then picks them up and flips them off or puts them into a rather alien context. I too have words such as *rachmones* and *chutzpah* in my vocabulary. However. . . .

Has he really given himself over to the words of Moses, Isaiah, Rabbi Akiva, Martin Buber, and many others—from the most devout and learned to the very simple souls like Tevyah the milkman—who have lived Judaism and—yes—have often been slaughtered for their Jewish beliefs? Judaism is a religion, a learning, a joy and a sorrow, a blessing and a curse, and a way of life for millions of people.

Does Mr. Cohen know any real Jews? Or are his Jewish examples the marginal Jews? Our rabbis, our Jewish teachers, refuse to accept the self-righteous and arrogant position that only Jews can be saved. Of course. Nothing in our Jewish teaching even hints at this. All people—Jews and non-Jews—must follow the commandments. And all are under one God. But Christians, Moslems, Jews, and others *do* have different ways to get at this one God, despite what Mr. Cohen says. This then is part of Judaism and Jewishness, a large part.

It's not easy to be a good Jew in a Christian or any other society. But I must say this, Betty. Over the years, Christians have not made it any easier for us. Many have tried to "show us the error of our ways" in sweet and melodious tones. Others have burned us at the stake or gassed us and then thrown us in the ovens. But we have survived—and we will survive.

Don't misunderstand me. When we have encountered Christians with a live-and-let-live attitude—fine. But I must say that my own experience has not made me all that optimistic, despite the recent attempts (rather flabby) at ecumenism. We often wait in vain for Christians who hear *their* still small voice to permit the Jews a little whisper of Grace. We often wait in vain for Christians to stand up and be counted when the Jew is in peril, when Israel is being threatened by genocide, when the Soviet Jews may be on the edge of the abyss.

> What does it really mean to be a Jew, Betty? Do you have any idea? One key word we use is *Shalom*. It means *Peace*, among other things. But basically it means *Harmony — Harmony* within and without. *Harmony*. Think of that and all its possible ramifications. Another key phrase is *L'Chaim — To Life*. But *Life* on our own terms. Not yours or Mr. Cohen's or anyone else's.

So went the letter never mailed. It had much more about Jews and Jewishness, but basically it touched on ideas about Jewishness that seemed to coincide with a number of things that Meyer Levin and Simon Halkin said. It even came close at times to Cynthia Ozick's chilling perception of the Jew and gentile worlds when she wrote "All the World Wants the Jews dead."[21] Or Barbara Tuchman's "They Poisoned the Wells" world view.[22]

I suppose what it comes down to is this: Levin, Halkin, Ozick, Tuchman, and others in their various ways have felt the dark Jewish tremors and the bright joys and have told us what they are. The question, therefore, still remains: Are the modern Jewish-American writers writing so that we can recognize a Jewish people in America with all their tremors and joys? With all the darkness and light? Is Bernard Malamud? And I suppose the answer for Malamud, at least, must be, well, yes and no and not really. Whitman saw life and celebrated it; Poe came to the abyss and plunged in. It may be said that Malamud, in his depiction of Jewish life, rarely did either. I now have some difficulty in reconciling my earlier and current views concerning Jewishness in Malamud's fiction. People like Grebstein and Knopp help bolster my former position. Halkin and Levin tend to support my "Dear Betty" approach. It may be that many Jewish-American writers are really writing about the fringes of the Jewish milieu or at least they write about Jews and the Jewish milieu while at the same time ignoring a good deal that seems to be significant about the Jew today.

To be sure, neither a Bellow nor a Roth nor a Malamud is a Mr. Cohen of the gratuitous and proselytizing tape. Nor can one deny that they haven't tapped and revealed important elements of Jewishness in the fictional worlds they have created. But can anyone in the world-wide Jewish community deny the fact that in modern times, to echo Meyer Levin once again, there are two events for the Jewish people of monumental importance, two events which flavor their thinking and feeling constantly, and that the fallout from these events has seeped into their very beings? The first is the European *Holocaust* in which six million Jews were exterminated, and the second, following close on the heels of the first, is the rebirth of the State of Israel.

Are these momentous events at the heart of Malamud's fiction? one may ask. Of course, the answer must be, *no*. Esthetically and intellectually, much of his fiction is unsurpassed. He renders a world filled with characters who must confront humanity—within themselves and others—in painful, pathetic, comic, or tragic ways. Overwhelmingly, these characters are Jewish, living within Jewish worlds imagined for them by their author. But one must go to a Chaim Potok[23] or a Charles Angoff to realize a real Jewish world. Or to an Elie Wiesel or S. Y. Agnon to reach the fully imagined Jewish world. Is Malamud, therefore, to be denied the title of Jewish-American Writer, which, ironically, he doesn't want anyway? No, I don't believe that's the point at issue.

What is the point then? Simply put, Malamud *is* timid. He *does* back off. When Morris explains his Jewishness and suffering to Frank, his explanations are the tip of the iceberg. Below the surface are anti-Semitism, pogroms, *The Holocaust*. Morris knows pogroms. He mentions them. But so quietly, so imperceptibly. We almost lose them in the telling. Morris, almost asphyxiated by gas in his upstairs flat, has a horrible dream. A Jewish nightmare. He sees the outsiders, the non-Jews closing in on him, his family, his home, his store, his life. It's as much the classic rape and defilement as when Helen is actually raped by Frank and she yells " 'Dog — uncircumcised dog!' "[24] Before our eyes Morris is constantly being revealed, undressed. From top to bottom. Sweater, shirt, trousers, drawers. Finally, the shoes. First one shoe. And then we wait. . . . The other never drops. And I'm afraid this is pretty much the case with Malamud's other characters, too. The second shoe never seems to drop. We may think it does with Yakov Bok. But we aren't sure. And so Malamud straightens out the record. It was the Beilis case. But it could have been Sacco and Vanzetti. "It could have been." A Malamud refrain. *Could have been* is marginality. *Is* is Jewishness.

One must finally realize that Malamud is a Jewish-American writer within the loose tradition of that special breed of hyphenated Jewish writer. He is a brother to the many intellectual and literary Jews who years ago left the *shtetl* and traditional Judaism to reach out into the world. They rejected the confines of their past as they accepted "enlightenment." In so doing they as people and the characters they gave us all took on the qualities of marginality as these writers ignored, skirted, homogenized, or rejected important concerns of the Jewish people.

NOTES

[1]Bernard Malamud, *The Assistant* (New York: Farrar, Straus and Giroux [Noonday]), 1971, pp. 123-125; first published, 1957.

[2]Bernard Malamud, *The Fixer* (New York: Farrar, Straus and Giroux, 1966), p. 335.

[3]These short stories are all from Bernard Malamud, *The Magic Barrel* (New York: Farrar, Straus and Giroux, 1971); first published, 1958.

[4]Philip Roth, *Reading Myself and Others* (New York: Farrar, Straus and Giroux, 1975), p. 168. See also pp. 9-10, and *passim*. Roth is often ambiguous on this subject. In his essay "Imagining Jews," for example, he says: ". . . It can safely be said that imagining what Jews are and ought to be has been anything but the marginal activity of a few American Jewish novelists. The novelistic enterprise — particularly in books like *The Victim, The Assistant,* and *Portnoy's Complaint* — might itself be described as imagining Jews *being* imagined, by themselves and by others." And a little later on he adds: "If he [the novelist] can, with conviction, assent to that appelation [i. e., Jew] and imagine himself to be such a thing at all. And that is not always easy to accomplish. For as the most serious of American-Jewish novelists seem to indicate — in those choices of subject and emphasis that lead to the heart of what a writer thinks — there are passionate ways of living that not even imaginations as unfettered as theirs are able to attribute to a character forthrightly presented as a Jew." (pp. 245-246)

[5]From a talk at the United States Cultural Center in Tel-Aviv, Israel, June 28, 1970; transcribed in *The Jerusalem Jost,* July 10, 1970, p. 12. Bellow has said and written much about himself as a writer and a

Jew. On this specific warm June evening he talked and fielded questions for almost two hours. At one point Bellow became expansive about the Jewishness of himself and fellow writers in America. They were not received well at first by the non-Jewish literary community he said. It was an uphill struggle. But after some minutes in which he defined himself as a separate (i.e., Jewish) but equal man of letters, he retreated by saying ". . . the Jewish writers are not so often—in their own minds—primarily Jewish writers; they are writers who happen to have this particular kind of experience, that is to say, the power of American society to absorb people is so enormous that you don't have time really to think of yourself in that [Jewish] way." (Transcribed in *The Jerusalem Post,* July 3, 1970, p. 12.)

⁶As quoted in *The Jerusalem Post* (Weekly Overseas Edition), March 2, 1976, p. 4. However, note also Bellow's *To Jerusalem and Back: A Personal Account* (New York: The Viking Press, 1976), which appeared while this Malamud symposium was being published.

⁷Leslie and Joyce Field, "Malamud, Mercy, and *Menschlechkeit,*" in Leslie and Joyce Fields, eds., *Bernard Malamud: A Collection of Critical Essays* (Englewood Cliffs, New Jersey: Prentice-Hall, Inc., 1974), p. 7. The excerpts from Malamud originally appeared as an interview in *The Jerusalem Post* (Weekly Overseas Edition), April 1, 1968, p. 13.

⁸Leslie and Joyce Field, "An Interview With Bernard Malamud," in *Bernard Malamud: A Collection of Critical Essays,* pp. 11-12.

⁹As reported by Lionel Koppman in *The J W B Circle,* February 1976, p. 1; see also pp. 4-5.

¹⁰From my talk at the Ethnic Studies Section of the Rocky Mountain Modern Language Association meeting at Tucson, Arizona, October 20, 1972. See also Leslie Field, "Ethnic Studies: Benefit or Boondoggle?" *Bulletin of the Rocky Mountain Modern Language Association,* XXVI (Winter 1972), p. 151.

¹¹Sheldon Norman Grebstein, *Bernard Malamud: A Collection of Critical Essays,* pp. 18-19. Originally published in *Contemporary American-Jewish Literature,* Irving Malin, ed., 1973.

¹²Grebstein, op. cit. pp. 18-44.

¹³See Leslie A. Field and Joyce W. Field, eds., *Bernard Malamud and the Critics* (New York: New York University Press, 1970), pp. 3-10. Rovit's essay was originally published in *Critique,* 3:2 (Winter-Spring 1960), pp. 3-10.

¹⁴Robert Alter, "Jewishness as Metaphor," in *Bernard Malamud and the Critics,* pp. 29-42. Originally published in Alter's *After the Tradition,* 1969.

¹⁵Samuel Irving Bellman, "Women, Children, and Idiots First: Transformation Psychology," in *Bernard Malamud and the Critics,* pp. 11-28. Originally published in *Critique,* 7:2 (Winter 1964-65), pp. 123-138.

[16]Cynthia Ozick, "Literary Blacks and Jews," in *Bernard Malamud: A Collection of Critical Essays*, pp. 80-98. Originally published in *Midstream*, 18:6 (June/July 1972), pp. 10-24.

[17]Josephine Zadovsky Knopp, *The Trial of Judaism in Contemporary Jewish Writing* (Urbana, Illinois: University of Illinois Press, 1975). Knopp's overall thesis is that the novelists she has selected for analysis have a "Jewish view" of the nature of man and destiny. In her concluding argument on Malamud she says of Yakov Bok: ". . . his ultimate acceptance of the uniquely Jewish moral code, despite a continued refusal to accept the Jewish God, demonstrates Yakov's absorption of the moral message of the Old Testament and, in the final analysis, justifies Judaism." (p. 125)

[18]The foregoing views by Levin come from "A Conversation With Meyer Levin," Purdue University, West Lafayette, Indiana, November 6, 1974. Note also Benno Weiser Varon's "The Haunting of Meyer Levin," *Midstream* 22:7 (August/September 1976), pp. 7-23, which appeared while this Malamud symposium was being published.

[19]Simon Halkin, *Modern Hebrew Literature: From the Enlightenment to the Birth of the State of Israel — Trends and Values* (New York: Schocken Books, 1950, 1970).

[20]Leslie and Joyce Field, *Bernard Malamud: A Collection of Critical Essays*, pp. 1-7.

[21]Cynthia Ozick, "All the World Wants the Jews Dead," *Esquire* LXXXII (November 1974), pp. 103-107, 207-210.

[22]Barbara W. Tuchman, "They Poisoned the Wells," *Newsweek* (February 3, 1975), p. 11.

[23]See Daphne Merkin, "Why Potok Is So Popular," *Commentary* 61 (February 1976), pp. 73-75. This review of Chaim Potok's latest novel, *In the Beginning*, also touches on fringe or marginal elements of Jewishness in the American Jewish writers. She does not claim greatness for Potok's fiction, but she does say "after the countless portrayals in American fiction of wandering and assimilated Jews—from Malamud's S. Levin to Bellow's Moses Herzog to Roth's Alexander Portnoy — the literary public, at least a large segment of it, would seem to be ready for Chaim Potok's version of the American Jew — one who has never left the traditional religious community." She goes on to say that "Potok's figures still live in exclusively Jewish worlds; their energy is spent on issues most contemporary Jews have abandoned." Potok, she feels, deals with issues that other Jewish-American novelists ignore. "Unlike more consequential Jewish writers whose heritage colors but does not dictate to their material, Potok writes both *as* a Jew and *because* he is a Jew; one aspect validates the other."

[24]Bernard Malamud, *The Assistant*, pp. 168, 173.

Ben Siegel

THROUGH A GLASS DARKLY:
BERNARD MALAMUD'S PAINFUL VIEWS OF THE SELF

From his beginnings, man has relied on dreams and fantasies to glean from higher or hidden powers some hint of cosmic plan. Every literature records visions or hallucinations that shape human destiny by causing the dreamer to reassess his character, values, and fate. Man's fancies (sleeping or waking), therefore, have moved him repeatedly to look at himself totally and anew. In his self-appraisals he is helped by his prophets and seers. But these worthies confine themselves generally to visions and visitations, trances and frenzies. His poets and storytellers, however, add to their tales the refractive surfaces of mirrors and windows, spectacles and paintings, photographs and the human eye—all to confront man with his inner compulsions, passions, frustrations.

Many peoples cherish that perception capable of glimpsing truth behind facade and countenance. Yet no people has had more historical need to discern between devotion and deceit, self and selfishness than the Jews, for whom, too often, such discernment has meant the difference between joy and sorrow, survival and death. Jewish concern with inner and outer truths is suggested by a familiar parable. A rabbi, having been refused a charitable contribution by a worldly Jew, an *allrightnik*, quietly asks his congregant to look through a window and then in a mirror and to report what he sees. The impatient *allrightnik* retorts that at the window he sees people and in the mirror his reflection. "Isn't it astonishing," the rabbi sighs, "that when you cover a clear glass with a little silver, you see only yourself."[1]

Should Bernard Malamud know this exemplum, he would agree undoubtedly with the rabbi. His novels and stories, however, do suggest a disclaimer—that for the man who needs to confront his deepest self or being, his mirror image may prove more significant than anything he can observe through the clearest glass. Yet few writers are more aware than Malamud of how elusive is self-knowledge, how man's perceptual senses and aids distort reality more often than they sharpen it. Darkened windows and cracked mirrors, failed paintings and misleading photographs abound in his fiction. Too frequently these things obscure rather than reveal the framed face or character. Much in Malamud hinges also on dreams or reveries. His heroes, mostly displaced failures pursuing visions of new lives, escape their harsh realities only in fancy and imagination. Every dream reveals not only their own and their society's moral condition but something of Malamud's thematic interest in men's ethical or non-ethical behavior.

His concentration on moral behavior has annoyed a few critics. Some years ago, David Stevenson complained of his inadequate "concern . . . with the tough, meaningful complexities of man's private destiny, with what William James once called 'the recesses of feeling, the darker, blinder strata of character.' " By avoiding "these strata in favor of thematic concept," Stevenson charged, Malamud had limited "his stature as a writer."[2] Stevenson's point is only partly valid. Malamud does focus strongly on moral or thematic concept, but his people never cease probing their deepest motives and acts, their hopes and dreams—those primal urges comprising their "private destinies" and "darker, blinder" inner forces. Vital to his solitary non-achievers then are those visual images exposing to them their most private expectations and guilts.

Malamud seldom misses a chance, therefore, to amplify a reflected truth or insight. Intending his novels and stories to be parables of possibility and regeneration, he reiterates his "commitment to redemption and renewal through suffering."[3] Hardly an original thinker, he acknowledges readily the prior claims of past masters to this literary construct; in fact, he en-

joys and encourages comparisons to them, especially to Hawthorne, James, and Faulkner.[4] Critics have been quick to com-
ply. Theodore Solotaroff, for instance, notes the numerous
"mirror and light images" in the "moral romances" of Hawthorne and Malamud. Both writers reveal, Solotaroff states, an
identical "preoccupation" with moments that suspend all dis-
tinctions "between the objective and imaginary" and thus enable the "individual spirit" to see itself clearly. Such "self-con-
frontation," however, hardly guarantees happiness. In glimpsing himself, the Malamud hero merely views "his chief adversary." It is what he learns from his revelation, Solotaroff cau-
tions, that "determines his life."[5]

Equally important is what he fails to learn. Roy Hobbs, in
The Natural, offers example. Blessed with large natural gifts,
and driven by a need to be baseball's "champ . . . the best there
ever was," he emerges from obscure origins to strike out fabled
Walter (the Whammer) Wambold and send that aging titan
into retirement. On his way to the major leagues, Roy wakes
confused and disoriented in a darkened pullman berth and is
confronted by a premonitory image. Kneeling in a near-fetal
position that suggests his infantile visions, he paws at the window before striking a match and holding up its flame to the
glass. When he realizes the train is passing through a tunnel, he
is less surprised by the "sight of himself holding a yellow light
over his head, peering back in."[6] What Roy can not realize,
however, is that his life has just been "translated into space,"[7]
with his fabulous career revealed to be only a brief segment of
its span.

Still, a vision so rich with "awakenings and illuminations"
should reveal more of himself to Roy. The struggle of his characters "against self," Malamud declares, is "basic."[8] Certainly
his heroes resist the truths conveyed by their reflections and
fears. Mostly losers, they opt invariably for defeat or failure,
even with success or happiness in view. They can thank ill luck,
moral flaw, or sheer stupidity. Roy is indebted to all three. Rejecting every inner and outer hint or portent, he is shot by a
demented woman and doomed to fifteen years in the minors;

surfacing a second time, he has a spectacular summer. Success brings not pleasure, however, but recurring nightmares of inevitable loss. In one dream, he observes himself holding a golden baseball from which sprouts a white rose, its fragile beauty reinforcing Roy's fears for his fame and fate. His worst premonitions are quickly realized: with pennant and immortality in his grasp, he succumbs to greed, gluttony, and lust. In addition, he contributes to the death of Bump Baily, the outfielder he has replaced on the New York Knights. His failure stems in part from his desire for Bump's mistress, Memo Paris, a desire causing Roy to wonder if he has willed his rival's death. Memo, as her name suggests, revengefully stirs his "memory." But so fearful is Roy of past defeats that he strains to repress his memories, to conceal his private being from others and himself. Any talk of past events or "inner self" is for him like "plowing up a graveyard" (*TN*, p. 155).

But in Malamud the past is never dead. It reasserts itself here through earlier baseball figures, who reappear only slightly altered to confuse Roy's true identity and to help him repeat past mistakes. Not only are sportswriters and fans bemused by Roy's strong resemblance to Bump Baily, but Roy even sees Bump when he looks in his mirror. Whammer Wambold proves, however, the pervasive ghost. In addition to dressing like the Whammer, Roy, in his final game, after striking out on three pitches by young Herman Youngberry, realizes that he is reliving, with roles reversed, their earlier encounter. But his transformation from hero to has-been is more sudden and crushing than the Whammer's. Roy agrees to throw the playoff game, shatters his magical bat, and leaves a discredited failure. As Roy sobs in the street at the crushing of his dreams, a fan observes, "He coulda been a king" (*TN*, p. 237).

True enough, yet every man approaches kingship in his dreams. So the rise and fall of Malamud's great athlete seems merely one more ironic version of the American Dream. A folk hero, after all, by personifying his society's aspirations, elevates and reassures its lesser mortals. "Without heroes," states Iris Lemon, "we're all plain people and don't know how far we can go" (*TN*, p. 154). Here this means that Roy's dreams are shared by so many Americans that his failure proves, as Jonathan Baumbach points out, "a tragic joke," not only on him but "on all of us." Yet for Malamud life never lacks paradox, and if *The Natural* evolves into a "nightmare of [the] frustration of defeat," it serves also as a "fantasy of heroism."[10]

Understandably, some reviewers, especially non-Americans, have had difficulty grasping the novel's "positive" aspects. English critic Alan Ross has seen in it echoes of Nathanael West's "savage mockery" and "surrealist cynicism."[11] Certainly Malamud's characters reveal a good deal more anger and bitterness than have been adequately acknowledged. (Most major Yiddish fictionists, incidentally, have exhibited a similar anger.) Still he intends essentially an upbeat view of human character and values. "Our fiction is loaded with sickness, homosexuality, [and] fragmented man," he has complained, when "it should be filled with love and beauty and hope."[12] His writings bear him out; if they make up an open-ended saga of unfortunate beings and events, they depict always grief and pity and obligation as affirmations of the sadly comic individual fate. "Suffering," the gentle Iris tells Roy Hobbs, "is what brings us toward happiness" (*TN*, p. 158).

Not all Malamud characters, of course, exhibit love or beauty or even hope. But many do reveal pride and strength and responsibility. One who does is Breitbart, the lightbulb peddler, who staggers through the opening and closing scenes of *The Assistant*.[13] Toting his two large cartons, he epitomizes every man's burdens and his need for the transient respite of even the most dimly lit room. Breitbart's lack of light and repose is shared by all the befuddled figures of *The Assistant* and *The Magic Barrel*. Mostly beleaguered Jews clinging to dignity and self-respect, they shuffle between dark, cramped tenements, and bare, depressing shops. Isolated and unlucky, they are denied even total commitment to God or faith. They hope only for better things for their children. For themselves, they will settle for less failure and diminished pain.

Unhappiness takes a heavy toll. Many are tiresome, self-pitying *nudniks* or pests[14] unable to forget they are wanderers in a hostile world. Yet they never cease trying to salvage small victories from large defeats. "Naturalized" rather than "assimilated," overwrought and determined to be heard, they share an inflected, idiomatic Yiddish-English and the melancholy discovery that America, the Golden Land, has not ended their exile. Morris Bober speaks for most when he laments that he "had hoped for much in America and got little" (*TA*, p. 27). Their only talents are for suffering and survival. "A Malamud character," Malamud himself has stated, "is someone who fears his fate, is caught up in it, yet manages to outrun it. He's the subject and object of laughter and pity."[15] Still this laughter and pity, as well as the isolation and defeat all his people experience, Malamud might have added, are intended as aids not barriers to grasping one's true identity.

Malamud's suffusion of his fiction with claustral and "imprisoning" images has been well documented.[16] Note also how thoroughly he has absorbed his literary texts. Such modernists as Dickens and Dostoevsky, Joyce and Kafka, Lionel Trilling has observed, have conceived of "modern culture as a kind of prison," wherein modern man finds fulfillment by experiencing "alienation." If admittedly a painful, paradoxical state, alienation does serve, Trilling rightly points out, as a means of "self-realization" for, among others, Dreiser, Hemingway, and Faulkner.[17] Agreeing totally, Malamud makes such self-discovery central to his fiction. His chief concern, he states, is that at critical moments his characters exhibit self-honesty and candor. Yet if each hapless figure often appears less than he can be, Malamud insists that he prove "more than he seems" by striving for order, dignity, value.[18] His Jews, therefore, despite setback and pain, remain convinced of the self's inviolability and invincibility. "There are unseen victories all around us," states Malamud; "it's a matter of plucking them down" with effort and courage.[19]

Such courage is needed when life's one constant is agony or pain. Jewish novelists have learned about human anguish from

Jewish history and from Dostoevsky. Suffering redeems life and gives it meaning, observes the Russian's Underground Man. Often the individual's "greatest misfortune," his suffering, is always his chief source of self-awareness and self-love.[20] For Malamud, personal distress and torment prove man's prime means of consciousness and the chief link between his Jews and gentiles. Equally vulnerable to human rage and pain, his non-Jews often become the "mirror image doubles" or "secret sharers" of his Jews.[21] But where Dostoevsky holds suffering to be a means of purification and salvation, Malamud treats it as an inexorable affliction to be endured with dignity and resolution. Unhappy Leo Finkle derives solace from the thought "that he was a Jew and a Jew suffered." The Jew, in Leo's parochial view, thus becomes a paradigm of Everyman, in that all men suffer. Like Dostoevsky, Malamud believes shared anguish should lead to mutual sympathy and brotherhood. But he rejects the Russian's conviction that men are innately vicious and cruel.[22]

How shared suffering, poverty, and sorrow can unify diverse beings is what Frank Alpine learns. He is the Italian Jew-hater and thief of *The Assistant* who robs grocer Morris Bober and then tries to expiate his crime.[23] Here again mirrors, windows, and dreams offer the harassed Bober and Frank Alpine opportunities for self-realization, identity, and guidance. Even the newspaper Morris Bober reads is titled *The Mirror* and reflects his daily expectation of finding in the social realities surrounding him some answers to his dilemmas. As for Frank Alpine, he is not only repelled and attracted by the Jew he has victimized, but he is rendered equally uncertain by his confused glances at his own emerging self. Torn by aspiring dreams and harsh realities, by lofty ideals and low fleshly desires, he repeatedly fails to see himself clearly. The partial, deflected glimpses he does catch intensify his inadequacies and frustrations. Washing before a cracked mirror, for example, he sees a distorted face that suggests to him a warped personality. Viewing his reflection after sexually forcing Helen Bober, he feels "a nose-thumbing revulsion." "Where have you ever been,

he ask[s] the one in the glass, except on the inside of a circle?
What have you ever done but always the wrong thing?" (*TA*,
pp. 174-75).

Uncertain and guilt-ridden, Frank does not allow others to
see him totally. "There was more to him than his appearance,"
observes Helen Bober. "Still, he hid what he had and he hid
what he hadn't. . . . You looked into mirrors and saw mirrors
and didn't know what was right or real or important." He only
pretends "to be frank about himself," she decides, when in fact
he hides "his true self" (*TA*, p. 121). Frank's reluctance to strip
himself of masks and poses is juxtaposéd against his climbing
the dumbwaiter shaft to peer at Helen in her bath. The dis-
comfitures of self-exposure are thereby contrasted to the pleas-
ures of seeing others uncovered.

His dreams and reveries also remind Frank Alpine of his
failures, especially his inability to reach others. In these dreams
his telephones turn into bananas and his bird and flower carv-
ings for Helen go into the garbage can. In other dreams he
stands barefoot in the snow awaiting a kind gesture from his
angry lady love. Like Roy Hobbs, Frank desires a woman he
has enjoyed but can no longer get. Malamud's women also
crave what they can not have. Memo Paris laments a dead
lover. Helen Bober aches so for a happier life that she bears a
"starved" look, "a hunger in her eyes." His hunger for Helen
and his deepening religious feelings result for Frank in reveries
of St. Francis of Assisi, whose selfless life fascinates him. Becoming Frank's imagined intercessor, the saint retrieves from
a garbage can the wooden cross Frank has made for Helen.
When the saint tosses the cross into the air, it turns into a flower. "Little sister," announces the bowing saint, "here is your
little sister the rose." From St. Francis she accepts the offering,
although it comes with Frank Alpine's "love and best wishes"
(*TA*, pp. 245-46).

Thus does Frank gain in dream the acceptance he has for-
feited in reality. His loss asserts itself in another "snow" dream.
This one has him nearly buried and alone, and it suggests the
story he tells Helen of St. Francis fashioning in his loneliness a

snow wife and children. But then Malamud's people generally find in nature or the seasons a psychological mirror for their mental or emotional states. Both Frank Alpine and the Bobers suffer through a depressing, isolating winter to greet eagerly the "relief-bringing" spring.[24] When at that time of renewal Frank does transform himself into a disciplined, moral being, he models himself after the recently deceased Morris Bober who, like St. Francis, had affirmed his obligations to others. To deny such responsibilities, Frank now recognizes, leads not to freedom but to denial of self. By taking on the old storekeeper's burdens, he redeems his own past of sins. The love or commitment an individual invests in others, Malamud again makes clear, measures his own grace.[25] When Frank has himself circumcised to become a Jew, he brings together his dreams and realities. Now unified, his life gives hope to a persistent loser.

Expectations of a better life motivate also the scurrying figures in *The Magic Barrel*.[26] Here Malamud fashions 13 story plots and their people into another collective drama of aloneness and frustration. But if yearning for brotherhood, his buffeted figures fear actual communion. Glimpsing themselves in mirrors, windows, or dreams, they only feel more intensely their traumas and inner pains. The sickly tailor Manischevitz, for example, is guilty merely of being man and Jew and cannot fathom his endless bad luck. Like Morris Bober, he scans his newspaper to glean from the life whirling about him some truth to help him in his time of need. Help does come, not from print but from on high (who else even listens?). All will be well if the tailor can accept as God's emissary a Black in a derby who calls himself Alexander Levine. Manischevitz, who resembles Job more than Jacob, wrestles with the dilemma posed by so unorthodox an envoy. "So if God sends to me an angel," he ponders, "why a black?" (*MB*, p. 47). His answer comes in a dream of Levine "standing before a faded mirror, preening small decaying opalescent wings" (*MB*, p. 51). For the desperate tailor this is sign enough, and he hails the Black as both Jew and angel. At this, Manischevitz's sick wife recovers, and he witnesses Levine's ascension. Even angels may need man's faith, it seems, to regain heaven.

That man's need for faith in self may be even more urgent is suggested by "The Lady of the Lake." Henry Levin, in Italy for romance and a new life, changes his name to Freeman and falls in love with the beautiful Isabella del Dongo. A girl with her own obscure past, she hints of aristocratic heritage. Believing a Levin unworthy so ethereal a creature and his own aspirations, he thrice disavows his Jewish identity. She then declares herself Isabella della Seta, a Jewish deathcamp survivor who must remain loyal to her past, and fades into a lake-island mist. Levin-Freeman is left to ponder the price of self-denial and deception. Taught also a better understanding of self is Leo Finkle, the would-be rabbi of "The Magic Barrel." Seeking a wife to improve his chances for a good congregation, Leo turns to marriage broker Pinye Salzman. A cynical dealer in "abortive dreams," the latter draws an endless flow of photographs from his magic barrel. If Salzman's ladies are all losers, several do force his client into painful reappraisal. Candidate Lily Hirshorn, for instance, questions Leo into recognizing his lack of love for God and virtually everyone else. Or perhaps, he muses, he loves God so little because he does not love man. Leo's confusion is compounded when he sees both "evil" and "his own redemption" in the photo of Salzman's prostitute daughter Stella. Now considering himself in no moral position to deny the most stained creature her humanity, Leo determines to convert Stella to goodness and himself to God.

To gain humility and insight through painful self-discovery is also the fate of Arthur Fidelman. Another Jewish innocent footloose in Italy, he moves from appearances in *The Magic Barrel* and *Idiots First* through the six vignettes that constitute *Pictures of Fidelman: An Exhibition.*[27] These are verbal montages of a pilgrim-artist yearning for creativity and acceptance; what he learns, however, is less how to paint than how to live. Malamud's goal in these stories, he has stated, is to have his comic hero "find himself both in art and self-knowledge."[28] Fidelman does so, but he also discovers that neither art nor self is what he thought it was. The honing of his underdeveloped sensibilities begins precisely with his arrival in Rome to study Giotto. He quickly experiences a sense of "seeing himself . . . to the pinpoint, outside and in," growing aware, at nearly the same moment, of an "exterior source" to this near "tri-dimensional reflection of himself" (*PF*, p. 4). A stranger has been watching him. This observer, the scavenging refugee Shimon Susskind, makes his life a near-nightmare, but he becomes Fidelman's immediate illuminator of his own vulnerability and humanity.

Here, too, dreams abet self-discovery. In one dream, the skeletal Susskind accosts Fidelman in a cemetery. After asking why art exists, he leads the art student to a ghetto synagogue containing a Giotto painting of St. Francis giving his gold cloak to an old knight. Thus does his pathetic Virgil render the newcomer more senstive to the interrelationship of art and artist and the human heart. Yet compassion does not come easily. Giving Susskind his one extra suit of clothes, the student finds the refugee has destroyed his Giotto manuscript. The celebrated tableau that closes "The Last Mohican"—with Fidelman in pursuit of Susskind—suggests a mocking reprise of Keats's "Grecian Urn." The American's education, however, as the other Fidelman stories reveal, is far from complete. Fall guy for an array of tough Italian pimps, prostitutes, and promoters, he roams from Rome to Milan, from Florence to Venice. At each stop, he is abused, cheated, reduced by gangsters to brothel menial and art forger, and even buggered by one mistress's husband. "Life is short if you don't hurry" (*PF*, p. 205), he cries; it is even shorter, he perceives, if you do not learn. Fidelman learns quickly. He not only transforms his encountered brutalities into creative expression, but he develops his own talent for roguery and duplicity. His art talent is less certain. His only successful canvases are self-portraits dredging up hidden needs and guilts. In these paintings Shimon Susskind remains a haunting spectre of his Jewish past, reappearing there either running or hanging from a gallows.

Admittedly a comic victim, Fidelman proves also a resilient one; he escapes each defeat with a modicum more of compassion and dignity and pain. For in Italy all are experts on life and art, and Fidelman, confronted by his personal and aesthetic shortcomings, suffers daily decisions of self-appointed arbiters like Beppo Fassoli, his mistress's husband. Despite the agonized American's pleas for "mercy," Beppo slashes his canvases and admonishes him, "If you can't invent art, invent life" (*PF*, p. 199). Fidelman returns to America and settles for blowing glass and loving both men and women. Seemingly, he has learned enough for a deeper, more open life. Reviewers have read these stories as parables of the artistic life and of the non-artistic in life. Some have seen in Fidelman the familiar "universal misfit," or the American innocent abroad, or the Jew beset in a Christian culture.[29] Less noted by them—due perhaps to the irreverent humor and pathos—have been Malamud's anger at the continuing plight of the Diaspora Jew and his evoking here of exilic irony and stubborn, if passive, resistance. Certainly few readers have seen in Arthur Fidelman a mocking self-portrait of Bernard Malamud, who borrows his mother's maiden name to burlesque his own ultra-serious themes of love and redemption, suffering and discipline.

While redemption for Malamud has its comic aspects, it remains his major concern in *A New Life*.[30] A singular example of the "quest" narratives that dominated Fifties fiction, the novel traces a perplexed New York Jew's West Coast search for personal worth, integrity, and a little "measurable" happiness. Having escaped Malamud's gloomy tenements, teacher Seymour Levin sees himself at thirty as still pursuing "last year's train" and being "far behind in the world." Frank Alpine's adventures had ended with conversion; Levin's begins with his. A reformed drunk and unreformed misfit, Levin has fled past failures to fashion a better future, one linked to the liberal tradition of learning and thought. His new existence does have a serious flaw. "It hangs," as Levin notes, "on an old soul" (*NL*, p. 58). It seems he still carries a battered suitcase of old ideals, a gift for disaster, and a bent for "dark, hallucinated dreams."[31]

In addition, he wears a concealing beard, having grown it, he confesses, "in a time of doubt," to prevent looking himself in the face (*NL*, p. 188).

No victory here is without defeat, "no gain . . . without loss."[32] Levin eludes poverty and despair to find himself amid intellectual mediocrity and indifference. Wanting friendship, he gets friendliness. Seeking love, he finds sex. Pursuing justice, he resorts to deceit, blackmail, breaking, and entering. If he laughs one minute, he groans the next. As do all Malamud loners, Levin learns too slowly that the self-worth and dignity he craves are best gained by responding to another's needs. People have much to offer each other, Malamud makes clear. Their eyes, expressions, responses can provide a "feedback" more helpful to the individual than any mirror reflection. Many Malamud figures serve as "doubles" or second images that enable the original to grasp an insight into self. Very often, however, his wanderers are too bemused by inner and external needs to see others clearly. They fail to comprehend dream warnings issued by their intuitive or subconscious selves. Yet these internal signals prove more reliable moral guides than do their willed judgments. A Frank Alpine or Seymour Levin who grasps this truth seems eligible for better things. A Roy Hobbs who rejects all inner portents invites more failure and frustration.

Yet Levin, too, can avoid difficulty and confusion by more carefully heeding intuition and instinct. He gazes at a birch tree and realizes that with "its symmetry spoiled by its bias" it is much like himself. He then falls asleep contemplating the future and dreams he has caught "an enormous salmon by the tail" and is hanging on desperately; "the furious fish," however, "threshing the bleeding water," breaks free. "Levin," it cries, "go home" (*NL*, p. 24). The advice seems especially sound when he involves himself with Pauline Gilley, whose husband has hired him at Cascadia College. He also relates the impact of an earlier reverie when revealing to Pauline his alcoholic past. Driven to near-suicide by drink and despair, he had awakened in a strange cellar one morning to see his "rotting shoes on a broken chair" bathed "in dim sunlight," as if in "a painting." Strongly affected by this interplay of light and dark, he had decided "that life is holy" and he had become, as he puts it, "a man of principle." Pauline, her own dream expectations met, replies, "I sensed it. I knew who you were" (NL, pp. 201-2). What she apparently has not realized is that even a man of principle may prove an unreliable lover. Levin neglects her, and at a basketball game guiltily observes her through binoculars. A watching student suggests that Levin sees her naked through the glasses; what the extra lenses do enable him to see are the ravages of his neglect.

His office window offers another vantage point, with its cracked glass "resembling a tree," emblematic of his changed setting. Fascinated by the "clouds drifting eastward," as well as by the nearby casting classes for youthful anglers, he muses wonderingly, "A new world, Levin" (NL, pp. 97-8). Yet while physically idyllic, his new setting offers disappointments, in particular his classes and colleagues. The one exception is Leo Duffy, a disgraced predecessor Levin is never to meet but whose reputation reminds him repeatedly of his own weaknesses. Inheriting Duffy's office, Levin feels himself linked to this shadowy double by Professor Fairchild, the department chairman. Informing the newcomer of his duties, Fairchild recalls Duffy and seems to Levin to strike unerringly at his own character. Fairchild deplores two types of teachers: "One is the misfit who sneaks in to escape his inadequacy elsewhere and . . . the other is the aggressive pest whose one purpose is to upset other people's applecarts." Sometimes both types appear in "the same person," Fairchild adds. "Leo Duffy comes to mind . . . irresponsible and perverse" (NL, pp. 41-2).

Duffy may hardly be the proper model for his new life, but Levin finds himself sharing not only his double's office but his mistress. To this last painful fact Levin owes even his job. Pauline, distressed by Duffy's suicide, had picked Levin's photo from a stack of faculty rejects. He looked, she had decided, in need of a friend; in addition, he resembled a Jewish boy who once had befriended her. Thus the camera again proved a re-

demptive aid. Leo Finkle, in search of a proper marriage partner, had seized upon Stella Salzman's suffering face, and the
compassionate Iris Lemon had reached out to Roy Hobbs after
seeing the anguish recorded in his newspaper photo. "So I was
chosen" (*NL*, p. 361), sighs Levin. Pauline had "marked him
x in a distant port" and joined him to her in a new life, a life
rooted in the suffering each has known. As for himself, had he
been moved to love her, he wonders, "because her eyes mirrored Levin when he looked?" (*NL*, p. 217).

     He shrinks from a future "chained" to her and to her two
sickly adopted children. With her he might resemble extern-
ally a free man, but anyone peering "into his eyes would see the
the lines of a brickwall . . . a windowless prison." Still, he admits he has brought it on himself, and this prison is "really himself, flawed edifice of failures, each locking up tight the one before" (*NL*, p. 362). His confined feeling derives partly from his
sense of retracing Leo Duffy's life and errors. Yet he proves as
committed to completing the dead man's unfulfilled life as was
Frank Alpine to that of Morris Bober. He is determined also not
to repeat his own past mistakes of flight and aloneness. Agreeing in the spring to marry the pregnant Pauline, he proves
morally superior to Roy Hobbs, who had abandoned the
pregnant Iris Lemon. "The times are bad," Levin early observes,
"but I've decided I'll have no other" (*NL*, p. 18). Levin and
Malamud both view true freedom then not as the rejection but
the acceptance of obligations and ties.

     Still Levin can not decide whether he is Pauline's savior
or victim, or whether his new responsibilities will redeem or
destroy him. Either way, he — as do all Malamud heroes — will
keep "paying for being alive" (*NL*, p. 336). "Goodbye to your
sweet dreams" (*NL*, p. 360), taunts Pauline's husband, Gerald
Gilley, who is doing his best to crush them. But Malamud expects all men to meet the tests of charity and compassion, disappointment and defeat; he seems to expect more, however, of his
college teachers, wanting them to function as secular priests.[33]
Yet his academics—Cronin in "A Choice of Profession," Orlando
Krantz in "The Maid's Shoes," or Gerald Gilley and the Cascadia

College faculty—score no higher on their moral exams than do his most unlettered tenement dwellers." "It's not easy to be moral," Cronin laments, after a petty act against a student. When a needy maid proves bothersome, Krantz fires her. Each sees himself as a moral, high-minded man. So does Gerald Gilley. Devoted to teaching-and-blackmailing by photograph, Gilley closes the novel by aiming his camera at the departing Levin and Pauline and exclaiming, "Got your picture!" (*NL,* p. 367). This act hardly suggests a better Gilley,[34] despite Malamud's interview contention. The latter's pleasure derives more logically from having caught their images "on shiny paper" for his orderly scrapbook and files.

At the last, then, Levin has acted responsibly. Despite his failings, he has realized that "life is holy" rather than happy and human frailties place none beyond redemption. If such recognition is important for teachers and humanists, it is even more so for writers, who are expected by Malamud to recognize and release what is human in man. To re-create man's humanity, to hold up the "mirror" to that inner "mystery" where dwell "poetry and possibility," though the individual has "endlessly betrayed them," is for him vital to the writer's art. The writer alone, Malamud insists, reminds man that by striving he invents "nothing less than freedom." The writer or reader cherishing this truth preserves not merely his own freedom but "his own highest value."[35]

Like Seymour Levin, the striving souls of the dozen *Idiots First* [36] stories also pay heavily for their humanity. Patterned to paired, symbiotic figures driven by contrasting inner voices, each plot evolves from a crucial act that leads to new hope or "diminished survival."[37] One figure's struggle to escape entanglements is countered by his partner's urgent need or pain. Their conflicts test the solitary human spirit, with most Malamud sufferers failing to pass; victims themselves, they vent anger and frustration on their fellows. Both "Black Is My Favorite Color" and "The Jewbird" point up their victims' need to brutalize others. Stripped to basic emotions and uncertainties, these losers enjoy little hope and less love. Short stories for Malamud are often early sketches to be expanded in his novels. Here "The Cost of Living," "Life Is Better Than Death,"[38] and "The Death of Me" try out characters and actions later developed more fully. In "The Death of Me," for instance, Marcus, an elderly Jewish tailor, suffers a fatal heart attack trying to separate his battling assistants. The final violence, with Polish presser and Sicilian tailor stabbing each other as the Jew pleads for peace and mercy, provides an obvious rehearsal for *The Tenants*.

Most shocking to mind and memory, however, is the title story, "Idiots First." A mini-drama of Malamud's themes of compassion, charity, and sacrifice, its bizarre figures and events suggest that even divine fate may be humanized and life snatched (if briefly) from death. They reveal also how man's eyes may mirror not only human terror but celestial shame. The Angel of Death materializes here as an arrogant, bulky figure named Ginzburg, "with hairy nostrils and a fishy smell," to pursue a dying Jew named Mendel. But the desperate Mendel determines to fend off his assailant until he can get his grown imbecile son, Isaac, on the train to a California kinsman. His frantic efforts to raise Isaac's fare culminate in violence when Ginzburg, reappearing as the station ticket-collector, informs the pleading father he has missed the train. "What will happen happens," Ginzburg smirks. "This isn't my responsibility. . . . I ain't in the anthropomorphic business." Nor, he adds, is pity his "commodity." "The law is the law . . . the cosmic universal law" (*IF*, p. 13). Seizing the collector by the throat, the pitiful Mendel, despite the freezing cold invading his body, refuses to release his grip. As the gasping father clings to Ginzburg, he sees in the collector's eyes "the depth" of his own terror. But Mendel sees also that Ginzburg, staring into his eyes, has glimpsed in them the depth of his "own awful wrath." Angel or not, the collector beholds darkness and "a shimmering, starry, blinding light" that astounds and shames him. "Who me?" (*IF*, p. 15) he asks and relinquishes his grip. Isaac is free to go. Neither the Angel of Death nor his "cosmic law" has proved a match for a dying father's love.

Mendel has now to accept his own fate, but this all men must do. Although much younger, Malamud's "fixer," Yakov Bok — like Mendel — has found his past "a wound in the head," and from his future, in Tsarist Russia, he expects little better. Well, he does and does not. He yearns for a fresh start, a new life to cancel past failures, with "a full stomach now and then" and, as he puts it, "A job that pays rubles, not noodles. Even some education."[39] To sum it up, Yakov states, he has little, but he does have plans. Failing to satisfy these yearnings in the *shtetl*, he shaves his beard and sets off to pursue his dream in Kiev. His aspirations, different only in details from those of Frank Alpine and Seymour Levin, prove also beyond attainment. As do all Malamud loners, Yakov Bok learns too slowly that self-worth and dignity are best won gy giving of one's self more freely. He also gleans from sufferings, fantasies, and dreams some knowledge, both intuitive and prophetic, of his fate and its agents. In an early dream, soon after he starts work at the Kiev brickyard, he finds he is followed along a grave-yard road by the thieving German driver Richter. When the fixer asks the German what he carries in the bag on his back, the latter winkingly responds, "You" (*IF*, p. 63). Yakov's dream reveals his awareness of the driver's hatred and how badly he and the other workers want revenge for his interfering with their thefts.

Falsely accused of ritual murder, Yakov Bok is confined to a Russian prison and brutally abused. His most harrowing moments, however, occur amid the despairing silences—an enforced quiet epitomizing the enclosed loneliness of all Malamud's Jews. During 26 solitary months, he finds release from hunger and torment in dreams and hallucinations, with the novel's important figures appearing more often in these fantasies than in the "realistic" action.[40] Shocked to discover the magistrate Bibikov, for example, hanging in an adjoining cell, Yakov is soon warned by that good man's ghost that the authorities plan a similar fate for him. Yet, only a follow-up dream convinces him of the value of listening to his intuitive self. Severely ill, he eats to recover his health but continues to feel bad. Dreaming again of

Bibikov, he awakes this time with a strong brassy taste in his mouth. Yakov has a flashing insight. "Poison," he cries. "My God, they're poisoning me!" (*TF*, p. 199). He has diagnosed his illness.

The grim nature of the fixer's plight becomes more clear when Tsar Nicholas II appears in a dream to chastise him for being a Jew. "There are too many Jews," the Little Father declares, "my how you procreate! Why should Russia be burdened with teeming millions of you? You yourself are to blame for your troubles. . . . The ingestion of this tribe has poisoned Russia" (*TF*, p. 251). Yakov Bok has a better grasp now of this ruler he has venerated and to whom he looked for justice and mercy. Nor can he find mercy or a soft word within the prison. A single inmate, an old man wearing cracked glasses, shows him kindness. This slop-pail man helps Yakov clean his scalp wound and wrap his hands and feet so he can crawl to the infirmary. Only a prisoner of distorted vision, it seems, will help another. Yakov's vision, too, has been limited: his only view of the outside is through a cracked cell window. Thus do Malamud's unfortunates often look at the life about them through flawed glass.

They often see farther by dream and fantasy. When the depressed and miserable Yakov decides to provoke his guards to kill him, he is constrained by a dream suggesting his death's broader consequences. In his dream, a rickety wagon approaches bearing a coffin that holds Shmuel Rabinovitch, his father-in-law. Crying, Yakov awakes. "Live, Shmuel," he groans, "live. Let me die for you." But he can hardly die for Shmuel if he takes his own life. Shmuel could be murdered as a result of his death if the Russians work up a celebrating pogrom. "What have I earned," he asks himself, "if a single Jew dies because I did? Suffering I can gladly live without, I hate the taste of it, but if I must suffer let it be for something. Let it be for Shmuel" (*TF*, pp. 272-73). His dreams not only sharpen Yakov's awareness of his true plight and of his real friends and enemies, but they strengthen his resolve and guide his behavior.

Even his nightmares are instructive. Most frightening are those in which his unfaithful Raisl appears amid Jewish slaughter, his castration, and her repeated rape. Astounded when she runs in fear from him, Yakov wonders if perhaps he, too, has victimized her, rather than the reverse. Often, he recalls, he showed more interest in Spinoza than in her bed. Even her persistent sadness and dissatisfaction seem now merely to have mirrored his own. "She was a pretty girl," he reminds himself, "intelligent and dissatisfied, with even then a sad face. At least the right eye was sad; the left was neutral, it reflected me" (*TF*, p. 209). Having softened toward Raisl, he gets a belated chance to nourish a "new life" by acknowledging her illegitimate son as his own. The lad's name, appropriately, is *Chaim* or "life." (Conversely, he can not even fantasize any bonds to Zhenia Golov. His dream-efforts to raise the murdered boy from the dead fail.)

If in Malamud no gain is without loss, neither is loss ever devoid of gain. Yakov's sufferings may have taught him, as he insists, "the uselessness of suffering," but they also have toughened his character and will, stripped him of arrogance and false pride, and increased his compassion and charity, thereby enabling him, as Shmuel has admonished, "to fix his heart." He again loves Raisl (or "Israel"), whom he has hated, and now hates the Tsar, whom he has admired. His humiliations inspire fantasies and hallucinations that renew his flagging courage and teach him "true" freedom's meaning. He fears for his life when he learns his trial is to begin. His anxieties evoke again the ghostly Bibikov, who assures him the authorities no longer dare to murder him. And should Yakov manage to win his release, the magistrate adds, he must keep in mind that freedom's purpose is "to create it for others." At this, Yakov experiences "an extraordinary insight." Something in him has changed. "I'm not the same man I was. I fear less and hate more" (*TF*, p. 319). Just how much he has changed, outside and in, shocks even him. Riding to court under military guard, he sees in the coach window the archetypal figure Yakov Bok has become, "a faded shrunken Jew" (*TF*, p. 328). Yakov looks away, but his gaunt image remains so painfully vivid that he weeps in self-pity.

This bitter glimpse shapes his final delusional encounter with a naked Nicholas, who pleads for understanding. Yakov denounces the Tsar for his deficient knowledge of his people and for his lack of that mercy which creates in a man "charity" and "respect for the most miserable" (*TF*, p. 334). Nicholas, the fixer charges, proves his kindness with pogroms. His denunciation is the more poignant because of Yakov's long reverence for the Tsar as God's representative if not as God himself. Like his namesake the Patriarch Jacob, Yakov has dreamed of wrestling with this god, "beard to beard." Now, unmoved by the Tsar's pleas, the fixer, declaring that to abuse human nature invites destruction, shoots him. For this "ritual murder" of a failed god (a murder that precedes history by five years), Yakov Bok is prepared to stand trial.

Novelist Harry Lesser in *The Tenants* encounters different trials and tribulations, but with consequences seemingly as dire.[41] Another loner in quest of redemptive experience, Lesser pursues fulfillment through art. He struggles with a novel for which, because it parallels his own life, he can find no ending. Dedicated totally to his craft, he has withdrawn into a prison of his own making while yearning for contacts of the spirit and flesh. As a result, the outer world has been shut out as totally as in *The Fixer*, with attention focused as narrowly on an individual mind and character. No city or "white Gentiles"[42] are seen beyond the tenement in which Lesser battles himself and his black adversary. Like Philip Roth's recent *My Life as a Man*, Malamud's book is a "mirror novel," another effort at reducing to plausible fiction the events narrated and being read. The heroes or narrators of these involuted fictions struggle generally to extract art from experience by observing themselves living, writing, coping with the complex interplay of literature and life, the individual, and society. Malamud doubles the refractions here with two writers locked in a love-hate embrace of art and manhood, creativity and destruction. Black Willie Spearmint invades Lesser's building and tries to throw off his tormented past by fictionalizing a black writer's efforts to do the same. Lesser has been struggling for a decade with a novel about a novelist writing a novel about a novelist writing about the same things bothering him, that is, a writer's deficiencies in compassion and love.[43] "Lesser writes his book," he observes, in a wry self-comment, "and his book writes Lesser" (*TT*, p. 193).

Malamud's circular structure is suggested by his opening words: "Lesser catching sight of himself in his lonely glass wakes to finish his book" (*TT*, p. 3). His hero rouses himself from the dreams and reveries that conclude both inner and outer narratives and which combine to create a "Chinese-box effect."[44] The grim mood and realistic tenement setting slip rapidly into fact-and-fantasy — with all action filtered through Lesser's fanciful thoughts and nightmares. Willie's internalizings remain shrouded. Much less in doubt are the wants and feelings of building owner Irving Levenspiel (another Levin). Malamud landlords generally want to eject their current tenants. Levenspiel is no exception. Lesser, however, refuses to leave. Declaring home is where his novel is, he insists on staying until his book is finished. Ironically titled *The Promised End*, his novel traces a writer's search for love. It embodies also Lesser's attempt to instruct his life through his art. He need only work out an ending, he is convinced, to discover what love is. His prospects are not promising; well named, Lesser is, at 36, as he admits, "short of love" in his nature. He does not know why.

Failure appears also Willie Spearmint's fate. Torn between being artist or activist, he strains to translate the brutalities of his life into fiction. Lacking any sense of form or structure, Willie relies on his blackness and his shattering past to give shape and meaning to his sprawling narrative. When Lesser helps him evade the landlord, Willie insists that he also criticize his book—his style, not his message. Lesser is reluctant. Dedicated to his own style and standards, he finds Willie's lack of craft offensive. Thinking of himself (as did Arthur Fidelman) almost totally as artist rather than Jew, Lesser considers ethnicity an inadequate basis for art. Black has to be made "more than color or culture," he in effect tells Willie, while "outrage" should prove larger than mere "protest or ideology" (*TT*, p. 67). For Willie such criticism is crushing: Lesser has denigrated him and black art. When Lesser later confesses that he and Willie's Jewish girlfriend, Irene Bell, are in love, Willie explodes into a seething hatred for Lesser and all Jews.

Serious novelists often probe the tangled motives of shared guilt and failed charity until differences are blurred and victim and victimizer prove equally culpable. Here Malamud does it too. A revengeful Willie burns Lesser's manuscript and Lesser retaliates by smashing Willie's typewriter. Tension and violence build to a "final" scene that seemingly spurts blood. But neither the blood nor the apocalyptic conclusion is real. Both are products only of Lesser's overwrought mind and imagination. Many reviewers, however, have missed this important twist.[45] In fact, Lesser tries out three dream endings for his novel. His first occurs as early as page 23, where Lesser imagines Levenspiel setting fire to the building and himself courageously refusing to stop writing. Later, trying to re-create his burned manuscript, he fantasizes two more conclusions. In the first, Lesser hallucinates a scene derived from the graffitti-jungle mural of an empty apartment: a village chieftain marries him to the black Mary Kettlesmith, with a rabbi performing the rites for Willie and Irene Bell. "Someday," the rabbi observes, "God will bring together Ishmael and Israel to live as one people. It won't be the first miracle." When Irene asks Harry to explain these happy events, he hints at what is happening. "It's something I imagined," he states, "like an act of love, the end of my book, if I dared." Unconvinced even in dream, Irene responds, "You're not so smart" (*TT*, pp. 216-17).

Apparently Lesser agrees. His second fantasy is far less happy and much more sly. For this dream, too, he has prepared the reader. "Some endings," he had observed earlier, "demand you trick the Sphinx" (*TT*, p. 184). This last "ending" seems one such "trick." It enables both Lesser and Malamud to "close" their novels. It suggests that the time is no more right for the dream rabbi's "miracle," for his "one-people" concept, than it was a decade earlier in "Black Is My Favorite

Color." There Nat Lime (Not Time?), a naive or "green" store-keeper, was beaten by Blacks for loving a black woman. Life since then, Malamud implies, has grown even more grim. So grim indeed has it become that fantasy seemingly provides the strongest possibility of reconciling the races, a reconciling imagined surreally amid hatred and violence. These negative tendencies, hitherto evident in Willie Spearmint, now are shared by Lesser. Once more his fervid imagination transforms Levenspiel's decaying tenement into a dark, damp "grassy clearing." Gone are the interracial miracles. Instead, he and Willie now stalk each other seeking revenge. They exchange not only killing blows but identities. Their blows prove, how-ever, symbolic and folkloristic. As Lesser drives a jagged ax into Willie's skull and brain, Willie castrates him with a razor-sharp saber. Through Lesser's mind flashes the painful sig-nificance of this imagined horror. "Each," he thinks, "feels the anguish of the other" (*TT*, pp. 229-30). (Through the reader's mind, perhaps, may flash the castration of Faulkner's Joe Christmas[46] and the final stabbings in Malamud's "A Pimp's Revenge" and "The Death of Me.")

The words "The End" follow this vision as they do the other two. Neither Lesser nor Malamud, however, is quite fin-ished. Earlier, Lesser laments that he looks for but is "missing something"; this "something," he decides, "begins in an end" (*TT*, p. 107). In other words, he expects any "ending" he finds to become a beginning. His "final" moment of shared anguish – followed by Levenspiel's echoing cry – therefore functions severally. The fight and cry not only enable Lesser to release his own dark emotions, but they allow Malamud to voice his recurrent plea for mutual compassion and *rachmones*, mercy.[47] Reverberating through Lesser's mind as a liturgical chant by Levenspiel, the entreaty evokes for the reader similar appeals by the agonized Fidelman witnessing his canvases being slashed, by the dying tailor Marcus, and by the hand-wring-ing Jews watching Yakov Bok ride to trial. The scene may also augur Lesser's successful non-completion of his narrative, for this grim incident does not conclude the story as much as it establishes its "circular"[48] plot and structure. Having found his elusive beginning-in-the-end, Lesser will again awake to confront his reflection and sit down to write. Fantastic? Not really: the paradoxes and comic ironies of life-in-death and death-in-life, after all, shape all life and art.

For some reviewers, not surprisingly, this ending is a melodramatic cop-out, an attempt by Malamud to resolve all narrative problems by the "mirror trick" of superimposing his failure on his hero.[49] "The book has no conclusion," argues Cynthia Ozick, "and stops in the middle of an incoherency."[50] Her reading is much too literal. Levinspiel's "mercy" cry is that of the innocent bystander. It underscores Malamud's conviction that no one escapes human involvements or needs, and that fanaticism[51] can never be an adequate answer to such needs. (The cry also responds to a Willie Spearmint "ending" in which "Blackness" [*TT*, p. 204] is endlessly repeated.) Finally, the ending serves a personal anxiety shared by Lesser and Malamud and by all who write. For if Lesser fears love and human ties, he fears death even more. Art has become his only way of controlling life, of keeping "death in place." So his concern that each book he writes "nudges" him "that much closer to death" (*TT*, p. 4) holds deep meaning for him and for a Bernard Malamud now in his sixties. Harry Lesser has strong cause to keep writing his novel, at least to keep it open-ended and circular.

Equally open-ended and ambiguous are the bizarre confrontations of the *Rembrandt's Hat*[52] stories. These stories center on the familiar acts of belief and doubt, commitment and withdrawal, courage and fear—interlocking the real and imaginary more tightly than earlier Malamud tales. Their "God-haunted" adversaries face identical crises of defeat and fatigue, loneliness and old age.[53] Here at his most elliptical and allusive, Malamud scores his thematic points by reversing previous story plots. He continues to rely for motives and consequences, however, on dreams, nightmares, and mirrors, as well as on letters and manuscripts (burned and unburned). One who suffers the consequences of failed courage and faith is Albert Gans, the skeptical young biology teacher with a dying father, in "A Silver Crown." Despite a wonder-rabbi's warnings that man redeems himself and others only by acting on faith alone, Gans doubts the healing powers of the rabbi's silver crown — even after seeing a crown glowing in a hypnotic mirror. Responding with hatred and disbelief to the rabbi's pleas for trust, he brings death to his father (or to God, or both) and proves himself, rather than the questionable rabbi, a despoiler of miracles or a charlatan.

Whereas Gans, by rejecting a possible messenger from on high, reverses the happy ending of "Angel Levine," the central figures of "Man in the Drawer" invert the outcome of "The Last Mohican." In Moscow, a Russian named Feliks Levitansky (what else?) badgers an American writer, Howard Harvitz, to smuggle his manuscript of dangerous stories from the Soviet Union for publication in America. Harvitz, who has sunk to writing on literary museums, has enjoyed enough troubles in his life. He rejects the Russian's entreaties. But a nightmare in which he exchanges himself imaginatively with Levitansky sparks a "flash of humane insight"[54] and stirs his sense of responsibility to free expression and a fellow writer. Summoning the courage to hide the manuscript in his luggage, he heads for the airport. He is last seen speculating on his fate should he fail and on that awaiting Levitansky should he succeed.

Events may stir occasionally the better instincts of a Howard Harvitz, but they arouse more often man's animal impulses. Fabulists, however, frequently ponder the possibilities of animals aspiring to the human. For Malamud, not surprisingly, a beast-fable enables him to raise allusive questions of art and commitment, degradation, and dignity. Enter Abramowitz, a "Talking Horse," who resembles strongly Yakov Bok's Jewish-looking nag. The fixer had sold his pathetic steed for ferry passage only to have the animal return in a dream to accuse him of being a murderer and horsekiller (*TF*, p. 249). Abramowitz, however, does speak, and this gift causes problems and questions. Is he, puzzles Abramowitz, "a man in a horse or a horse that talks like a man?" (*RH*, p. 177). Forced to be a circus performer, he often wishes, as does every artist, that he were like his fellow creatures, ordinary, inarticulate, contented. At other times he dreams of the thoroughbred's style and dignity and of being free of his deaf-mute, unpredictable master, Goldberg, who determines his fate. After severe struggles and pains, Abramowitz half-frees the man within him to gallop off "a free centaur" (*RH*, p. 204). What has he accomplished? Cynics may argue that he is still, like all aspiring beings, a mixed creature—crassly put, a horse's ass. But then, Abramowitz may well ask, "Who isn't?"

Such metaphysical questions are better left to philosophers and theologians. Less debatable is Bernard Malamud's commitment to absurd man and his comic condition. No matter how pathetic or foolish, the individual can, by suffering, compassion, and self-scrutiny, Malamud insists, assert his humanity.[55] Seldom failing to do so, his embattled figures, in their painful views of inner selves and realities, form a revealing chronicle of modern life. The sense of human truth and collective responsibility surfacing in his fiction differs little from that expressed centuries ago in the Talmudic debates of the students of Rabbi Shammai and Rabbi Hillel. Man would be better off, contended Shammai's students, had he never been created. Hillel's followers disagreed; man's creation, they insisted, despite disappointments and defeats, has proven beneficial to him and the universe. Inevitably the two groups compromised. Man would have been better off, they agreed, had he *not* been created. Since he is on earth, however, he should make the best of it, by living compassionately.[56] Bernard Malamud has in his fiction nodded assent to this decision.

Notes

[1]See Leo Rosten, *The Joys of Yiddish* (New York: McGraw-Hill, 1968), p. 13.

[2]David Stevenson, "The Strange Destiny of S. Levin," *New York Times Book Review*, 8 October 1961, p. 1.

[3]Marc L. Ratner, "Style and Humanity in Malamud's Fiction," *Massachusetts Review*, 5 (Summer 1964), 670.

[4]See, for example, Curt Leviant, " 'My Characters Are God Haunted': An Interview with Bernard Malamud," *Hadassah Magazine*, 55 (June 1974), 19.

[5]Theodore Solotaroff, "Bernard Malamud's Fiction: The Old Life and the New," *Commentary*, 33 (March 1962), 199.

[6]Bernard Malamud, *The Natural* (New York: Harcourt, Brace and Company, 1952), p. 9. Subsequent references will be incorporated into the text with the abbreviation *TN*.

[7]Earl R. Wasserman, "*The Natural*: Malamud's World Ceres," *Centenniel Review*, 9 (Fall 1965), 444.

[8]See Leviant, p. 19.

[9]Malamud has claimed that *The Natural* was suggested by an Arthur Daly sports column on "Why does a talented man sell out?" See "A Talk with B. Malamud," *New York Times Book Review*, 8 October 1961, p. 28.

[10]Jonathan Baumbach, "All Men Are Jews," *The Landscape of Nightmare: Studies in the Contemporary American Novel* (New York: New York University Press, 1965), p. 102. This essay appeared originally as "The Economy of Love: The Novels of Bernard Malamud," *Kenyon Review*, 25 (Summer 1963), 438-57.

[11]Alan Ross, "Special Notices: *The Natural*," *London Magazine*, 3 (June 1963), 86-87.

[12]See Ronald Z. Sheppard, "About Bernard Malamud," *Book Week*, 13 October 1963, p. 5.

[13]Bernard Malamud, *The Assistant* (New York: Farrar, Straus and Cudahy, 1957). Subsequent references will be incorporated into the text with the abbreviation *TA*.

[14]See David Boroff, "Losers, But Not Lost," *Saturday Review*, 12 October, 1963, p. 33.

[15]See Israel Shenker, "For Malamud It's Story," *New York Times Book Review*, 3 October 1971, p. 18.

[16]See, for example, Robert Alter, "Malamud as Jewish Writer," *Commentary*, 42 (September 1966), 71-76.

[17]Lionel Trilling, Preface to *The Opposing Self: Nine Essays in Criticism* (New York: Viking, 1955), p. xiii; see also "Wordworth and the Rabbis," p. 150. And for Trilling's expanded discussion of prison imagery in nineteenth-century literature, see "Little Dorrit," pp. 50-65.

[18]See Sheppard, p. 5.

[19]*New York Times Book Review*, 13 October 1963, p. 5.

[20]Fyodor Dostoevsky, *Notes from Underground*, trans. Constance Garnett, in *Classics of Modern Fiction: Ten Short Novels*, ed. Irving Howe (New York: Harcourt Brace Jovanovich, 1972), p. 37.

[21]Sam Bluefarb, "Bernard Malamud: The Scope of Caricature," *English Journal*, 53 (May 1964), 319-20.

²²See Philip Rahv, Introduction to *A Malamud Reader,* ed. Philip Rahv (New York: Farrar, Straus and Giroux, 1967), pp. x-xi.

²³Malamud has made only one fleeting reference to the fiction of Yiddish writer Sholem Asch (see Leviant, p. 18). But he may have derived the basic plot and character elements for *The Assistant* from Asch's story "De Profundis" — with added details from the latter's novel *East River.* In "De Profundis" (which Asch occasionally referred to as "Out of the Depths"), Stash Grabski, a lonely young Polish anti-Semite, kills a Jewish neighbor in whose house he had played as a child. Soon stricken with remorse, Stash befriends his victim's widow and children and later is killed defending them from his former comrades. See *Children of Abraham: The Short Stories of Sholem Asch,* trans. Maurice Samuel (New York: Putnam's, 1942), pp. 181-235. In *East River,* trans. H. H. Gross (New York: Putnam's, 1946), Asch centers attention on the kindly grocer Moses Wolf Davidowsky, his cranky wife Deborah, and his sons Nathan and Irving (who marries the daughter of a drunken, Jew-hating Catholic neighbor). Malamud also seems to have borrowed Asch's emphasis on the mutual concern of Judaism and Christianity for personal guilt, penance, and redemption.

²⁴See Baumbach, p. 120.

²⁵See Baumbach, p. 122.

²⁶Bernard Malamud, *The Magic Barrel* (New York: Farrar, Straus and Cudahy, 1958). Subsequent references will be incorporated into the text with the abbreviation *MB.*

²⁷Bernard Malamud, *Pictures of Fidelman: An Exhibition* (New York: Farrar, Straus and Giroux, 1969). Subsequent references will be incorporated into the text with the abbreviation *PF.*

²⁸*New York Times Book Review,* 13 October 1963, p. 5.

²⁹See John Gross, "Lieutenants and *Luftmenschen,*" *New York Review of Books,* 24 April 1969, p. 42.

³⁰Bernard Malamud, *A New Life* (New York: Farrar, Straus and Cudahy, 1961). Subsequent references will be incorporated into the text with the abbreviation *NL.*

³¹Baumbach, p. 106.

³²Baumbach, p. 105.

³³See Stanley Edgar Hyman, "Bernard Malamud's Moral Fables," *New Leader,* 28 October 1963, p. 21.

³⁴See Ruth B. Mandel, "Bernard Malamud's *The Assistant* and *A New Life:* Ironic Affirmation," *Critique,* 7 (Winter 1964-65), 118.

³⁵Malamud expressed these sentiments in his 1959 National Book Award acceptance speech; see Ratner, p. 677.

³⁶Bernard Malamud, *Idiots First* (New York: Farrar, Straus and Company, 1961). Subsequent references will be incorporated into the text with the abbreviation *IF.*

[37]Theodore Solotaroff, "Showing Us 'What It Means Human,'" *Book Week*, 13 October 1963, p. 12.

[38]Morris Bober's bleak world is evoked in "The Cost of Living," where a guilty landlord drives old grocer Sam Tomashevsky out of business and into despair by renting an adjoining store to a supermarket. A clever widower in "Life Is Better Than Death" gets pregnant a mourning widow and deserts her—a situation confronted by Roy Hobbs and Seymour Levin.

[39]Bernard Malamud, *The Fixer* (New York: Farrar, Straus and Giroux, 1966), p. 12. Subsequent references will be incorporated into the text with the abbreviation *TF*.

[40]See Edwin M. Eigner, "Malamud's Use of the Quest Romance," *Genre*, 1 (January 1968), 69. This essay has been reprinted as "The Loathly Ladies," in *Bernard Malamud and the Critics*, eds. Leslie A. and Joyce W. Field (New York: New York University Press, 1970), pp. 85-108.

[41]Bernard Malamud, *The Tenants* (New York: Farrar, Straus and Giroux, 1971). Subsequent references will be incorporated into the text with the abbreviation *TT*.

[42]Cynthia Ozick, "Literary Blacks and Jews," *Midstream*, 18 (June/July 1972), 23.

[43]See John Alexander Allen, "The Promised End: Bernard Malamud's *The Tenants*," *Hollins Critic*, 8 (December 1971), 4.

[44]Morris Dickstein, "Malamud's Best Book in Years About a Black and a Jew: *The Tenants*," New York Times Book Review, 3 October 1971, p. 17.

[45]See, for example, Roger Sale, "What Went Wrong?," *New York Review of Books*, 12 October 1971, p. 3. See also Peter S. Prescott, "Yin, Yang and Schlemiel," *Newsweek*, 27 September 1971, p. 110. "There is a Yin and Yang structure to Malamud's novels," Prescott observes, "a polarity that is one of the most attractive qualities in his fiction, but in this story the conjunction of opposites leads not to unity but to annihilation."

[46]See Jack Ludwig, "The Dispossessed," *Partisan Review*, 39 (Fall 1972), 601.

[47]See Allen, p. 4.

[48]For a detailed analysis of Malamud's verbal and narrative "circularity" in *The Tenants*, see Brita Lindberg-Seyersted, "A Reading of Malamud's *The Tenants*," *American Studies* (Great Britain), 9, No. 1, 85-102.

[49]See William B. Hill, "The Tenants," *Best Sellers*, 15 October 1971, p. 316.

[50]"Literary Blacks and Jews," p. 13.

[51]See Shenker, p. 18.

⁵²Bernard Malamud, *Rembrandt's Hat* (New York: Farrar, Straus and Giroux, 1973). Subsequent references will be incorporated into the text with the abbreviation *RH*.

⁵³See Robert Kiely, "In Each Story an Impossible Wish," *New York Times Book Review*, 3 June 1973, p. 7.

⁵⁴Renee Winegarten, "Malamud's Head," *Midstream*, 19 (October 1973), 78.

⁵⁵See Ratner, p. 683.

⁵⁶See Robert R. Kirsch, "This Wise Fool Is a Real Shlemiel," *Los Angeles Times Calendar*, 15 October 1961, p. 18.

Leslie Fiedler

THE MANY NAMES OF S. LEVIN:
AN ESSAY IN GENRE CRITICISM

When i first accepted your invitation, I was not sure what
aspect of Malamud's work I wanted to talk about, or indeed if I
wanted to talk about Malamud at all. I have the sense of having said long ago whatever it is I have to say about his books
and the generation of Jewish-American writers to which he and
I both belong. Frankly the whole subject begins to bore me a
little. But contemplating a return to the Northwest, a trip
across the Mississippi, the Great Plains, and finally a passage
through the mountains, over the Divide and down the Western
Slope — a journey into what had once seemed to me an almost
unimaginable future and now has become a nostalgically re-
membered past — I knew that I must address the subject after
all.

There is only one book I should talk about without betray-
ing my own early adult life and the piety I feel toward it as I
enter my sixtieth year. In *A New Life* Malamud evokes and
fictionalizes *his* first journey into a West that had begun for
him as for me, as someone else's fiction (goyish images in our
Jewish heads) and had to become a part of his own life — a
New Life for an Easterner, reborn, as all Easterners are reborn
in this world — before it could become a part of his fiction.

In the pages of that fiction, the West itself was reborn as
(if you'll pardon the expression) a Jewish West, the American
West as a facet of Jewish-American culture, or at least a standard theme of the Jewish-American novel as it had defined itself just after World War II. Though Malamud's book was

published in the Sixties, it is set in that earlier period. Indeed, it is *about* the Fifties almost as much as it is about the West: the age of McCarthyism and the Cold War. I have, therefore, presumed to come to Corvallis to deal with that book, which was conceived here, in total disregard of the ancient adage which warns that in the hangman's noose one doesn't mention the rope. But, after all, it was your idea to organize this Malmudian occasion, a clear sign that for most if not all of you a figure once thought of as a pain-in-the-ass or a loveable misfit has been transformed into a Cultural Monument. And this is a final irony, Corvallis's revenge on Malamud, as *A New Life* was once Malamud's revenge on Corvallis for having failed, as the West always does, his dream, its own dream. But perhaps there is a super-irony undercutting the easier ironies with which I have begun, an irony which makes all acts of revenge finally acts of love. It is in that faith, at any rate, that I consider Malamud today.

A New Life is a Western, or more accurately a neo- or meta-Western, which is to say, a Western written by an author (typically in a university, where such literature is studied) aware of the tradition, the genre, and therefore a book about that genre as well as about life in the West. It is helpful, I think, to remind ourself that at the same moment at which Malamud's meta-Western was appearing, another book was being published, very different in every other aspect, but like *A New Life* academic in its origins and its relationship to the tradition of the classic or pop Western. Moreover, like Malamud's novel it, too, is set in the landscape of Oregon, and Oregonians move through its pages.

I am thinking of Ken Kesey's *One Flew Over the Cuckoo's Nest*, which in 1976, fifteen years after its conception, has been quite deliberately detached from the name of its original begetter and re-invented, re-presented by Milos Forman and Jack Nicholson as a Hollywood Western. I have in fact just seen it in that form, in which it is being discovered by an immensely larger audience than ever read it (or even bought it) in print. I hear that even as I speak a film version of a *New Life* is also being planned and cast. Yet I am convinced, for reasons which should be clear to you before I am through, that it will never touch as large and varied a group of viewers as Kesey's book.

The mass audience is able to respond to *One Flew Over the Cuckoo's Nest* at the deepest psychic levels because in the end it proves to be a real Western as well as a meta-Western, or perhaps because it was from the start a real Western merely disguised as a meta-Western. What I intend to suggest (assuming that every genre embodies an archetype, at whose heart is a characteristic myth of love) is that the erotic center of Kesey's novel re-embodies the archetypal Eros which underlies the most American of all fictional forms. I have spent a good deal of my life writing about that myth, from my early essay "Come Back to the Raft Ag'in, Huck Honey" to a relatively late study called *The Return of the Vanishing American,* and I like to think there remains scarcely a literate American who is not aware of its structure and meaning. It seems to me, therefore, sufficient at this point to say merely that it is a myth of transitory and idyllic love between two males in the Wilderness, one a White refugee from White civilization, the other a non-White member of a group which has been exploited or persecuted by his White lover's people. White Women, who represent the world of Law and Order from which the renegade White Man is in flight, when they appear in this myth at all, appear as the Ultimate Enemy. Whenever we find such pairs at the center of a fiction, whether they be Twain's Huck and Jim, Cooper's Natty Bumppo and Chingachgook, Melville's Ishmael and Queequeg, Saul Below's Henderson and Dafu, or Kesey's Patrick McMurphy and Chief Bromden, we are in the presence of the true Western.

Never mind the geographical setting. The West is a metaphor for, a mythic name of, the Unexplored wherever it may be: the retreating horizon, the territory that always lies just ahead of where we happen to be, waiting to be penetrated by anyone willing to light out ahead of the rest. Writing just before the Cultural Revolution that peaked in the late Sixties, and prophetically aware of its imminence as Malamud was not,

Kesey realized that *Inner* Space, the new areas of consciousness revealed by experiments with hallucinogenic drugs, represented the Unexplored Territory for the dying twentieth century better than *Outer* Space, those lands beyond the Mississippi once identified as the ultimate West. Only a naif like Malamud's S. Levin could still in the Fifties take the woods used
for experiment by a School of Forestry (most of whose grad-
uates would end up behind desks in Washington, D. C.) as the
Primeval Wilderness. But Kesey knew that the logging industry, along with scientific forestry, had long since subdued all
American forests and that a new West would have to be discovered, if the Western were to be preserved as a living mythic
form, rather than a subject for irony or sentimentality. The West
beyond the ultimate geographical West he located in Schizo-
phrenia, which made the Madhouse the Wilderness beyond the
last wilderness, a place in which the Indian Comrade would
wait still for his refugee White Brother, as he was waiting when
the first White Europeans set foot on American soil.

Moreover, in Kesey the enemy of that Red-White male
union and everything it represents is identified, as in all classic
Westerns, with the White Woman. In older versions of the
archetypal form, it was "sivilization" which she advocated
against the Code of the West with its celebration of flight, violence, and loneliness tempered only by occasional male bond-
ing: Christian Humanism, which is to say, Church and School,
marriage and the family—and behind them all a sustaining ideal
of civil order, social accommodation and self-control. In Kesey's
novel, it is "sanity" and accommodation to a "rational" world,
which makes heroism impossible and for which the super-White
Big Nurse stands. And he hates her as passionately as he does
her program. Malamud, however, is not sufficiently misogynist
to write a real Western. Indeed, no one can truly understand or
love the West, as it has been mythologized in hundreds of novels and thousands of films and T.V. scripts, who does not hate
Respectable White Women, the enforcers of civility and nor-
mality—for Kesey, the Nurse, and for most of his forerunners,
the Schoolmarm.

But S. Levin *is* a schoolmarm who likes to think of himself as bringing Culture and Liberal Humanism to the Barbar-
ian West, meanwhile dreaming of promotion and tenure, making it as a Professor, and, who knows, maybe even someday as
Chairman of a Department of English. But this means to imagine a West replete with books and short on guns, a West different from the East only in lower density of population and
greater beauty of scenery. He has no vision of the West as an
alternative way of life, an altered mode of consciousness, radically different from all we had imported from Europe and re-
constructed in the old urban East: the High Genteel Culture
preserved (however inadequately) in the College of the City
of New York, as well as in the Ivy League, but disconcertingly
undercut by the populist ideals of the Land Grant College. Levin ends up, therefore, not by riding off alone, as in the Western
movies of my childhood, or dying in the liberating, murderous
embrace of his Indian buddy, as in Kesey's book but by marry-
ing Madame Bovary and heading out for San Francisco (i.e.,
the East in the West, or more precisely imaginary Bohemian
Europe in ultimate America) to live happily—or unhappily—
ever after. It remains a little unclear which, but it doesn't matter, since what happens to him, good or bad, is presented as inevitable, a necessary consequence of what the timid Fifties defined as "maturity" or "responsibility."

Malamud's novel is in this sense an anti-Western disguised
as a meta-Western, or at least a travesty Western. It is a tale
about failed Westering, the failure of a refugee Easterner to become a Westerner because he could not abide being reborn in
heroic loneliness; but who aspiring to become a lover, a husband,
and a father, ended up making it only as a fall-back lover, a
second husband, and a stepfather. What remains obscure in *A
New Life* is whether it is the West which fails S. Levin or S.
Levi who fails the West, or both. In any case, Malamud's novel is, or at least tries to become comic. It belongs, therefore, not,
like Kesey's, to the sentimental tradition of Owen Wister, Jack
London, and Zane Grey, but to one whose first eminent practitioner was Mark Twain, who also had gone west hopefully,

then retreated in amused despair to write a book, get married, and make his fortune. The hero or rather anti-hero of such travesty Westerns is the dude or tenderfoot who can never even learn the language much less the ground rules which govern the strange territory in which he finds himself, whether drawn there by dreams of gold or tenure.

Indeed, as long as *A New Life* remains a burlesque account of a buffoon with a fedora hat on his head, an umbrella in his hand, and a copy of James Joyce's *Ulysses* under his arm, a *shlemiel* who cannot really believe that the Pacific is really out there over the next range of mountains, and who has never seen a mountain ash or heard of a potluck picnic, a *nebechel* who, in a world where men have gone from horse to automobile to airplane without ever touching the ground, cannot even *drive* (which is to say, is by the definitions of the place, impotent), it is not just hilarious, but moving and true. Its fable, moreover, reflects the essential comedy of the West after it has been mythicized by one generation of immigrants and is invaded by the next and the next and the next, being an account of two provincialities meeting head-on in a kind of mutual incomprehension which makes tragedy impossible, since the greatest catastrophe which can eventuate is a pratfall.

As long as S. Levin remains the absurd anti-hero on whom kids pee and nervous housewives spill tuna-fish casseroles, I love him and believe in him; as I do, too, when he fails to make it with a barmaid in a barn, or with his aging and anxious officemate on a desk — fleeing bare-assed and flustered, while sexual defeat piles on sexual defeat. The archetypal eros of the travesty Western is *coitus interruptus*, the unconsummated act of love. I stay with S. Levin, and with Malamud, even when Levin has an offstage, approximately satisfactory climax with a B-/C+ co-ed in a motel, because *en route* to their rendezvous he is scared into a ditch by a logging truck and stopped by a mule which he tries to lure off the road with Life Savers — clearly arriving too late and too undone for anything more fulfilling than a quick orgasm and a long troubled sleep. But when Levin finally makes it under the trees with a faculty wife, my credulity grows strained, my interest wanes, and disconcertingly, the West even as a physical setting begins to disappear from the book—along with anything like a genuine confrontation of East and West.

Self-pity, self-righteousness, and a sneaky kind of self-adulation take over from a healthy irony and sense of the ridiculous as the book slips into what may well be the least rewarding of all American fictional sub-genres, the Academic Novel. In this kind of book, some sensitive representative of the liberal tradition typically finds himself embattled in a world controlled by mindless, callous bureaucrats: Deans and Department Chairmen in the Academic Novel proper, though Big Business or Madison Avenue or Hollywood or the Armed Forces can be substituted for the university without making any essential difference. When he seems at the point of defeat, however, he revenges himself on his persecutors by screwing or running off with the wife of one of them, then retreating to write the very novel the reader holds in his hands.

Up until the cop-out point, *A New Life* had provided for me, who have never seduced or decamped with the wife of a Dean or Chairman, real vicarious satisfaction. When it appeared, I was close to the end of my own nearly quarter-century long exile in the West, and it seemed to me at that point that I would never write my own anti-Western. Yet I felt very much the need for *someone* to get into print an account of the most absurd and touching of all the waves of migration that have ever moved across this country from East to West: the migration of certain upwardly mobile, urban, Eastern young academics, chiefly Jews, into remote small-town State Universities, Cow Colleges, and Schools of Education.

For various reasons, including a sudden unforeseen growth in enrollment, such institutions were just then rather grudgingly opening their doors to those they would have refused a little while before on ethnic grounds. Yet the moment at which that first Jewish wave of academics reached such alien campuses was the heyday of McCarthyism, when they were most likely to be suspect on political grounds. Indeed, anyone urban and

Eastern, much less Jewish, was likely in those hysterical times to be suspected of being a troublemaker or a Communist or both, until he had proved otherwise, though he may in fact have left the East with the cry of "Red-Baiter" or "Escapist" ringing in his ears.

All in all, that particular westward migration seems at this point even funnier than the two hilarious ones that followed it: the Beatnik march on the Pacific (memorialized without much sense of humor in Jack Kerouac's *On the Road*), and the Hippie Back-to-the-Land Movement, whose ebbing has left rusting farm equipment and great patches of cultivated pot everywhere in its wake. It was inadvertent, since most of those involved (including me) did not realize that they were "going West" in any traditional mythic sense. We were just taking what jobs were available in bad times or simply getting the hell out of a world forever associated for us with the Great Depression, which had exacerbated our normal adolescent *angst* and impatience with a world we never made. Certainly we had not the slightest suspicion that in a little while some of us would be hunting and fishing like old-time country-bred WASPs or wearing string ties and Stetson hats; much less that our consciousnesses (or failing that, those of the kids we begot in that Strange Land) might be altered in ways less visible and more profound. What compounded the comic aspect of the whole adventure even more was that the Inadvertent Pioneers of the Fifties tended to be not just Jews but classic Jewish *shlemiels*. By a process of negative selection which I do not quite understand, it was the *nebechal*, the loser, that fled to provincial American campuses from the working class or petty bourgeois communities of Chicago or New York or Brooklyn or Newark, New Jersey. The sharper ones went into business or became doctors, lawyers, or at least wangled their way into more prestigious universities on the Eastern Seaboard, or at the very least, in California, which is not what I mean by the West at all.

S. Levin is not untypical in his total schlemielhood, though there can have been few who came like him to an Ag School

without knowing it, or for that matter, without knowing quite
what an Ag School was. But he is typical of more than the westward bound academics of the Fifties; indeed, insofar as *A New
Life* records the misadventures of luckless bumbler, it belongs
to a genre with which Jewish writers were concerned long before any of them had heard of Tom Mix or Gary Cooper or
John Wayne, a genre with roots in Yiddish folk culture, whose
most eminent old world practitioner was Sholem Aleichem.
Moreover, it has influenced the Jewish-American novel, especially in its comic erotic scenes ever since the time of Daniel
Fuchs and Nathaniel West. But this means that insofar as *A
New Life* is about the Schlemiel in Love or Out West or in the
University, it belongs to the mainstream of Jewish-American
fiction.

So why then is S. Levin not a Jew, not really, *really* a Jew,
either in his own consciousness, or in that of his colleagues, students, goyish lovers, and haters? He seems in this respect less
like Malamud's earlier and later protagonists, and more like,
say, the leading character in Arthur Miller's *After the Fall,* of
whom I once heard a departing spectator remark, "If his mother
is Jewish and his father is Jewish, how come he ain't Jewish?"
We learn quite early in the novel that Levin's father is not just
a thief, but a *gonif* (interestingly, the only other Yiddish word
in the book is *luftmensch*), and that he himself used to be a
drunkard, for which there is no evidence whatsoever beyond
the simple assertion. But perhaps this is an encoded reference
to his Jewishness as a stigma he now carefully conceals, even
as he tries to live it down. But in another sense, it is surely a
denial of that Jewishness, since mythologically speaking — as
I myself learned on my grandfather's knee — *a shiker is a goy.*
Or maybe the identification of Levin as an "urban Easterner"
is intended to say it all since that phrase in such a Western
small town as Levin inhabits is often a euphemism for "Jew,"
when not for "Jew bastard." Be that as it may, nobody uses the
word on him in rage or anger or simple description up to page
361 of the book's 367 pages. And when it occurs, it is used so

obliquely and cagily that nothing could be proved against him in court.

"Your picture," Pauline, with whom he is about to run away, says tenderly, "reminded me of a Jewish boy I knew in college who was kind to me." There is a hint here, perhaps, of the often embarrassing ritual philosemitism common just after World War II among some liberal academics (and particularly among their wives), who plunged into a crisis of bad conscience after the Death of the Six Million under Hitler was no longer a secret. Yet our anti-hero's name, after all, is Levin, S. Levin, Seymour Levin as he calls himself, or Lev as Pauline calls him (only the hostile, indifferent, and insensitive call him "Sy" in an attempt to acclimatize him). A Jewish name in all its changes, one is tempted to say, if there ever was one. But the epigraph from *Ulysses* with which Malamud prefaces his book, sends us off on what seems a deliberately planted false scent: by equating the name with a perfectly good old English word meaning "lightning"; and directing us to a novel about Dublin written by an Irishman. "Lo, Levin leaping lightens/ in eye-blink Ireland's western welkin."

Upon further consideration, however, the Joycean allusion turns out not to be so false a scent after all—suggesting that the ambiguous Jew at the center of this American parable of a Stranger in a Strange Land is derived from a goy's portrait of his own aging, foolish self as an Imaginary Jew, or if you like, a mythological one. And there turn out to be stream-of-consciousness passages attributed to S. Levin in this academic novel which sound like pastiches or parodies of L. Bloom's reminations on his way from and to home on Eccles Street. Moreover, the word "westward" in the passage cited provided Malamud, I am convinced, a clue for the geographical translation of Bloom lost in Ireland to Levin disoriented in the American West. It is a notion that smacks of the Graduate School, but it is as fraught with pathos and pure comedy as that other classroom inspiration of Malamud's to replay T. S. Eliot's version of the Grail Legend in Ebbets Field, which makes for all the best effects (and they are very good, indeed) in *The Natural.*

If there is another place in the world besides Ireland where the immemorial conflict of Jew and Gentile can be played out as comedy, burlesque, farce rather than tragedy, it is precisely the American West. Here, quite as in Ireland, the mythological hostility of two cultures joined and separated by a common myth, is not associated with a long history of bloody pogroms as in Russia or Poland or the Middle East, or with an attempt at total genocide as in Germany. It can therefore be presented in a tone scarcely more serious than vaudeville skits like Gallagher and Shean or hits of the popular comic theatre like *Abie's Irish Rose*. The very notion of the Western Jew is like that of the Irish Jew a joke in itself. And to understand the sense in which this is true it is enough, perhaps, just to think of that most absurd of recent American aspirants to the Presidency, that Jewish Westerner, or even better, crypto-Jewish Westerner, Barry Goldwater, or to reflect on the fact that any traditional catch phrase out of Western literature becomes hilariously funny the minute it is spoken with a Yiddish accent: "Smile ven you say dot, strrengerr!"

In the early chapters of *A New Life*, Malamud seems on the verge of blending successfully the comic folk traditions of the shlemiel-shlimazl and the tenderfoot-dude, and combining both with Joyce's burlesque version of the Wandering Jew as cuckold, masturbator, and peeper at underdrawers: a culturally displaced person, who in a world of drinkers cannot drink, only talk on soberly as everyone else proceeds to get joyously smashed or laid or both. But finally Malamud fails, as his book fails to be funny enough, perhaps out of timidity or pedanticism or squeamishness, or perhaps because (influenced not by what *Ulysses* is, but what it had come to seem in the hands of the academic critics) he wanted to write an Art Novel, a Great Book, instead of an Entertainment or a Travesty. At any rate, out of lack of nerve or excess of ambition, he turns S. Levin into a cuckolder rather than a cuckold, a successful lover of women rather than a beater of his own meat, a heroic defender of the Liberal Tradition, which is to say an insufferable prig like

Stephen Dedalus rather than an unloved, loveable victim like Leopold Bloom.

The giveaway, the final offense against the original conception of the book, and its potentiality for becoming the first real Jewish anti-Western (true ancestor of *Blazing Saddles*) is that there is neither anti-semitism nor an ironical defense against it to be found in its pages. And how can there be, if there are no Jews, and for that matter, no real goyim either, which is to say, no mythological Westerners. There is not even an ultimately and dangerously appealing *shikse*, in a deadly sexual encounter with whom ("her invitation wasn't to pleasure, but to struggle, hard and sharp, closer to murder than love . . .") the protagonist of the Jewish American Novel must test his manhood and his Jewishness. Think of the murderous gentile bitches in Ludwig Lewisohn, Ben Hecht, Nathaniel West, Philip Roth, Norman Mailer and then of Pauline in *A New Life*. Poor Pauline. She cannot ever really become the Deadly Stranger Woman, that Faye who always seems Greener on the other side but has to be satisfied with the role of the Loathly Lady — if big feet and no tits are enough to qualify her for even that mythological role.

After she speaks the magic word "Jewish", however, and it is only she who is permitted to say it, the action promises to turn around, the tone of the book to change from that of condescending satire (the sort of goyish satire endemic to all academic novels), which only puts down the other, to true Jewish irony, which is directed first of all against oneself and one's people, and, at its most intense, against one's God. It is tone of the Book of Jonah, prototype of all Jewish humor, with its wry comment on the ambiguous meaning of being chosen, i.e., having no choice. When Pauline has finished explaining to Levin that she needed him, wanted him because, however he may have avoided that label, he *looked* Jewish, Levin responds dryly, "So I was chosen," and for the first time in many pages I am moved to laugh. But I am puzzled a little as well since in context the phrase is equivocal. I am left uncertain about whether in using it Levin is mocking himself for having once been schmuck enough to believe that he *was* chosen as an Apostle to the Gentiles of Corvallis, Oregon, or whether he is super-schmuck enough to believe it still as his story comes to a close.

Immediately thereafter, in any case, he gives himself a new name, or rather reclaims an old one, but this strange re-baptism is even more ambiguous. "God bless you, Lev," the woman he has chosen goes on to say in real or burlesque or merely trivialized benediction. And at that point, he chooses to disavow the name he has allowed her to call him unchallenged throughout, rejecting along with it the cryptic initial S., by which his author has designated him, and "Seymour" as well—that ridiculous pseudo-Anglo-Saxon appellation, which like Irving, stirs a snigger in polite anti-semites. Nor does he want any longer to be known as "Sy," an assimilationist nickname, as American as apple pie. "Sam, they used to call me at home," he says; and "God bless you, Sam," she responds in a kind of continuing litany.

The conjunction of "call me" and "Sam" — short, of course, for Samuel — seems too apt to be unplanned, evoking for me the image (as if, in typical fashion, Malamud is raising the symbolic ante of his fiction just before he runs out of space) of the first of the Hebrew Prophets, who when God called him by name, answered, "*Hineni*, here I am." *No*, I want to say, don't do it! It's too pat, too easy, too slick, somehow, too *Christian* a conversion. And then I tell myself, "Come on, Malamud knows what he's doing. If his hand is on his heart a little melo-dramatically, his tongue is firmly in his cheek, to take the curse off by undercutting the pretentiousness of the Biblical allusion." But I'm not sure, even though S. Levin does say "Sam" and not "Samuel," making it possible for us to recall, as we close the book, not the solemn passage in *Kings* but the jocularly anti-semitic song, "Sam, you made the pants too long." I certainly would prefer to take it this way, for such a reading makes *A New Life* in conclusion what it promised to be at the start, really Jewish and funny as hell.

DONALD RISTY

A COMPREHENSIVE CHECKLIST
OF MALAMUD CRITICISM

I. BOOKS ON MALAMUD'S WORK

Cohen, Sandy. *Bernard Malamud and the Trial by Love.* Melville Studies in American Literature, No. 1, ed. Robert Brainsard Pearsall. Amsterdam: Rodopi N. V., 1974.

Field, Leslie A., and Joyce W. Field, eds. *Bernard Malamud and the Critics.* New York: New York Univ. Press, 1970.

Pp. 3-10: "The Jewish Literary Tradition" by Earl H. Rovit. Originally appeared as "Bernard Malamud and the Jewish Literary Tradition." *Critique,* 3, No. 2 (Winter-Spring 1960), 3-10.

Pp. 11-28: "Women, Children, and Idiots First: Transformation Psychology" by Samuel Irving Bellman. Originally appeared as "Women, Children, and Idiots First: The Transformation Psychology of Bernard Malamud." *Critique,* 7, No. 2 (Winter 1964-1965), 123-38.

Pp. 29-42: "Jewishness as Metaphor" by Robert Alter. Originally appeared as "Bernard Malamud: Jewishness as Metaphor." *After the Tradition: Essays on Modern Jewish Writing.* New York: Dutton, 1969, pp. 116-30.

Pp. 45-66: "*The Natural:* World Ceres" by Earl R. Wasserman. Originally appeared as "*The Natural:* Malamud's World Ceres." *Centennial Review,* 9 (1965), 438-60.

Pp. 67-84: "Four Versions of Pastoral" by James M. Mellard. Originally appeared as "Malamud's Novels: Four Versions of Pastoral." *Critique,* 9, No. 2 (1967), 5-19.

Pp. 85-108: "The Loathly Ladies" by Edwin M. Eigner. Originally appeared as "Malamud's Use of the Quest Romance." *Genre,* 1 (1968), 55-75.

Pp. 109-119: "Myth Inside and Out: *The Natural*" by Frederick W. Turner, III. Originally appeared as "Myth Inside and Out: Malamud's *The Natural.*" *Novel,* 1 (Winter 1968), 133-39.

Pp. 123-36: "Victims in Motion: The Sad and Bitter Clowns" by Ben Siegel. Originally appeared as "Victims in Motion: Bernard Malamud's Sad and Bitter Clowns." *Northwest Review*, 5, No. 2 (Spring 1962), 69-80. Reprinted in Waldmei;, Joseph J., ed. *Recent American Fiction: Some Critical Views*. Boston: Houghton Mifflin, 1963, pp. 203-14.

Pp. 137-50: "The Scope of Caricature" by Sam Bluefarb. Originally appeared as "Bernard Malamud: The Scope of Caricature." *English Journal*, 53 (1964), 319-26.

Pp. 151-70: "Comic Vision and the Theme of Identity" by Mark Goldman. Originally appeared as "Bernard Malamud's Comic Vision and the Theme of Identity." *Critique*, 7, No. 2 (Winter 1964-1965), 92-109.

Pp. 171-84: "The New Romanticism" by Charles Alva Hoyt. Originally appeared as "Bernard Malamud and the New Romanticism." Moore, Harry Thornton, ed. *Contemporary American Novelists*. Carbondale: Southern Illinois Univ. Press, 1964, pp. 65-79.

Pp. 185-95: "Mythic Proletarians" by Max F. Schulz. Originally appeared as "Bernard Malamud's Mythic Proletarians." *Radical Sophistication: Studies in Contemporary Jewish-American Novelists*. Athens, Ohio: Ohio Univ. Press, 1969, pp. 56-68.

Pp. 199-206: "The Qualified Encounter" by Ihab Hassan. Originally appeared as "The Qualified Encounter: Three Novels by Buechner, Malamud, and Ellison." *Radical Innocence: Studies in the Contemporary American Novel*. Princeton: Princeton Univ. Press, 1961, pp. 161-68.

Pp. 207-18: "Culture Conflict" by Walter Shear. Originally appeared as "Culture Conflict in *The Assistant*." *Midwest Quarterly*, 7 (Summer 1966), 367-80.

Pp. 219-33: "The Complex Pattern of Redemption" by Peter L. Hays. Originally appeared as "The Complex Pattern of Redemption in the Assistant." *Centennial Review*, 13 (1969), 200-14.

Pp. 235-48: "The Old Life and the New" by Theodore Solotaroff. Originally appeared as "Bernard Malamud's Fiction: The Old Life and the New." *Commentary*, 33 (March 1962), 197-104. Reprinted in *The Red Hot Vacuum and Other Pieces on the Writing of the Sixties*. New York: Atheneum, 1970, pp. 71-86.

Pp. 249-60: "The Sadness of Goodness" by Marcus Klein. Originally appeared as "Bernard Malamud: The Sadness of Goodness." *After Alienation*. Cleveland: World Publishing Co., 1964, pp. 247-93.

Pp. 261-74: "Ironic Affirmation" by Ruth B. Mandel. Originally appeared as "Bernard Malamud's *The Assistant* and *A New Life*: Ironic Affirmation." *Critique*, 7, No. 2 (Winter 1964-1965), 110-22.

Pp. 275-84. "History and Imagination—Two Views of the Beiliss Case" by Maurice Friedberg. Originally appeared in *Midstream*, 12, No. 9 (1966), 71-76.

Pp. 285-303: "The Hero as Schnook" by Alan Warren Friedman. Originally appeared as "Bernard Malamud: The Hero as Schnook." *Southern Review,* NS 4 (1968), 927-44.

Pp. 305-31: "The Stories" by Sidney Richman. Originally appeared in *Bernard Malamud.* Twayne's U. S. Authors Series, No. 109. New York: Twayne Publishers, 1967, pp. 98-123.

Field, Leslie A., and Joyce W. Field. *Bernard Malamud: A Collection of Critical Essays.* Twentieth Century Views. Englewood Cliffs, N. J.: Prentice-Hall, 1975.

Pp. 8-17: "An Interview with Bernard Malamud" by Leslie and Joyce Field.

Pp. 18-44: "Bernard Malamud and the Jewish Movement" by Sheldon Norman Grebstein. Originally appeared in Malin, Irving, comp. *Contemporary American-Jewish Literature.* Bloomington: Indiana Univ. Press, 1973, pp. 175-212.

Pp. 45-71: "Bernard Malamud's Ironic Heroes" by Sansford Pinsker. Originally appeared as "The Schlemiel as Moral Bungler: Bernard Malamud's Ironic Heroes." *The Schlemiel as Metaphor: Studies in the Yiddish and American Jewish Novel.* Carbondale: Southern Illinois Univ. Press, 1971, pp. 87-124.

Pp. 72-79: "The Syncretism of Bernard Malamud by Sam Bluefarb.

Pp. 80-98: "Literary Blacks and Jews" by Cynthia Ozick. Originally appeared in *Midstream,* June/July 1972, 10-24.

Pp. 99-103: "Malamud's Head (*Rembrandt's Hat*)" by Renee Winegarten. Originally appeared as "Malamud's Head." *Midstream,* Oct. 1973, pp. 76-79.

Pp. 104-16: "The Promised End: Bernard Malamud's *The Tenants*" by John Alexander Allen. Originally appeared in *Hollins Critic,* 8, No. 5 (1971), 1-15.

Pp. 117-29: "Portrait of the Artist as *Schlemiel (Pictures of Fidelman)*" by Leslie Field.

Pp. 130-42: "Malamud's Trial: *The Fixer* and the Critics" by Gerald Hoag. Originally appeared in *Western Humanities Review,* 24 (1970), 1-12.

Pp. 143-55: "In the Heart of the Valley: Bernard Malamud's *A New Life*" by Richard Astro.

Pp. 156-165: "From Bernard Malamud, with Discipline and with Love (*The Assistant* and *The Natural*)" by William Freedman. Originally appeared as "From Bernard Malamud, With Discipline and With Love." French, Warren, ed. *The Fifties: Fiction, Poetry, Drama.* Deland, Fla.: Everett/Edwards, 1970, pp. 133-43.

Kosofsky, Rita Nathalie. *Bernard Malamud: An Annotated Checklist.* Serif Series of Bibliographies and Checklists, No. 7, ed. William White. Kent, Ohio: Kent State Univ. Press, 1969.

Meeter, Glenn. *Bernard Malamud and Philip Roth: A Critical Essay.* Contemporary Writers in Christian Perspective Series, ed. Roderick Jellema. Grand Rapids: William B. Eerdmans, 1968.

Richman, Sidney. *Bernard Malamud.* Twayne's U. S. Authors Series, No. 109. New York: Twayne Publishers, 1967.

II.   GENERAL BOOKS CONTAINING DISCUSSION OF MALAMUD'S WORK

Aldridge, John W. "Notes on the Novel II." *Time to Murder and Create: The Contemporary Novel in Crisis.* New York: D. McKay Co., 1966, pp. 52-94.

Allen, Walter. *The Modern Novel in Britain and the United States.* New York: E. P. Dutton, 1964, pp. 322, 330-32.

Alter, Robert. "Bernard Malamud: Jewishness as Metaphor." *After the Tradition: Essays on Modern Jewish Writing.* New York: Dutton, 1969, pp. 116-30. Reprinted as "Jewishness as Metaphor." Field, Leslie A., and Joyce W. Field, eds. *Bernard Malamud and the Critics.* New York: New York Univ. Press, 1970, pp. 29-42.

Baumbach, Jonathan. "All Men Are Jews: *The Assistant* by Bernard Malamud." *The Landscape of Nightmare: Studies in the Contemporary American Novel.* New York: New York Univ. Press, 1965, pp. 101-22.

Bryant, Jerry H. *The Open Decision: The Contemporary American Novel and Its Intellectual Background.* New York: Free Press, 1970, pp. 324-40.

Burgess, Anthony. "American Themes." *The Novel Now: A Guide to Contemporary Fiction.* New York: Norton, 1967, pp. 197-98.

Burrows, David J. "The American Past in Malamud's *A New Life.*" *Private Dealings: Eight Modern American Writers.* Stockholm: Almqvist and Wiksell, 1970, pp. 86-94.

Ducharme, Robert. "Myth and Irony in *The Fixer.*" Good, Stephen H., and Olaf P. Tollefsen, eds. *Interdisciplinary Essays.* Emmitsburg, Md.: St. Mary's College, 1971. II, 31-36.

Duehl, John. "Characterization and Structure: Bernard Malamud." *Creative Writing and Rewriting: Contemporary American Novelists at Work.* New York: Appleton-Century-Crofts, 1967, pp. 69-96.

Dupee, Frederick Wilcox. "Malamud: The Uses and Abuses of Commitment." *"The King of the Cats," and Other Remarks on Writers and Writing.* New York: Farrar, Straus, and Giroux, 1965, pp. 156-63.

Fiedler, Leslie A. "Jewish Americans, Go Home!" *Waiting For the End.* New York: Stein and Day, 1964, pp. 89-104.

Fiedler, Leslie A. *Love and Death in the American Novel.* New York: Criterion, 1960, pp. 469-70.

Fiedler, Leslie A. "Three Jews, III: Malamud: The Commonplace as Absurd." *No! In Thunder: Essays on Myth and Literature.* Boston: Beacon Press, 1960, pp. 101-10.

Fiedler, Leslie. *The Jew in the American Novel.* New York: Herzl Press, 1959, pp. 57-58.

Finkelstein, Sidney. *Existentialism and Alienation in American Literature.* New York: International Publishers, 1965, pp. 268-69.

Freedman, William. "From Bernard Malamud, With Discipline and With Love." French, Warren, ed. *The Fifties: Fiction, Poetry, Drama.* Deland, Fla.: Everett/Edwards, 1970, pp. 133-43. Reprinted as "From Bernard Malamud, with Discipline and with Love (*The Assistant* and *The Natural*)" in Field, Leslie A., and Joyce W. Field, eds. *Bernard Malamud: A Collection of Critical Essays.* Twentieth Century Views. Englewood Cliffs, N. J.: Prentice-Hall, 1975, pp. 156-65.

Grebstein, S. N. "Bernard Malamud and the Jewish Movement." Malin, Irving, comp. *Contemporary American-Jewish Literature.* Bloomington: Indiana Univ. Press, 1973, pp. 175-212. Reprinted in Field, Leslie A., and Joyce W. Field, eds. *Bernard Malamud: A Collection of Critical Essays.* Twentieth Century Views. Englewood Cliffs, N. J.: Prentice-Hall, 1975, pp. 18-44.

Gunn, Giles B. "Bernard Malamud and the High Cost of Living." Scott, Nathan A., Jr., ed. *Adversity and Grace: Studies in Recent American Literature.* Chicago: Univ. of Chicago Press, 1968.

Guttman, Allen. *The Jewish Writer in America: Assimilation and the Crisis of Identity.* New York: Oxford Univ. Press, 1968, pp. 59-85.

Handy, William J. "Malamud's *The Fixer.*" *Modern Fiction: A Formalist Approach.* Carbondale: Southern Illinois Univ. Press, 1972, pp. 131-58.

Harap, Louis. *The Image of the Jew in American Literature: From Early Republic to Mass Immigration.* Philadelphia: The Jewish Publication Society of America, 1974, pp. 389, 526.

Hassan, Ihab. "The Qualified Encounter: Three Novels by Buechner, Malamud, and Ellison." *Radical Innocence: Studies in the Contemporary American Novel.* Princeton: Princeton Univ. Press, 1961, pp. 161-68. Reprinted as "The Qualified Encounter." Field, Leslie A., and Joyce W. Field, eds. *Bernard Malamud and the Critics.* New York: New York Univ. Press, 1970, pp. 199-206.

Hicks, Granville. "Bernard Malamud." *Literary Horizons: A Quarter Century of American Fiction.* New York: New York Univ. Press, 1970, pp. 65-83.

Hicks, Granville. "Generations of the Fifties: Malamud, Gold, and Updike." Balakanian, Nona, and Charles Simmons, eds. *The Creative Present: Notes on Contemporary American Fiction.* Garden City: Doubleday, 1963, pp. 217-37.

Hoffman, Frederick J. "Marginal Societies in the Novel." *The Modern Novel in America.* 3rd ed. Chicago: Henry Regnery, 1963, pp. 224-55.

Hoyt, Charles A. "Bernard Malamud and the New Romanticism." Moore, Harry Thornton, ed. *Contemporary American Novelists*. Carbondale: Southern Illinois Univ. Press, 1964, pp. 65-79. Reprinted as "The New Romanticism." Field, Leslie A., and Joyce W. Field, eds. *Bernard Malamud and the Critics*. New York: New York Univ. Press, 1970, pp. 171-84.

Hyman, Stanley Edgar. "A New Life for a Good Man." *Standards: A Chronicle of Books for Our Time*. New York: Horizon, 1966, pp. 33-37. Originally appeared in *New Leader*, 2 Oct. 1961, pp. 24-25. Reprinted in Kostelanetz, Richard, ed. *On Contemporary Literature*. New York: Avon, 1969, pp. 442-46.

Kazin, Alfred. "The Magic and the Dread." *Contemporaries*. Boston: Little, Brown, 1962, pp. 202-07. Reprinted in Kostelanetz, Richard, ed. *On Contemporary Literature*. New York: Avon, 1969, pp. 437-41.

Kempton, Kenneth Payson. "For Plot Read Idea." *Short Stories for Study*. Cambridge: Harvard Univ. Press, 1953, pp. 316-21.

Klein, Marcus. "Bernard Malamud: The Sadness of Goodness." *After Alienation*. Cleveland: World Publishing Co., 1964, pp. 247-93. Reprinted as "The Sadness of Goodness." Field, Leslie A., and Joyce W. Field, eds. *Bernard Malamud and the Critics*. New York: New York Univ. Press, 1970, pp. 249-60.

Kort, Wesley A. "*The Fixer* and the Death of God." *Shriven Selves: Religious Problems in Recent American Fiction*. Philadelphia: Fortress Press, 1972, pp. 90-115.

Kostelanetz, Richard. *The End of Intelligent Writing: Literary Politics in America*. New York: Sheed and Ward, 1974.

Liptzin, Solomon. *The Jew in American Literature*. New York: Bloch, 1966, pp. 226-28.

Ludwig, Jack Barry. *Recent American Novelists*. Univ. of Minnesota Pamphlets on American Writers, No. 22. Minneapolis: Univ. of Minnesota, 1962, pp. 39-41.

Malin, Irving. *Jews and Americans*. Carbondale: Southern Illinois Press, 1965.

Malin, Irving, and Irvin Stark. Introduction to *Breakthrough: A Treasury of Contemporary American-Jewish Literature*. New York: McGraw-Hill, 1964, p. 20.

Mudrick, Marvin. "Malamud, Bellow, and Roth." *On Culture and Literature*. New York: Horizon, 1970, pp. 200-30. Originally appeared as "Who Killed Herzog? Or, Three American Novelists." *Univ. of Denver Quarterly*, 1, No. 1 (Spring 1966), 61-97.

Mueller, Lavonne. "Malamud and West: Tyranny of the *Dream Dump*." Madden, David, ed. *Nathaniel West: The Cheaters and the Cheated: a Collection of Critical Essays*. Deland, Fla.: Everett/Edwards, 1973, pp. 221-34.

Nyren, Dorothy. "Bernard Malamud." *A Library of Literary Criticism: Modern American Literature.* New York: F. Ungar, 1960, pp. 315-18.

Olderman, Raymond M. *Beyond the Wasteland: A Study of the American Novel in the Nineteen-Sixties.* New Haven: Yale Univ. Press, 1972, pp. 14-15, 20, 92.

Pinsker, Sanford. "The Schlemiel as Moral Bungler: Bernard Malamud's Ironic Heroes." *The Schlemiel as Metaphor: Studies in The Yiddish and American Jewish Novel.* Carbondale: Southern Illinois Univ. Press, 1971, pp. 87-124. Reprinted as "Bernard Malamud's Ironic Heroes." Field, Leslie A., and Joyce W. Field, eds. *Bernard Malamud: A Collection of Critical Essays.* Twentieth Century Views. Englewood Cliffs, N. J.: Prentice-Hall, 1975, pp. 45-71.

Podhoretz, Norman. "The New Nihilism in the American Novel." *Doings and Undoings: The Fifties and After in America.* New York: Farrar, Straus, and Giroux, 1964, pp. 176-78. Originally appeared in *Partisan Review,* 25 (1958), 476-90.

Rahv, P. "A Note on Bernard Malamud." *Literature and the Sixth Sense.* Boston: Houghton Mifflin, 1960, pp. 280-88.

Roth, Philip. "Imagining Jews." *Reading Myself and Others.* New York: Farrar, Strauss and Giroux, 1975, pp. 215-46.

Rupp, Richard H. "Bernard Malamud: A Party of One." *Celebration in Postwar American Fiction, 1945-67.* Coral Gables, Fla.: Univ. of Miami, 1970, pp. 165-88.

Rubin, Louis D., Jr. *The Curious Death of the Novel: Essays in American Literature.* Baton Rouge: Louisiana State Univ. Press, 1967.

Samuels, C. T. "The Fixer." Harrison, Gilbert A., ed. *The Critic as Artist: Essays on Books 1920-1970.* New York: Liveright, 1972, pp. 291-98.

Schulz, Max F. "Bernard Malamud's Mythic Proletarians." *Radical Sophistication: Studies in Contemporary Jewish-American Novelists.* Athens, Ohio: Ohio Univ. Press, 1969, pp. 56-68. Reprinted as "Mythic Proletarians." Field, Leslie A., and Joyce W. Field, eds. *Bernard Malamud and the Critics.* New York: New York Univ. Press, 1970, pp. 185-95.

Sheed, Wilfrid. "Bernard Malamud: Pictures of Fidelman." *The Morning After: Selected Essays and Reviews.* New York: Farrar, Straus, and Giroux, 1971, pp. 59-61.

Sherman, Bernard. *The Invention of the Jew: Jewish-American Education Novels (1916-1964).* New York: Thomas Yoseloff, 1969.

Siegel, Ben. "Victims in Motion: Bernard Malamud's Sad and Bitter Clowns." Waldmeir, Joseph J., ed. *Recent American Fiction: Some Critical Views.* Boston: Houghton Mifflin, 1963, pp. 203-14. Originally appeared in *Northwest Review,* 5, No. 2 (Spring 1962), 69-80. Reprinted as "Victims in Motion: The Sad and Bitter Clowns." Field, Leslie A., and Joyce W. Field, eds. *Bernard Malamud and the Critics.* New York: New York Univ. Press, 1970, pp. 123-34.

Solotaroff, Theodore. "Bernard Malamud's Fiction: The Old Life and the New." *The Red Hot Vacuum and Other Pieces on the Writing of the Sixties.* New York: Atheneum, 1970, pp. 71-86. Originally appeared in *Commentary*, 33 (March 1962), 197-204. Reprinted as "The Old Life and the New" in Field, Leslie A., and Joyce W. Fields, eds. *Bernard Malamud and the Critics.* New York: New York Univ. Press, 1970, pp. 235-48.

Syrkin, Marie. "Jewish Awareness in American Literature." Janowsky, Oscar I., ed. *The American Jew: A Reappraisal.* Philadelphia: Jewish Publication Society of America, 1974, pp. 211-33.

Tanner, Tony. "A New Life." *City of Words: American Fiction, 1950-70.* New York: Harper and Row, 1971, pp. 322-43.

Teller, Judd. "From Yiddish to Neo-Brahmin." *Strangers and Natives— The Evolution of the American Jew from 1921 to the Present.* New York: Delacorte Press, 1968, pp. 251-72.

Trilling, Lionel. *The Experience of Literature: Fiction.* New York: Holt, 1967, pp. 371-73.

Ulanov, Barry. *The Two Worlds of American Art: The Private and the Popular.* New York: Macmillan, 1965, pp. 205, 232-33.

Wager, Willis. *American Literature: A World View.* New York: New York Univ. Press, 1968, p. 261.

Weinberg, Helen. *The New Novel in America: The Kafkan Mode in Contemporary Fiction.* Ithaca: Cornell Univ. Press, 1970, pp. 165-85.

Wisse, Ruth R. *The Schlemiel as Modern Hero.* Chicago: Univ. of Chicago Press, 1971, pp. 110-18.

III.   ARTICLES AND REVIEWS CONTAINING DISCUSSION OF
MALAMUD'S WORK

NOTE: The difficulty of categorizing many items as "article" or "review" has necessitated the inclusion of both types of mention within this section. In the case of discussion appearing as part of an article or review, page numbers refer to the entire item.

Adams, Phoebe. "The Burdens of the Past." *Atlantic*, Nov. 1961, pp. 184-85.

Adelman, George. Review of *Idiots First*. *Library Journal*, 88 (1963), 4238.

Adelman, George. Review of *Pictures of Fidelman*. *Library Journal*, 94 (1969), 1899.

Adler, Dick. "The Magician of 86 Street." *Book World*, 29 Oct. 1967, p. 8.

Allen, John Alexander. "The Promised End: Bernard Malamud's *The Tenants*." *Hollins Critic*, 8, No. 5 (1971), 1-15. Reprinted in Field, Leslie A., and Joyce W. Field, eds. *Bernard Malamud: A Collection of Critical Essays*. Twentieth Century Views. Englewood Cliffs, N. J.: Prentice-Hall, 1975, pp. 104-16.

Alley, Alvin D., and Hugh Agee. "Existential Heroes: Frank Alpine and Rabbit Angstrom." *Ball State University Forum*, 9, No. 1 (Winter 1968), 3-5.

Alter, Robert. "Malamud as Jewish Writer." *Commentary*, 42 (1966), 71-76.

Alter, Robert. "Out of the Trap." *Midstream*, 9, No. 4 (1963), 88-90.

Alter, Robert. "The Tenants." *Commentary*, 54 (October 1972), 68-74.

Alter, Robert. "Updike, Malamud, and the Fire in This Time." *Commentary*, 54 (1972), 68-74.

Angoff, Charles. "Jewish-American Imaginative Writings in the Last Twenty-Five Years." *Jewish Book Annual*, 25 (1967), 129-39.

Axthelm, Pete. "Holes in the Ground." *Newsweek*, 5 May 1969, pp. 110F, 111, 112.

Bailey, Anthony. "Insidious Patience." *Commonweal*, 66 (1957), 307-308.

Baker, W. Review of *The Fixer*. *World Jewry*, 10 (May/June 1967), 25.

Balliett, Whitney. "Rub-a-Dub-Dub." *New Yorker*, 10 Dec. 1966, pp. 234-235.

Bamberger, H. Review of *A Malamud Reader*. *Dimensions*, 2 (Spring 1968), 60-61.

Bannon, Barbara. Review of *A Malamud Reader*. *Publishers' Weekly*, 192, No. 10 (4 Sept. 1967), 50.

Barsness, John A. "*A New Life:* The Frontier Myth in Perspective." *Western American Literature*, 3 (1969), 297-302.

Baumbach, Jonathan. "The Economy of Love: The Novels of Bernard Malamud." *Kenyon Review*, 25 (1963), 438-57.

Baumbach, Jonathan. "Malamud's Heroes: The Fate of Fixers." *Commonweal*, 85 (1966), 97-99.

Bell, Pearl K. "Morality Tale Without Mercy." *New Leader*, 18 Oct. 1971, pp. 17-18.

Bellman, Samuel Irving. "Fathers and Sons in Jewish Fiction." *Congress Biweekly*, 22 May 1967, pp. 18-20.

Bellman, Samuel Irving. "Henry James's 'The Madonna of the Future' and Two Modern Parallels." *California English Journal*, 1, No. 3 (1965), 47-53.

Bellman, Samuel Irving. "Women, Children, and Idiots First: The Transformation Psychology of Bernard Malamud." *Critique*, 7, No. 2 (Winter 1964-1965), 123-38. Reprinted in Field, Leslie A., and Joyce W. Field, eds. *Bernard Malamud and the Critics*. New York: New York Univ. Press, 1970, pp. 11-28.

Ben-Asher, N. "Jewish Identity and Christological Symbolism in the Work of Three Writers." *Jewish Frontier*, 39 (November 1972), 9-15.

Berman, R. S. "Totems of Liberalism." *Modern Age*, 6 (Spring 1962), 212-24.

Blackman, R. C. Review of *The Magic Barrel*. *Christian Science Monitor*, 15 May 1958, p. 11.

Bluefarb, Sam. "Bernard Malamud: The Scope of Caricature." *English Journal*, 53 (1964), 319-26. Reprinted in Field, Leslie A., and Joyce W. Field, eds. *Bernard Malamud and the Critics*. New York: New York Univ. Press, 1970, pp. 137-50.

Blumberg, A. Review of *The Fixer*. *Jewish Life*, 34 (March/April 1967), 73-79.

"Books They Liked Best." *Book World*, 3 Dec. 1967, p. 6.

Boroff, D. "American Judaism Looks at the Living Arts Finest Flowering." *American Judaism*, 13 (Winter 1963/1964), 18.

Boroff, David. "Losers, But Not Lost." *Saturday Review*, 12 Oct. 1963, p. 33.

Bowen, Robert O. "The View from Beneath." *National Review*, 11 (2 Dec. 1961), 383-84.

Bradbury, M. Review of *The Fixer*. *Manchester Guardian Weekly*, 96 (13 April 1967), 11.

Bresler, Riva T. Review of *The Fixer*. *Library Journal*, 91 (1966), 3470.

Breslin, J. B. Review of *Rembrandt's Hat*. *America*, 129 (1973), 15.

Brooke, Joselyn. "New Novels." *The Listener*, 69 (9 May 1963), 801.

Broyard, Anatole. "If the Hat Doesn't Fit . . ." *New York Times*, 17 May 1973, 41.

Broyard, Anatole. Review of *Pictures of Fidelman*. *New York Times Book Review*, 4 May 1969, pp. 5, 45.

Broyard, Anatole. "The View from the Tenament: I." *New York Times*, 20 Sept. 1971, p. 23.

Broyard, Anatole. "The View from the Tenament: II." *New York Times*, 21 Sept. 1971, p. 35.

Bryden, Ronald. "I Cincinnatus." *Spectator*, 204 (3 June 1960), 810.

Burgess, Anthony. "Blood in the Matzos." *Spectator*, 14 April 1967, 424-25.

Cadle, Dean. "Bernard Malamud." *Wilson Library Bulletin*, 33 (1958), 266. Reprinted in *Current Biography Yearbook*. New York: H. H. Wilson Co., 1958.

Catinella, Joseph. Review of *The Tenants*. *Saturday Review*, 25 Sept. 1971, p. 36.

Cevasco, George. Review of *The Fixer*. *The Sign*, Dec. 1966, p. 19.

Charles, Gerda. "Bernard Malamud—the 'Natural' Writer." *Jewish Quarterly*, 9 (Spring 1962), 5-6.

Charles, Gerda. "Elizabethan Age of Modern Jewish Literature—1950-1960: Decade of the Great Breakthrough." *World Jewry*, 4 (September 1961), 15-17.

Charles, Gerda. Review of *The Fixer*. *Conservative Judaism*, 21 (Spring 1967), 80-81.

Charles, Gerda. Review of *Rembrandt's Hat*. *Jewish Observer and Middle East Review*, 23 (18 January 1974), 25.

Corke, Hilary. Review of *The Fixer*. *Listener*, 77 (1967), 501.

"A Correct Compassion." (London) *Times Literary Supplement*, 1 April 1960, p. 205.

Craib, Roderick. Review of *The Tenants*. *Commonweal*, 95 (1971), 309, 311.

Daniels, Sally. "Recent Fiction: Flights and Evasions." *Minnesota Review*, 2 (Summer 1962), 546-57.

Davenport, Guy. "Elegant Botches." *National Review*, 21 (1969), 549-50.

Davenport, Guy. Review of *Idiots First*. *National Review*, 15 (1963), 450, 52.

Davis, Leila. "Bernard Malamud." *Hollins Critic*, 8, No. 5 (1971), 7.

Davis, Leila. "Bibliography of Malamud." *Hollins Critic*, 8, No. 5 (1971), 9.

Davis, Robert Gorham. "Invaded Selves." *Hudson Review*, 19 (Winter 1966-1967), 659-68.

Deemer, Charles. "Ole Masters' New Stories." *New Leader*, 17 Sept. 1973, pp. 19-20.

Degnan, James P. "The Ordeal of Yakov Bok." *The Critic*, 25, No. 2 (1966), 102-104.

DeMott, Benjamin. "Fiction Chronicle." *Hudson Review*, 14 (Winter 1961-1962), 622-29.

Desmond, J. F. "Malamud's Fixer—Jew, Christian, or Modern?" *Renascence*, 27 (Winter 1975), 101-10.

Dickstein, Morris. "Cold War Blues: Notes on the Culture of the Fifties." *Partisan Review*, 41 (1974), 30-53.

Dickstein, Morris. "The Tenants." *New York Times Book Review*, 3 Oct. 1971, pp. 1, 14, 16, 18, 20.

Dollard, Peter A. "A Clash Between Two Writers, a Jew and a Black." *Library Journal*, 96 (1971), 3346.

Dollard, Peter A. Review of *Rembrandt's Hat*. *Library Journal*, 98 (1973), 1601.

Donoghue, Denis. "Both." *Listener*, 82 (1969), 607-08.

Ducharme, Robert. "Structure and Content in Malamud's *Pictures of Fidelman*." *Connecticut Review*, 5, No. 1 (1971), 26-36.

Dupee, F. W. "The Power of Positive Sex." *Partisan Review*, 31 (1964), 425-30.

Edelman, L. Review of *The Fixer*. *Jewish Heritage*, 9 (Fall 1966), 3-4.

Edelman, L. Review of *Pictures of Fidelman*. *National Jewish Monthly*, 84 (January 1970), 48-49.

Edelman, L. Review of *Rembrandt's Hat*. *National Jewish Monthly*, 87 (June 1973), 54-56.

Edelstein, J. M. "Binding Variants in Malamud's *The Natural*." *American Notes and Queries*, 1 (May 1963), 133-34.

Eigner, Edwin M. "Malamud's Use of the Quest Romance." *Genre*, 1 (1968), 55-75. Reprinted as "The Loathly Ladies" in Field, Leslie A., and Joyce W. Field, eds. *Bernard Malamud and the Critics*. New York: New York Univ. Press, 1970, pp. 85-108.

Elkin, Stanley. Review of *The Fixer*. *Massachusetts Review*, 8 (Spring 1967), 388-92.

Elliott, George P. "Yakov's Ordeal." *New York Times Book Review*, 4 Sept. 1966, pp. 1, 25-26.

Elman, Richard M. Review of *The Fixer*, *Congress bi-Weekly*, 33 (24 October 1966), 10-12.

Elman, Richard M. "Malamud on Campus." *Commonweal*, 75 (1961), 114-15.

Fanger, Donald. "*The Fixer* in Another Country." *The Nation*, 203 (1966), 389-90.

Farber, Stephen. "*The Fixer*." *Hudson Review*, 22 (1969), 134-38.

Featherstone, Joseph. "Bernard Malamud." *Atlantic*, March 1967, pp. 95-98.

Feinstein, Elaine. "Guilt." *London Magazine*, NS 12, No. 2 (June/July 1972), 166-68.

Feinstein, Elaine. "Unashamed Humanism." *London Magazine*, NS 13, No. 6 (February/March 1974), 137-40.

Fenton, James. "Simple and Classic." *New Statesman*, 78 (1969), 542.

Fiedler, Leslie A. "In the Interest of Surprises and Delight." *Folio*, 20 (Summer 1955), 17-20.

Fiedler, Leslie A. "The Commonplace as Absurd." *Reconstructionist*, 24, No. 1 (1958), 22-24.

Fiedler, Leslie A., "The Jew as Mythic American." *Ramparts*, (2 Autumn 1963), 32-48.

Field, Katherine. Review of *Rembrandt's Hat*. *Christian Science Monitor*, 1 Aug. 1973, 8.

Fineman, Irving. "The Image of the Jew in Fiction of the Future." *National Jewish Monthly*, 82 (December 1967), 48-51.

Fineman, Irving. "The Image of the Jew in Our Fiction." *Tradition*, 9 (Winter 1966), 19-47.

Finkelstein, Sidney. "The Anti-Hero of Updike, Bellow, and Malamud." *American Dialog*, 7, No. 2 (1972), 12-14, 30.

Fitzgerald, Edward J. Review of *The Natural*. *Saturday Review*, 6 Sept. 1952, 32.

Fleischer, L. Review of *Pictures of Fidelman*. *Congress bi-Weekly*, 36 (26 May 1969), 20-22.

Foff, Arthur. Review of *The Magic Barrel. Northwest Review,* 1 (Fall-Winter 1958), 63-67.

Foreman, J. D. Review of *Pictures of Fidelman. Best Sellers,* 29 (15 May 1969), 67.

Francis, H. E. "Bernard Malamud's Everyman." *Midstream,* 7, No. 1 (Winter 1961), 93-97.

Frankel, Haskel. Interview with Malamud. *Saturday Review,* 10 Sept. 1966, pp. 39-40.

Freedman, William. "American Jewish Fiction: So What's the Big Deal?" *Chicago Review,* 19, No. 1 (1966), 90-107.

Fremont-Smith, Eliot. "Yakov's Choice." *New York Times,* 29 Aug. 1966, p. 27.

Friedberg, Maurice. "History and Imagination—Two Views of the Beiliss Case." *Midstream,* 12, No. 9 (1966), 71-76. Reprinted in Field, Leslie A., and Joyce W. Field, eds. *Bernard Malamud and the Critics.* New York: New York Univ. Press, 1970, pp. 275-84.

Friedman, Alan Warren. "Bernard Malamud: The Hero as Schnook." *Southern Review,* NS 4 (1968), 927-44. Reprinted as "The Hero as Schnook" in Field, Leslie A., and Joyce W. Field, eds. *Bernard Malamud and the Critics.* New York: New York Univ. Press, 1970, pp. 285-303.

Friedman, Alan Warren. "The Jew's Complaint in Recent American Fiction: Beyond Exodus and Still in the Wilderness." *Southern Review,* 8 (1972), 41-59.

Friedman, Richard. "Worlds Apart." *Book World,* 19 Sept. 1971, p. 4.

Fuller, Edmund. "Malamud's Novel Aims High but Falls Short." *Wall Street Journal,* 9 Sept. 1966, p. 12.

Geismar, Maxwell. "The American Short Story Today." *Studies on the Left,* 4, No. 2 (Spring 1964), 21-27.

Geismar, Maxwell. "The Jewish Heritage in Contemporary American Fiction." *Ramparts,* 2 (Autumn 1963), 5-13.

Geltman, Max. "Irrational Streams of Blood." *National Review,* 18 (1966), 1117-19.

Glanville, Brian. "Speaking of Books: Anglo-Jewish Writers." *New York Times Book Review,* 17 April 1966, pp. 2, 40.

Glanville, Brian. "The Sporting Novel." *New York Times Book Review,* 18 July 1965, pp. 2, 18.

Glassgold, Peter. "Malamud's Literary Ethic." *Nation,* 213 (1971), 504-05.

Glicksberg, Charles I. "A Jewish American Literature?" *Southwest Review,* 53 (1968), 196-205.

Gold, Herbert. "Dream to Be Good." *Nation,* 184 (1957), 350.

Goldman, Mark. "Bernard Malamud's Comic Vision and the Theme of Identity." *Critique,* 7, No. 2 (Winter 1964-1965), 92-109. Reprinted as "Comic Vision and the Theme of Identity" in Field, Leslie A., and

Joyce W. Field, eds. *Bernard Malamud and the Critics.* New York: New York Univ. Press, 1970, pp. 151-70.

Golub, Ellen. "The Resurrection of the Heart." *English Review,* 1, No. 2 (1973), 63-78.

"The Good Grocer." *Time,* 29 April 1957, p. 100.

"Goodbye Old Paint." *Time,* 9 May 1969, p. 108.

Goodheart, Eugene. "Fantasy and Reality." *Midstream,* 7, No. 4 (Autumn 1961), 102-05.

Goodman, Oscar B. "There Are Jews Everywhere." *Judaism,* 19 (1970), 283-94.

Goyen, William. "A World of Bad Luck." *New York Times Book Review,* 28 April 1957, p. 4.

Graber, Ralph S. "Baseball in American Fiction." *English Journal,* 56 (1967), 1107-14.

Greenberg, Alvin. "A Sense of Place in Modern Fiction: The Novelist's World and the Allegorist's Heaven." *Genre,* 5 (1972), 353-66.

Greenfeld, J. Review of *The Tenants. American Zionist,* 62 (January 1972), 41-42.

Greenfeld, Josh. "Innocence and Punishment." *Book Week,* 4 No. 1 (1966), 1, 10.

Greiff, Louis K. "Quest and Defeat in *The Natural.*" *Thoth,* 8 (1967), 23-34.

Griffith, John. "Malamud's *The Assistant.*" *Explicator,* 31 (Sept. 1972), item. 1.

Gross, John. "Lieutenants and Luftmenschen." *New York Review of Books,* 24 April 1969, pp. 40-43.

Guerin, Ann. "The Tormented Tale of an Innocent." *Life,* 16 Feb. 1968, pp. 88-92.

Halio, Jay L. "Fantasy and Fiction." *Southern Review,* NS 7 (1971), 635-47.

Halley, Anne. "The Good Life in Recent Fiction." *Massachusetts Review,* 3 (Autumn 1961), 190-96.

Handy, William J. "Malamud's *The Fixer:* Another Look." *Northwest Review,* 8, No. 3 (Spring 1967), 74-82.

Hardwick, Elizabeth. "*The Fixer,* 'Novel of Startling Importance.'" *Vogue,* 1 Sept. 1966, p. 208.

Harper, Howard M., Jr. "Trends in Recent American Literature." *Contemporary Literature,* 12 (1971), 204-29.

Hartt, N. N. "The Return of Moral Passion." *Yale Review,* 51 (Winter 1962), 300-308.

Hassan, Ihab. "The Hopes of Man." *New York Times Book Review,* 13 Oct. 1963, p. 5.

Hassan, Ihab. Letter concerning omission within his review of *Idiots First*. *New York Times Book Review*, 27 Oct. 1963, p. 65.

Hayes, E. Nelson. Review of *The Assistant*. *The Progressive*, 21, No. 7 (1957), 29.

Hays, Peter L. "The Complex Pattern of Redemption in *The Assistant*." *Centennial Review*, 13 (1969), 200-14. Reprinted as "The Complex Pattern of Redemption" in Field, Leslie A., and Joyce W. Field, eds. *Bernard Malamud and the Critics*. New York: New York Univ. Press, 1970, pp. 219-34.

Henderson, R. W. Review of *The Natural*. *Library Journal*, 77 (1952), 1408.

Hentoff, Nat. "Bernard Malamud." *Commonweal*, 79 (1963), 328-29.

Hicks, Granville. "American Fiction in 1958." *Saturday Review*, 27 Dec. 1958, pp. 11-12.

Hicks, Granville. "Hard Road to the Good Life." *Saturday Review*, 7 Oct. 1961, p. 20.

Hicks, Granville. "His Hopes on the Human Heart." *Saturday Review*, 12 Oct. 1963, pp. 31-32.

Hicks, Granville. "A Note on Literary Journalism, and Good Novels by Moore and Malamud." *The New Leader*, 29 April 1957, pp. 21-22.

Hicks, Granville. "One Man to Stand for Six Million." *Saturday Review*, 10 Sept. 1966, pp. 37-39.

Hicks, Granville. "The Uprooted." *Saturday Review*, 17 May 1958, p. 16.

Hill, John S. "Malamud's 'The Lady of the Lake': A Lesson in Rejection." *University Review*, 36 (1969), 149-50.

Hill, William B. Review of *The Fixer*. *America*, 115 (1966), 706.

Hill, William B. Review of *The Tenants*. *America*, 125 (1971), 430.

Hill, William B. Review of *The Tenants*, *Best Sellers*, 31 (1971), 316.

Hirsch, David. "Jewish Identity and Jewish Suffering in Bellow, Malamud, and Philip Roth." *Jewish Book Annual*, 29 (1971-72), 17.

Hirsch, F. Review of *The Tenants*. *Judiasm*, 21 (Spring 1972), 247-49.

Hoag, Gerald. "Malamud's Trial: *The Fixer* and the Critics." *Western Humanities Review*, 24 (1970), 1-12. Reprinted in Field, Leslie A., and Joyce W. Field, eds. *Bernard Malamud: A Collection of Critical Essays*. Twentieth Century Views. Englewood Cliffs, N. J.: Prentice-Hall, 1975, pp. 130-42.

Hollander, John. "To Find the Westward Path." *Partisan Review*, 29 (1962), 137-39.

Horne, Lewis B. "Yakov Agonistes." *Research Studies*, 37 (1969), 320-26.

Howe, Irving. "Mass Society and Post-Modern Fiction." *Partisan Review*, 26 (1959), 420-36.

Howes, Victor. "I Dig a Different Drum". *Christian Science Monitor*, 20 Jan. 1972, p. 6.

Hruska, Richard J. "My Grandfather and Morris Bober." *CCC: The Journal of the Conference of College Composition and Communication,* 13 (May 1962), 32-34.

Hyman, Stanley Edgar. "A New Life for a Good Man." *New Leader,* 2 Oct. 1961, pp. 24-25. Reprinted in *Standards: A Chronicle of Books for Our Time.* New York: Horizon, 1966, pp. 33-37. Also Reprinted in Kostelanetz, Richard, ed. *On Contemporary Literature.* New York: Avon, 1969, pp. 442-46.

"I Paint with my Paint." (London) *Times Literary Supplement,* 16 Oct. 1969, p. 1177.

Igoe, William J. "More Than One America." *The Tablet,* 217 (1963), 513-14.

Inge, M. Thomas. "The Ethnic Experience and Aesthetics in Literature: Malamud's *The Assistant* and Roth's *Call It Sleep." Journal of Ethnic Studies,* Winter 1974, pp. 45-50.

Jackson, Katherine Gauss. Review of *The Fixer. Harper's,* Oct. 1966, pp. 127-28.

Jackson, Katherine Gauss. Review of *Pictures of Fidelman. Harper's,* June 1969, pp. 92-93.

Jacobson, Dan. "Magic and Morality." *Commentary,* 26 (1958), 359-61.

Jacobsen, Dan. "The Old Country." *Partisan Review,* 34 (1967), 307-309.

Jebb, Julian. "As Good as the Blurbs Say." *Time and Tide,* 43, No. 13 (1962), 40.

Johnson, Marigold. "Small Mercies." *New Statesman,* 86 (1973), 433.

Johnson, Richard A. Review of *Idiots First. Studies in Short Fiction,* 1 (1964), 171-72.

Jones, G. William. "Current Novelists and 'Entering into the World.' " *Southwest Review,* 49 (1964), 91-96.

Josipovici, G. "Freedom and Wit, the Jewish Writer and Modern Art." *European Judaism,* 3, No. 1 (1968), 41-50.

Kaminsky, Alice R. "The American Jew in the Academic Novel." *Midwest Quarterly,* 3 (Summer 1962), 305-18.

Kapp, Isa. "A Therapeutic Plainness." *New Leader,* 52 (26 May 1969), 7-9.

Kauffman, Stanley. "Greatness as a Literary Standard." *Harper's,* Nov. 1965, pp. 151-56.

Kauffman, Stanley. "Some of Our Best Writers." *New York Times Book Review,* 30 May 1965, 1, 16-17.

Kazin, Alfred. "Fantasist of the Ordinary." *Commentary,* 24 (1957). 89-92.

Keller, Marcia. Review of *The Tenants. Library Journal,* 97 (1972), 791.

Kennedy, William. "The Frightening Beiliss Case in Fictional Scholarly Perspective." *National Observer,* 5 Sept. 1966, p. 19.

Kennedy, William. "Malamud Finds Renewal in a Fidelman College." *National Observer,* 12 May 1969, p. 23.

Kermode, Frank. "Bernard Malamud." *New Statesman,* 63 (1962), 452-53.

Kiely, Robert. *"Rembrandt's Hat." New York Times Book Review,* 3 June 1973, p. 7.

Kilby, C. S. Review of *The Assistant. New York Herald Tribune Book Review,* 28 April 1957, p. 8.

Killinger, John, Jr. "Is Anybody There?" *Christian Herald,* 90, No. 3 (March 1967), 49, 56-57.

Kirby, David K. "The Princess and the Frog: The Modern American Short Story as Fairy Tale." *Minnesota Review,* NS 4 (Spring 1973), 145-49.

Kitching, Jessie. Review of *The Fixer. Publishers' Weekly,* 189, No. 26 (27 June 1966), 96.

Klein, Marcus. "Imps from Bottles, Etc." *Hudson Review,* 11 (Winter 1958-1959), 620-25.

Knopp, Josephine Z. "The Ways of *Mentshlekhkayt*: A Study of Morality in Some Fiction of Bernard Malamud and Philip Roth." *Tradition,* 13, No. 3 (Winter 1973), 67-84.

Korg, Jacob. "Ishmael and Isreal." *Commentary,* May 1972, pp. 82, 84.

Kostelanetz, Richard. "The Short Story in Search of Status." *Twentieth Century,* 174 (Autumn 1965), 65-69.

Lamdin, Lois S. "Malamud's Schlemiels." *Carnegie Series in English,* 11 (1970), 31-42.

Landis, Joseph C. "Reflections on American-Jewish Writers." *Jewish Book Annual,* 25 (1967), 140-47.

Lask, Thomas. "The Creative Itch." *New York Times,* 3 May 1969, p. 33.

Lasson, Robert. "The Story of a Professional Giver." *Book World,* 4 May 1969, p. 4.

Leer, Norman. "The Double Theme in Malamud's *Assistant*: Dostoevsky with Irony." *Mosaic,* 4, No. 3 (Spring 1971), 89-102.

Leer, Norman. "Escape and Confrontation in the Short Stories of Philip Roth." *Christian Scholar,* 49 (1966), 132-46.

Leer, Norman. "Three American Novels and Contemporary Society: A Search for Commitment." *Wisconsin Studies in Contemporary Literature,* 3, No. 3 (1962), 67-86.

Lefcowitz, Barbara F. "The *Hybris* of Neurosis: Malamud's *Pictures of Fidelman." Literature and Psychology,* 20 (1970), 115-20.

Leff, Leonard J. "Malamud's Ferris Wheel." *Notes on Contemporary Literature,* 1, No. 1, 14-15.

Leff, Leonard J. "Utopia Reconsidered: Alienation in Vonnegut's *God Bless You, Mr. Rosewater." Critique,* 12, No. 3 (1970), 29-37.

Lehan, Richard. "The American Novel—A Survey of 1966." *Wisconsin Studies in Contemporary Literature*, 8 (1967), 437-49.

Leibowitz, Herbert. "Malamud and the Anthropomorphic Business." *New Republic*, 21 Dec. 1963, pp. 21-23.

Lemon, Lee T. "Working Quietly." *Prairie Schooner*, 47 (Fall 1973), 270.

Leonard, John. "Cheever to Roth to Malamud." *Atlantic*, June 1973, pp. 112-16.

Leviant, Curt. "Bernard Malamud: My Characters Are God-haunted." *Hadassah*, 56 (June 1974), 18-19.

Leviant, Curt. " 'The Fixer' Fixation." *Jewish Frontier*, 34, No. 1 (Jan. 1967), 24-25.

Levin, Meyer. "Growth in Brooklyn." *Saturday Review*, 15 June 1957, p. 21.

Levine, Norman. "Stockpot." *Spectator*, 210 (1964), 802-03.

Lewis, Stuart A. "The Jewish Author Looks at the Black." *Colorado Quarterly*, 21 (Winter 1973), 317-30.

Lindberg-Seyersted, B. "Reading of Bernard Malamud's *The Tenants*." *Journal of American Studies*, 9 (April 1975), 85-102.

Lindroth, James R. Review of *The Tenants*. *America*, 125 (1971), 561.

Lockerbie, D. Bruce. Review of *The Fixer*. *Eternity*, Feb. 1967, p. 56.

Lodge, David. "Home Run." *Spectator*, 10 May 1963, pp. 608, 610.

Ludlow, Francis. Review of *The Fixer*. *Book Buyer's Almanac*, Sept. 1966, p. 121.

Ludwig, Jack. "The Dispossessed." *Partisan Review*, 39 (1972), 596-602.

Luttwak, E. N. Review of *Rembrandt's Hat*. *National Review*, 25 (1973), 1191.

Maddocks, Melvin. "Life Is Suffering But . . ." *Atlantic*, Nov. 1971, pp. 132, 134, 136.

Maddocks, Melvin. "Malamud's Heroic Handyman." *Christian Science Monitor*, 8 Sept. 1966, p. 13.

Malcolm, Donald. "The Grooves of Academe." *New Yorker*, 27 January 1962, pp. 105-07.

Malin, I. Review of *The Tenants*. *Congress bi-Weekly*, 38 (10 December 1971), 20.

Malin, Irving. Review of *Idiots First*. *Reconstructionist*, 29 (29 Nov. 1963), 25-28.

Maloff, Saul. "Betwen the Real and the Absurd." *Nation*, 193 (1961), 407-408.

Maloney, J. J. Review of *The Natural*. *New York Herald Tribune Book Review*, 24 Aug. 1952, p. 8.

Mandel, Ruth B. "Bernard Malamud's *The Assistant* and *A New Life*: Ironic Affirmation." *Critique*, 7, No. 2 (Winter 1964-1965), 110-

22. Reprinted as "Ironic Affirmation" in Field, Leslie A., and Joyce W. Field, eds. *Bernard Malamud and the Critics*. New York: New York Univ. Press., 1970, pp. 261-74.

Manning, Olivia. "Under the Influence." *Spectator*, 208 (30 March 1962), 421.

Mano, D. Keith. "A Balanced Ticket." *National Review*, 23 (1971), 1358-59.

Marcus, Mordecai. Review of *The Tenants*. *Prairie Schooner*, 46 (Fall 1972), 275.

Marcus, Mordecai. "The Unsuccessful Malamud." *Prairie Schooner*, 41 (Spring 1967), 88-89.

Marcus, Steven. "The Novel Again." *Partisan Review*, 29 (1962), 171-95.

Mathewson, Joseph. Review of *The Fixer*. *Harper's Bazaar*, Nov. 1966, pp. 116, 118.

May, Charles E. "Bernard Malamud's 'A Summer's Reading.' " *Notes on Contemporary Literature*, 2, No. 4, 11-13.

May, Charles E. "The Bread of Tears: Malamud's 'The Loan.' " *Studies in Short Fiction*, 7 (1970), 652-54.

Meixner, John A. "Morrison, Kirk, Malamud." *Sewanee Review*, 72 (1964), 540-42.

Mellard, James M. "Malamud's Novels: Four Versions of Pastoral." *Critique*, 9, No. 2 (1967), 5-19. Reprinted as "Four Versions of Pastoral" in Field, Leslie A., and Joyce W. Field, eds. *Bernard Malamud and the Critics*. New York: New York Univ. Press, 1970, pp. 67-84.

Mellard, James M. "Malamud's *The Assistant*: The City Novel as Pastoral." *Studies in Short Fiction*, 5 (Fall 1967), 1-11.

Merrick, Gordon. "The Attachment to Misery." *New Republic*, 1 July 1958, pp. 20-21.

Mesher, D. R. "Remembrance of Things Unknown: Malamud's 'The Last Mohican.' " *Studies in Short Fiction*, 12 (Fall 1975), 397-404.

Michaels, Leonard. Review of *Rembrandt's Hat*. *New York Review of Books*, 20 Sept. 1973, p. 37.

Miller Karl. "Sporting Life." *New Statesman*, 65 (1963), 602.

Miller, Theodore C. "The Minister and the Whore: An Examination of Bernard Malamud's 'The Magic Barrel.' " *Studies in the Humanities*, 3, No. 1 (1972), 43-44.

Mitgang, Herbert. "Fiction Fantasies by Malamud (and Chagall)." *New York Times*, 14 Oct. 1963, p. 27.

Mudrick, Marvin. "Who Killed Herzog? Or, Three American Novelists." *Univ. of Denver Quarterly*, 1, No. 1 (Spring 1966), 61-97. Reprinted as "Malamud, Bellow, and Roth." *On Culture and Literature*. New York: Horizon, 1970, pp. 200-30.

Murray, J. G. Review of *Idiots First*. *Critic*, 22 (Dec. 1963-Jan 1964), 77.

Novak, W. Review of *The Tenants*. *Response*, 7 (1973), 147-51.

Oboler, Eli M. Review of *A New Life*. *Library Journal*, 86 (1961), 3302.

"Old Men of the Sea." *Time*, 12 May 1958, pp. 102, 104.

"The Outsider." *Time*, 9 Sept. 1966, pp. 106, 108.

Ozick, Cynthia. "Literary Blacks and Jews." *Midstream*, June/July 1972, pp. 10-24. Reprinted in Field, Leslie A., and Joyce W. Field, eds. *Bernard Malamud: A Collection of Critical Essays*. Twentieth Century Views. Englewood Cliffs, N. J.: Prentice-Hall, 1975, pp. 80-98.

"Passions and Dilemmas." *Newsweek*, 9 Oct. 1961, p. 105.

Peden, William. "Dogged by a Sense of Injustice and Grief." *New York Times Book Review*, 11 May 1958, p. 5.

Pendleton, Elsa. "Fantasy in Fiction." *Progressive*, Feb. 1972, pp. 49-50.

Perrine, Laurence. "Malamud's 'Take Pity.'" *Studies in Short Fiction*, 2 (1964), 84-86.

Peterson, Virgilia. "Fact of the Matter." *The Reporter*, 35, No. 6 (1966), 57-58.

Phillips, Robert. Review of *Rembrandt's Hat*. *Commonweal*, 99 (1973), 245-46.

Phillopson, J. S. Review of *The Fixer*. *Best Sellers*, 36 (1966), 211.

Pickrel, Paul. Review of *A New Life*. *Harper's*, Nov. 1961, p. 120.

Pickrel, Paul. "Selected Shorts." *Harper's*, Nov. 1963, pp. 130, 132.

Pinsker, Sanford. "The Achievement of Bernard Malamud." *Midwest Quarterly*, 10 (1969), 379-89.

Pinsker, Sanford. "Christ as Revolutionary/Revolutionary as Christ: The Hero in Bernard Malamud's *The Fixer* and William Styron's *The Confessions of Nat Turner*." *Barat Review*, 6, No. 1 (1971), 29-37.

Pinsker, Sanford. "The 'Hassid' in Modern American Literature." *Reconstructionist*, 30 (6 March 1970), 7-15.

Pinsker, Sanford. "A Note on Bernard Malamud's "Take Pity.'" *Studies in Short Fiction*, 6 (Winter 1969), 212-13.

Pinsker, Sanford. "Salinger, Malamud, and Wallant: The Jewish Novelist's Quest." *Reconstructionist*, 32 (25 Nov. 1966), 7-14.

Podhoretz, Norman. "Achilles in Left Field." *Commentary*, 15 (1953), 321-26.

Podhoretz, Norman. "The New Nihilism in the American Novel." *Partisan Review*, 25 (1958), 476-90. Reprinted in *Doings and Undoings: The Fifties and After in America*. New York: Farrar, Straus, and Giroux, 1964, pp. 176-78.

"Poor in Spirit." (London) *Times Literary Supplement*, 5 Oct. 1973, p. 1158.

Poore, Charles. Review of *The Assistant*. *New York Times*, 9 May 1957, p. 29.

Poore, Charles. Review of *The Magic Barrel*. *New York Times,* 10 May 1958, p. 19.

Popkin, Henry. "Jewish Stories." *Kenyon Review,* 20 (1958), 637-41.

Porter, Peter. "Really Black." *New Statesman,* 83 (1972), 397-98.

Poss, Stanley. "Serial Form and Malamud's Schlemihls." *Costerus,* 9 (1973), 109-16.

Pradham, S. V. "The Nature and Interpretation of Symbolism in Malamud's *The Assistant.*" *Centennial Review,* 16 (1972), 394-407.

Prescott, Peter S. "The Horse's Mouth." *Newsweek,* 4 June 1973, pp. 101-02.

Prescott, Peter S. Review of *The Tenants. Newsweek,* 27 Dec. 1971, p. 57.

Prescott, Peter S. "Yin, Yang, and Schlemiel." *Newsweek,* 27 Sept. 1971, pp. 110, 112.

Price, R. G. G. Review of *The Natural. Punch,* 244 (1 May 1963), 645-46.

Price, R. G. G. Review of *A New Life. Punch,* 242 (9 May 1962), 733-34.

Pritchett, V. S. "A Pariah." *New York Review of Books,* 22 Sept. 1966, pp. 8, 10.

Pritchett, V. S. "That Time and That Wilderness." *New Statesman,* 64 (1962), 405-06.

Rabinowitz, Dorothy. Review of *Rembrandt's Hat. World,* 5 June 1973, p. 66.

Raffel, B. "Bernard Malamud." *Literary Review,* 13 (Winter 1969-1970), 149-55.

Rao, A. V. Krishna. "Bernard Malamud's *The Assistant*: The American Agonistes." *Triveni,* 42, No. 2 (July/Sept. 1973), 28-34.

Ratner, Marc L. "Style and Humanity in Malamud's Fiction." *Massachusetts Review,* 5 (Summer 1964), 663-683.

Ratner, Marc. "The Humanism of Malamud's *The Fixer.*" *Critique,* 9, No. 2 (1967), 81-84.

"Realistic Fabulist." *Time,* 15 Nov. 1963, pp. 123, 126.

Review of *The Assistant. Kirkus Bulletin,* 25 (1 Feb. 1957), 101.

Review of *The Assistant. New Yorker,* 13 July 1957, pp. 86-87.

Review of *The Fixer. Booklist,* 63 (1966), 237.

Review of *The Fixer. Choice,* 3 (1966), 771.

Review of *The Fixer. Kirkus Bulletin,* 34 (1 July 1966), 102.

Review of *The Fixer. Library Journal,* 91 (1966), 5268.

Review of *The Fixer. Newsweek,* 19 Dec. 1966, pp. 117A, 117D.

Review of *The Fixer. Publishers' Weekly,* 24 July 1967, p. 57.

Review of *The Fixer. Teachers College Record,* 68 (1966), 185-86.

Review of *Idiots First. American Jewish Archives,* 19 (April 1967), 86.

Review of *The Magic Barrel. Booklist,* 54 (1958), 586.

Review of *The Magic Barrel. Kirkus Bulletin,* 26 (1958), 245.

Review of *A Malaud Reader. Booklist,* 64 (1967), 425.

Review of *A Malamud Reader. Choice,* 4 (1968), 1382.

Review of *The Natural. Best Sellers,* 33 (1973), 550.

Review of *The Natural. Book Week,* 1 Aug. 1965, p. 14.

Review of *The Natural. Kirkus Bulletin,* 20 (15 July 1952), 420.

Review of *The Natural. New Yorker,* 6 Sept. 1952, p. 106.

Review of *A New Life. Best Sellers,* 33 (1973), 258.

Review of *A New Life. Virginia Quarterly Review,* 38 (1962), x.

Review of *Pictures of Fidelman. American Jewish Archives,* 22 (November 1970), 178.

Review of *Pictures of Fidelman. Booklist,* 65 (1969), 1112.

Review of *Pictures of Fidelman. Choice,* 6 (1969), 818.

Review of *Pictures of Fidelman. Commonweal,* 91 (5 Dec. 1969), 314-315.

Review of *Pictures of Fidelman. Kenyon Review,* 37 (1 March 1969), 269.

Review of *Pictures of Fidelman. Publishers' Weekly,* 16 Feb. 1970, p. 75.

Review of *Pictures of Fidelman. Publishers' Weekly,* 24 Feb. 1969, p. 63.

Review of *Pictures of Fidelman. Spectator,* 223 (1969), 908.

Review of *Pictures of Fidelman. Virginia Quarterly Review,* 45 (1969), R88.

Review of *Rembrandt's Hat. Booklist,* 70 (1973), 31.

Review of *Rembrandt's Hat. Kenyon Review,* 41 (1 April 1973), 409.

Review of *Rembrandt's Hat. Kenyon Review,* 41 (15 April 1973), 468.

Review of *Rembrandt's Hat. Listener,* 90 (11 Oct. 1973), 491.

Review of *Rembrandt's Hat. New Republic,* 9 June 1973, p. 32.

Review of *Rembrandt's Hat. Publishers' Weekly,* 26 March 1973, p. 69.

Review of *The Tenants. American Jewish Archives,* 26 (April 1974), 83.

Review of *The Tenants. American Libraries,* 3 (1972), 87.

Review of *The Tenants. Antioch Review,* 31 (Fall 1971), 438.

Review of *The Tenants. Best Sellers,* 32 (1972), 315.

Review of *The Tenants. Booklist,* 68 (1971), 231.

Review of *The Tenants. Choice,* 9 (1972), 369.

Review of *The Tenants. Economist,* 13 May 1972, pp. 73, 95.

Review of *The Tenants. Kenyon Review,* 39 (1 Sept. 1971), 964.

Review of *The Tenants. New Yorker,* 2 Oct. 1971, pp. 130-31.

Review of *The Tenants. Publishers' Weekly,* 10 July 1972, p. 47.

Review of *The Tenants. Publishers' Weekly,* 23 Aug. 1971, p. 74.

Review of *The Tenants. Virginia Quarterly Review,* 48 (1972), R19.

Reynolds, Richard. "The Magic Barrel': Pinye Salzman's Kadish." *Studies in Short Fiction*, 10 (1973), 100-102.

Ribalow, Harold U. "What's This Jewish Book Craze All About?" *National Jewish Monthly*, 81 (November 1966), 50, 52.

Ribalow, Harold U. "A Collection of Malamud Short Stories." *Congress Bi-Weekly*, 18 Nov. 1963, pp. 18-19.

Ribalow, Harold U. "A Genuine Jewish Novel." *Congress Weekly*, 13 May 1957, p. 16.

Ribalow, Harold U. "Bernard Malamud: 'The Suffering of Jews.' " *Reconstructionist*, 33 (9 June 1967), 12-16.

Richey, Clarence W. " 'The Woman in the Dunes': A Note on Bernard Malamud's *The Tenants*." *Notes on Contemporary Literature*, 3, No. 1 (1973), 4-5.

Richler, Mordecai. "Malamud's Race War." *Life*, 22 Oct. 1971, p. 10.

Richler, Mordecai. "Write, Boychick, Write." *New Statesman*, 73 (1967), 473-74.

Ridley, Clifford A. "Malamud Weaves a Fable in Black." *National Observer*, 30 Oct. 1971, p. 21.

Ridley, Clifford A. "Short Stories Extinct? Don't Believe It." *National Observer*, 2 June 1973, p. 21.

Riemer, Jack. Review of *The Tenants*. *Commonweal*, 95 (1972), 504.

Rosenfeld, Alvin H. "The Progress of the American Jewish Novel." *Response*, 7 (1973), 115-30.

Rosenfeld, Alvin H. Review of *Pictures of Fidelman*. *Judaism*, 18 (Fall 1969), 504-08.

Rosenthal, Raymond. "A Christian Problem." *New Leader*, 49, No. 18 (1966), 18-19.

Ross, Alan. Review of *The Natural*. *London Magazine*, 3, No. 3 (1963), 86-87.

Roth, H. L. Review of *The Assistant*. *Library Journal*, 82 (1957), 1067.

Roth, Philip. "Writing American Fiction." *Commentary*, 31 (1961), 223-33. Reprinted in Klein, Marcus, ed. *The American Novel Since World War II*. Greenwich, Conn.: Fawcett Publications, 1969, pp. 142-58.

Rothstein, R. "Sight and Sound." *Hadassah*, 52 (October 1970), 34.

Rovit, Earl H. "Bernard Malamud and the Jewish Literary Tradition." *Critique*, 3, No. 2 (Winter-Spring 1960), 3-10. Reprinted as "The Jewish Literary Tradition" in Field, Leslie A., and Joyce W. Field, eds. *Bernard Malamud and the Critics*. New York: New York Univ. Press, 1970, pp. 3-10.

Rubin, Louis D., Jr. "The Curious Death of the Novel: or, What to Do About Tired Literary Critics." *Kenyon Review*, 28 (1966), 305-25.

Rubin, Louis D., Jr. "Six Novels and S. Levin." *Sewanee Review*, 70 (1962), 504-14.

Rugoff, Milton. "Making Everyday Life Glow." *New York Herald Tribune Book Review,* 25 May 1958, p. 3.

Russell, Mariann. "White Man's Black Man: Three Views." *College Language Association Journal,* 17 (1973), 93-100.

Sale, Roger. "The Newness of the Novel." *Hudson Review,* 16 (Winter 1963-1964), 601-609.

Sale, Roger. "What Went Wrong?" *New York Review of Books,* 21 Oct. 1971, pp. 3-6.

Samuels, Charles Thomas. "The Career of Bernard Malamud." *New Republic,* 10 Sept. 1966, pp. 19-21.

Schickel, Richard. "Decline of the Short Story." *The Progressive,* 22, No. 9 (1958), 50-51.

Schlueter, Paul. "Seeds of Destruction." *Christian Century,* 88 (1971), 1448.

Scholes, Robert. "Malamud's Latest Novel." *Northwest Review,* 8, No. 2 (Fall/Winter 1966-1967), 106-108.

Scholes, Robert. "Portrait of Artist as 'Escape-Goat.'" *Saturday Review,* 10 May 1969, pp. 32-34.

Schott, Webster. "A Small Man Uncrushed by Brutal Power." *Life,* 16 Sept. 1966, p. 14.

Schroth, Raymond A. "The Fixer." *America,* 115 (1966), 284.

Schulz, Max F. "Malamud's *A New Life*: The New Wasteland of the Fifties." *Western Review,* 6, No. 1 (Spring 1969), 37-44.

"Schwartz, the Bird." *Newsweek,* 7 Oct. 1963, p. 112.

Scharfman, William. "Inside and Outside Malamud." *Rendezvous,* 7, No. 1 (Spring 1972), 25-38.

Sharma, D. R. "*The Natural:* A Nonmythical Approach." *Panjab University Research Bulletin,* 5, No. 2 (1974), 3-8.

Shear, Walter. "Culture Conflict in *The Assistant.*" *Midwest Quarterly,* 7 (Summer 1966), 367-80. Reprinted as "Culture Conflict" in Field, Leslie A., and Joyce W. Field, eds. *Bernard Malamud and the Critics.* New York: New York Univ. Press, 1970, pp. 207-18.

Sheed, Wilfred. "A Portrait of the Artist as Schlemiel." *Life,* 9 May 1969, p. 12.

Shenker, Israel. "For Malamud It's Story." *New York Times Book Review,* 3 Oct. 1971, pp. 20, 22. Reprinted as "Bernard Malamud on Writing Fiction: An Interview." *Writer's Digest,* July 1972, pp. 22-23.

Sheppard, Ronald Z. "About Bernard Malamud." *Book Week,* 1, No. 5 (13 Oct. 1963), 5.

Sheppard, Ronald Z. "Condemnation Proceedings." *Time,* 27 Sept. 1971, pp. 96-97.

"Shlemiel Triumphant." *Newsweek,* 12 Sept. 1966, pp. 109-10.

Shrubb, Peter. "About Love and Pity—The Stories of Bernard Malamud." *Quadrant,* 9, No. 6 (1965), 66-71.

Shulman, Robert. "Myth, Mr. Eliot, and the Comic Novel." *Modern Fiction Studies,* 12 (Winter 1966-1967), 395-403.

Siegel, Ben. "Victims in Motion: Bernard Malamud's Sad and Bitter Clowns." *Northwest Review,* 5, No. 2 (Spring 1962), 69-80. Reprinted in Waldmeir, Joseph J., ed. *Recent American Fiction: Some Critical Views.* Boston: Houghton Mifflin, 1963, pp. 203-14. Also reprinted as "Victims in Motion: The Sad and Bitter Clowns" in Field, Leslie A., and Joyce W. Field, eds. *Bernard Malamud and the Critics.* New York: New York Univ. Press, 1970, pp. 123-34.

Skolnik, N. Review of *The Tenants. Jewish Spectator,* 36 (December 1971), 30-31.

Skow, John. "Ending the Pane." *Time,* 28 May 1973, pp. 99-100.

Solotaroff, Theodore. "Bernard Malamud's Fiction: The Old Life and the New." *Commentary,* 33 (March 1962), 197-204. Reprinted in *The Red Hot Vacuum and Other Pieces on the Writing of the Sixties.* New York: Atheneum, 1970, pp. 71-86. Reprinted as "The Old Life and the New" in Field, Leslie A., and Joyce W. Field, eds. *Bernard Malamud and the Critics.* New York: New York Univ. Press, 1970, pp. 235-48.

Solotaroff, Theodore. "Philip Roth and the Jewish Moralists." *Chicago Review,* 13, No. 4 (Winter 1959), 87-99. Reprinted in Malin, Irving, and Irwin Stark, eds. *Breakthrough: A Treasury of Contemporary American-Jewish Literature.* Philadelphia: The Jewish Publication Society of America, 1965, pp. 354-66.

Solotaroff, Theodore. "Showing Us 'What It Means Human.'" *Book Week,* 1, No. 5 (13 Oct. 1963), 5.

"Sons of Perdition." (London) *Times Literary Supplement,* 6 April 1967, p. 286.

Spiegel, Moshe. Review of *The Fixer. Chicago Jewish Forum,* 25 (Winter 1966-67), 152-54.

Stampfer, J. Review of *A Malamud Reader. Congress bi-Weekly,* 35 (8 April 1968), 20-21.

Standley, Fred L. "Bernard Malamud: The Novel of Redemption." *Southern Humanities Review,* 5 (1971), 309-18.

Stanton, Robert. "Outrageous Fiction: *Crime and Punishment, The Assistant,* and *Native Son.*" *Pacific Coast Philology,* 4 (1969), 52-58.

Stegner, Page. "Stone, Berry, Oates—and Other Grist from the Mill." *Southern Review,* NS 5 (1969), 273-83.

Stern, Daniel. "The Art of Fiction: Bernard Malamud" [Interview]. *Paris Review,* No. 61 (Spring 1975), 40-64.

Stern, Daniel. "Commonplace Things, and the Essence of Art." *Nation,* 217 (1973), 181-82.

Stern, Daniel. Review of *The Fixer. Hadassah,* 48 (September 1966), 15.

Stern, Milton R. "All Men Are Jews." *Nation,* 197 (1963), 243-44.

Stetler, Charles. Review of *Pictures of Fidelman*. *Studies in Short Fiction*, 8 (1971), 341-43.

Stevenson, David L. "The Strange Destiny of S. Levin." *New York Times Book Review*, 8 Oct. 1961, pp. 1, 28.

Stevenson, David L. "The Activists." *Daedalus*, 92 (1963), 238-49.

Stone, Richard. "Malamud: Exposing Racial Fraud?" *Wall Street Journal*, 12 Oct. 1971, p. 20.

Sullivan, Walter. " 'Where Have All the Flowers Gone?' Part II: The Novel in the Gnostic Twilight." *Sewanee Review* 78 (1970), 654-64.

"The Sustaining Stream." *Time*, 1 Feb. 1963, 81-84.

Swados, Harvey. "The Emergence of An Artist." *Western Review*, 22 (1958), 149-51.

Sylvester, Harry. Review of *The Natural*. *New York Times Book Review*, 24 Aug. 1952, p. 5.

Syrkin, Marie. "From Frank Alpine to Willie Spearmint . . ." *Midstream*, Nov. 1971, pp. 64-68.

"A Talk With B. Malamud." *New York Times Book Review*, 8 Oct. 1961, p. 28.

Tanner, Tony. "Bernard Malamud and the New Life." *Critical Quarterly*, 10 (1968), 151-68.

Taubman, Robert. "People of the Law." *New Statesman*, 67 (5 June 1964), 883-84.

"Tenement for Two." (London) *Times Literary Supplement*, 24 March 1972, p. 325.

Tracy, Robert. "A Sharing of Obsessions." *Southern Review*, NS 6 (1970), 890-904.

Tucker, Martin. "A Pluralistic Place." *Venture*, 3 Nos. 1 & 2 (1959), 69-73.

Tucker, Martin. Review of *The Fixer*. *Commonweal*, 85 (1966), 272.

Tucker, Martin. Review of *Pictures of Fidelman*. *Commonweal*, 90 (1969), 420-21.

Turner, Frederick W., III. "Myth Inside and Out: Malamud's *The Natural*." *Novel*, 1 (Winter 1968), 133-39. Reprinted in Field, Leslie A., and Joyce W. Field, eds. *Bernard Malamud and the Critics*. New York: New York Univ. Press, 1970, pp. 109-19.

Vanderbilt, Kermit. "Writers of the Troubled Sixties." *Nation*, 217 (1973), 661-65.

Voss, Arthur W. M. Review of *A New Life*. *Books Abroad*, 36 (1962), 79.

Wagner, Mary Hagel. Review of *Idiots First*. *America*, 109 (1963), 488, 490-91.

Waldmeir, Joseph J. "Only an Occasional Rutabaga: American Fiction Since 1945." *Modern Fiction Studies*, 15 (Winter 1969-70), 467-81.

Wasserman, Earl R. *"The Natural:* Malamud's World Ceres." *Centennial Review,* 9 (1965), 438-60. Reprinted in Field, Leslie A., and Joyce W. Field, eds. *Bernard Malamud and the Critics.* New York: New York Univ. Press, 1970, pp. 45-65.

Waterhouse, Keith. "New Short Stories." *New Statesman,* 59 (1960), 725-26.

Waugh, Aubeson. Review of *The Tenants. Spectator,* 228 (1972), 549-50.

Weales, Gerald. Review of *The Tenants. Hudson Review,* 24 (Winter 1971-72), 726-27.

Weales, Gerald. "The Sharing of Misery." *New Leader,* 41 (1 Sept. 1958), 24-25.

Wechsler, Diane. "Analysis of 'The Prison' by Bernard Malamud." *English Journal,* 59 (1970), 782-84.

Wegelin, Christof. "American Schlemiel Abroad: Malamud's Italian Stories and the End of American Innocence." *Twentieth Century Literature,* 19 (1973), 77-88.

Weintroub, Benjamin. Review of *A New Life. Chicago Jewish Forum,* 24 (Winter 1965-66), 165-66.

Weiss, Samuel A. "Notes on Bernard Malamud." *Chicago Jewish Forum,* 21 (Winter 1962-63), 155-58.

Weiss, Samuel A. "Passion and Purgation in Bernard Malamud." *Univ. of Windsor Review,* 2, No. 1 (Fall 1966), 93-99.

Wermuth, Paul C. Review of *The Magic Barrel. Library Journal,* 83 (1958), 1933.

West, Jessamyn. Review of *A New Life. New York Herald Tribune Book Review,* 8 Oct. 1961, p. 4.

Whitbread, Jane. "The Best of the Current Short Story Crop." *Good Housekeeping,* March 1960, pp. 54-56.

White, Robert L. "The English Instructor as Hero: Two Novels by Roth and Malamud." *Forum* (Univ. of Houston), 4 (Winter 1963), 16-22.

Widmer, Kingsley. "The American Road: The Contemporary Novel." *Univ. of Kansas City Review,* 26 (June 1960), 309-17.

Wiesel, E. Review of *Idiots First. Hadassah,* 44 (November 1963), 18.

"The Wild Man from the East." *Time,* 6 Oct. 1961, p. 96.

Winegarten, Renee. "Malamud's Head." *Midstream,* Oct. 1973, pp. 76-79. Reprinted as "Malamud's Head *(Rembrandt's Hat)*" in Field, Leslie A., and Joyce W. Field, eds. *Bernard Malamud: A Collection of Critical Essays.* Twentieth Century Views. Englewood Cliffs, N. J.: Prentice-Hall, 1975, pp. 99-103.

Winegarten, Renee. Review of *The Fixer. Jewish Observer and Middle East Review,* 16 (7 April 1967), 17-18.

Wohl, A. "On Seeing *The Fixer*—Some Reflections." *American Zionist,* 59 (March 1969), 44-45.

Wohlgelernter, M. Review of *The Fixer*. *Tradition*, 8 (Fall 1966), 62-72.

Wohlgelernter, M. Review of *Pictures of Fidelman*. *American Zionist*, 60 (October 1969), 42-43.

Wyndham, Francis. "Putting It Down in Black and White." *Listener*, 87 (1972), 390.

Yardley, Jonathan. "The Obscure Sufferers." *New Republic,* 16 Oct. 1971, pp. 24, 26.

DATE		